About *Fundame* *of Strategy*

Based on the twelfth edition of the market-leading *Exploring Strategy*, this book concentrates on the fundamental issues and techniques of strategy. The book will particularly suit those on short courses in strategy focused on strategy analysis, or studying strategy as part of a wider degree, perhaps in the sciences or engineering. This fifth edition of *Fundamentals of Strategy* reflects contemporary business issues and is updated to reflect the covid-19 pandemic. Concepts that are particularly relevant given the recent crisis include PESTEL and scenario analysis (Chapter 2), dynamic capabilities (Chapter 4), stakeholders and corporate social responsibility (Chapter 5) and strategic change (Chapter 9).

Readers of *Fundamentals of Strategy* can be sure that they have the core concepts of strategy in this book, while knowing that they can easily go deeper into particular topics by referring to the complete twelfth edition of *Exploring Strategy*. There they will find extended treatments of the issues covered here, as well as greater attention to issues of strategy development and change and the role of the strategist. *Exploring Strategy* also offers more cases and deeper exploration of issues through 'Thinking Differently' modules, 'strategy lenses' and 'commentaries'. A brief contents of *Exploring Strategy* can be found on p. v. Teachers familiar with *Exploring Strategy* will find that the definitions, concepts and the content of *Fundamentals of Strategy* are entirely consistent, making it easy to teach courses using the different books in parallel.

Fundamentals of Strategy now has nine chapters, with the emphasis on what *Exploring Strategy* terms the 'strategic position' and 'strategic choices' facing organisations. Under 'strategic position', *Fundamentals* introduces macro-environmental and industry analysis, resource and capability analysis, stakeholders and culture. Under 'strategic choices', the book addresses business-level strategy, business models, corporate-level strategy, international strategy, strategic entrepreneurship, innovation and mergers and acquisitions. The final ninth chapter, 'Strategy in action', raises implementation issues such as organisational structure, managerial systems and strategic change.

We believe that *Fundamentals of Strategy* brings the proven benefits of *Exploring Strategy* to the growing number of students on shorter courses. We hope that you will enjoy using it too.

A guide to getting the most from all the features and learning materials of *Fundamentals of Strategy* follows this preface.

Richard Whittington
Patrick Regnér
Duncan Angwin
Gerry Johnson
Kevan Scholes
April 2020

Richard Whittington, MA, MBA, PhD is Professor of Strategic Management at the Saïd Business School and Millman Fellow at New College, University of Oxford. He researches Strategy-as-Practice and is and author of ten books, including *Opening Strategy: Professional Strategists and Practice Change, 1960 to Today* (2019). He has had full or visiting positions at the Harvard Business School, HEC Paris, Imperial College London, the University of Toulouse and the University of Warwick. He is active in executive education and consulting internationally.

Patrick Regnér, BSc, MSc, PhD is Professor of Strategic Management at Stockholm School of Economics. He has published in leading journals like *Strategic Management Journal, Journal of International Business, Human Relations,* etc. and serves on several editorial boards including *Academy of Management Review, Journal of Management Studies* and *Strategic Organization*. He has extensive teaching experience on all academic levels at several international institutions. He does executive teaching and consulting with organisations active worldwide and is senior advisor at strategy advisory firm Value Formation. His current research focuses on strategy and institutions.

Duncan Angwin, MA, MPhil, MBA, PhD is the Dean of Nottingham University Business School. He was previously the Sir Roland Smith Professor of Strategic Management and Head of Department for Entrepreneurship and Strategy at Lancaster University. He has authored twelve books, over forty refereed articles in journals such as *Academy of Management Learning & Education, British Journal of Management California Management Review, Journal of World Business, MIT Sloan Management Review, and Organization Studies* and is on the editorial boards of several journals. He teaches strategy to executives internationally. He has won in excess of €10m in research grants and currently focuses on international M&A and strategy practices. See **http://www.duncanangwin.com**

Gerry Johnson, BA, PhD is Emeritus Professor of Strategic Management at Lancaster University School of Management. He has also taught at Strathclyde Business School, Cranfield School of Management, Manchester Business School and Aston University. He is the author of numerous books and his research has been published in many of the foremost management research journals in the world. He also works with senior management teams on issues of strategy development and strategic change.

Kevan Scholes, MA, PhD, DMS, CIMgt, FRSA is Principal Partner of Scholes Associates – specialising in strategic management. He is also Emiritus Professor of Strategic Management and formerly Director of the Sheffield Business School, UK. He has extensive experience of teaching strategy to undergraduate and postgraduate students inside and outside the UK, as well as of management development work in private and public sector organisations. He has been an advisor on management development to a number of national bodies and is a Companion of The Chartered Management Institute.

FUNDAMENTALS OF STRATEGY

FIFTH EDITION

Richard Whittington
Saïd Business School, University of Oxford

Patrick Regnér
Stockholm School of Economics

Duncan Angwin
Nottingham University Business School

Gerry Johnson
Lancaster University Management School

Kevan Scholes
Sheffield Business School

Pearson

Harlow, England • London • New York • Boston • San Francisco • Toronto • Sydney • Dubai • Singapore • Hong Kong
Tokyo • Seoul • Taipei • New Delhi • Cape Town • São Paulo • Mexico City • Madrid • Amsterdam • Munich • Paris • Milan

PEARSON EDUCATION LIMITED
KAO Two
KAO Park
Harlow CM17 9SR
United Kingdom
Tel: +44 (0)1279 623623
Web: www.pearson.com/uk

_____

First published 2009 (print)
Second edition published 2012 (print)
Third edition published 2015 (print and electronic)
Fourth edition published 2018 (print and electronic)
Fifth edition published 2021 (print and electronic)

© Pearson Education Limited 2009, 2012 (print)
© Pearson Education Limited 2015, 2018, 2021 (print and electronic)

ISBN: 978-1-292-35137-7 (print)
          978-1-292-35139-1 (PDF)
          978-1-292-35138-4 (ePub)

British Library Cataloguing-in-Publication Data
A catalogue record for the print edition is available from the British Library

Library of Congress Cataloging-in-Publication Data
Names: Whittington, Richard, 1958- author. | Angwin, Duncan, author. |
  Regnér, Patrick, author. | Johnson, Gerry, author. | Scholes, Kevan,
  author.
Title: Fundamentals of strategy / Richard Whittington, Duncan Angwin,
  Patrick Regnér, Gerry Johnson, Kevan Scholes.
Description: Fifth edition. | Hoboken : Pearson, 2021. | Previous edition
  entered under: Gerry Johnson. | Includes bibliographical references and
  index. | Summary: "Fundamentals of Strategy builds on the established
  strengths of Exploring Strategy, proven over twelve best-selling
  editions. A range of in-text features and supplementary resources have
  been developed to enable you and your students to gain maximum added
  value to the teaching and learning of strategy"-- Provided by publisher.
Identifiers: LCCN 2020037969 (print) | LCCN 2020037970 (ebook) | ISBN
  9781292351377 (print) | ISBN 9781292351391 (PDF) | ISBN 9781292351384
  (ePub)
Subjects: LCSH: Business planning. | Strategic planning. | Business
  planning--Case studies. | Strategic planning--Case studies.
Classification: LCC HD30.28 .J6495 2021 (print) | LCC HD30.28 (ebook) |
  DDC 658.4/012--dc23
LC record available at https://lccn.loc.gov/2020037969
LC ebook record available at https://lccn.loc.gov/2020037970

10 9 8 7 6 5 4 3 2 1
23 22 21 20

Cover: © Otto Steininger/Ikon Images/Getty Images

Print edition typeset in 9/12.5pt Frutiger Neue LT W1G by SPi Gobal
Print edition printed in Slovakia by Neografia

NOTE THAT ANY PAGE CROSS REFERENCES REFER TO THE PRINT EDITION

Brief contents

Contents

Getting the most from *Fundamentals of Strategy*

Fundamentals of Strategy builds on the established strengths of *Exploring Strategy,* proven over twelve best-selling editions. A range of in-text features and supplementary resources have been developed to enable you and your students to gain maximum added value to the teaching and learning of strategy.

- **Outstanding pedagogical features.** Each chapter has clear learning outcomes, definitions of key concepts in the appendix, practical questions associated with real-life Illustrations, and concise end-of-chapter case examples through which students can easily apply what they have learned.

- **Up-to-date materials.** *Fundamentals of Strategy* is based on the latest twelfth edition of *Exploring Strategy*. Our references are up to date, so that you can easily access the latest research. Cases and examples are fresh and engage with student interests and day-to-day experience. We refer to the challenges raised by the covid-19 crisis.

- **Range of examples.** This edition maintains the wide range of examples used in the text, Illustrations and cases. We draw from all over the world, with no bias to North America, and use examples from the public and voluntary sectors as well as the private.

  Fundamentals of Strategy does not include any longer cases. If you wish to supplement the book with any of the case studies included in *Exploring Strategy*, please consult your local Pearson Education representative to find out what their Custom Publishing programme can do for you.

- **Attractive text layout and design.** We make careful use of colour and photography to improve clarity and ease of 'navigation' through the text. Reading the text should be an enjoyable and straightforward process.

- **Resources for students**
  - A dynamic eText
  - Self-assessment questions
  - Key concept audio summaries
  - Video cases and author videos
  - Revision flashcards
  - A multi-lingual glossary
  - Links to relevant websites
  - Classic cases
  - The Strategy Experience Simulation

Resources for lecturers

- Instructor's manual
- Powerpoint slides
- A testbank of assessment questions

- **Video resources** are available on line. These have been specially created for in-class use and contains briefings on key concepts by the authors, and material to support video assignments identified at the end of each chapter of *Fundamentals of Strategy*.

  You can order and find out more about these resources from your local Pearson Education representative (**www.pearsoned.co.uk/replocator**).

- **Teachers' workshop.** We run an annual workshop to facilitate discussion of key challenges and solutions in the teaching of strategic management. Details of forthcoming workshops can be found at **www.pearsoned.co.uk/strategyworkshop**.

- **Complementary textbook.** *Exploring Strategy* provides deeper and more extensive coverage of the theory and practice of strategy. A brief table of contents from the twelfth edition is listed below:

Part I
The strategic position — 31

[handwritten annotations: "PESTEL", "5 Forces", "VRIO SWOT"]

Part II
Strategic choices

199

Part III
Strategy in action

367

Fundamentals of Strategy Online

A wide range of supporting resources are available at: http://go.pearson.com/uk/he/resources
Register to create your own personal account using the access code supplied with your copy of the book,* and access the following teaching and learning resources:

Resources for students

- **A dynamic eText** of the book that you can search, bookmark, annotate and highlight as you please
- **Self-assessment questions** that identify your strengths before recommending a personalised study plan that points you to the resources which can help you achieve a better grade
- **Key concept audio summaries** that you can download or listen to online
- **Author videos** explaining key concepts in the book
- **Video cases** that show managers talking about strategic issues in their own organisations
- **Revision flashcards** to help you prepare for your exams
- **A multi-lingual online glossary** to help explain key concepts
- Guidance on **how to analyse a case study**
- **Links** to relevant sites on the web so you can explore more about the organisations featured in the case studies
- **Classic cases** – over 30 case studies from previous editions of the book
- **The Strategy Experience Simulation** gives you hands-on experience of strategic analysis and putting strategy into action

Resources for instructors

- **Instructor's manual**, including extensive teaching notes for cases and suggested teaching plans
- **PowerPoint slides**, containing key information and figures from the book
- Support for **The Strategy Experience Simulation** with guidance on the aims and objectives of the simulation, and instructions on how to set up simulation groups that enable you to monitor your students' performance

For more information, please contact your local Pearson Education sales representative.

---

*If you don't have an access code, you can still access the resources by purchasing access online. A sample selection of these resources is also available at **http://go.pearson.com/uk/he/resources**

Chapter 1
Introducing strategy

Key terms

Learning outcomes

After reading this chapter, you should be able to:

- Summarise the strategy of an organisation in a '*strategy statement*'.
- Distinguish between *corporate, business* and *functional* strategies.
- Identify key issues for an organisation's strategy using the *Exploring Strategy* Framework.

1.1 Introduction

The Chief Executive Officer (CEO) of a medium-sized family business knew they had a problem. New aggressive competition in their main European markets was threatening their performance just as demand was softening. To help him address this major problem the CEO invited in a consultancy firm to assess whether this was the right time for his business to find new international markets for growth or to invest more in product innovation to stimulate demand. Claudia, the junior consultant in the team, heard the consulting partner explain how they would carry out a systematic analysis of the company's situation to understand its success, assess the challenges posed by the competition and shifting markets and identify broader opportunities and threats from the wider environment. It would be her task to assemble key data and conduct analysis to generate future possible options for the business. These would help inform the CEO's decision about how his business could improve its competitive position. The consulting firm would assist with implementation if needed.

The problem presented by the CEO to the consultants is one of strategy. It is concerned with key issues for the future of the organisation. For instance, how should the company compete in the future with aggressive new entrants? What growth options are there for the company? If further internationalisation is a good strategy, what would be the optimal method to achieve this outcome and what might be the resourcing implications? All of these strategy questions are vital to the future survival of the organisation.

Strategy questions naturally concern entrepreneurs and senior managers at the top of their organisations. But these questions matter more widely. Outside of the organisation, stakeholders such as investors, suppliers and customers influence the strategy. Inside the organisation, middle managers also have to understand the strategic direction, both to know how to get top management support for their initiatives and to explain it to the people they are responsible for. Anybody looking for a management-track job needs to be ready to discuss strategy with their potential employer. Indeed, anybody taking a job should first be confident that their new employer's strategy is actually viable. There are even specialist career opportunities in strategy, for example like Claudia, as a strategy consultant or as an in-house strategic planner, often key roles for fast-track young managers.

This book is relevant to any kind of organisation responsible for its own direction into the future. Thus the book refers to large private sector multinationals and small entrepreneurial start-ups; to family businesses, both large and small; to public-sector organisations such as schools and hospitals; and to not-for-profits such as charities or sports clubs. Strategy matters to almost all organisations, and to everybody working in them.

1.2 What is strategy?[1]

Strategy is the long-term direction of an organisation. Thus the long-term direction of Amazon is from book retailing to internet services in general. This section examines the practical implication of this definition of strategy; distinguishes between different levels of strategy; and explains how to summarise an organisation's strategy in a 'strategy statement'.

1.2.1 Defining strategy

Defining strategy as the long-term direction of an organisation implies a more comprehensive view than some influential definitions. Figure 1.1 shows the strategy definitions of several leading strategy theorists: Alfred Chandler and Michael Porter, both from the Harvard

Figure 1.1 Definitions of strategy

'. . . the determination of the long-run goals and objectives of an enterprise and the adoption of courses of action and the allocation of resources necessary for carrying out these goals'
Alfred D. Chandler

'Competitive strategy is about being different. It means deliberately choosing a different set of activities to deliver a unique mix of value'
Michael Porter

'a firm's theory about how to gain competitive advantages'
Peter Drucker

'a pattern in a stream of decisions'
Henry Mintzberg

'the long-term direction of an organisation'
Exploring Strategy

Sources: A.D. Chandler, *Strategy and Structure: Chapters in the History of American Enterprise*, MIT Press, 1963, p. 13; M.E. Porter, 'What is strategy?', *Harvard Business Review*, November–December 1996, p. 60; P.F. Drucker, 'The theory of business', *Harvard Business Review*, September–October 1994, pp. 95–106; H. Mintzberg, *Tracking Strategies: Towards a General Theory*, Oxford University Press, 2007, p. 3.

Business School, Peter Drucker from Claremont University, California and Henry Mintzberg, from McGill University, Canada. Each points to important elements of strategy. Chandler emphasises a logical flow from the determination of goals and objectives to the allocation of resources. Porter focuses on deliberate choices, difference and competition. Drucker suggests that it is a theory about how a firm will win.[2] Mintzberg, however, takes the view that strategy is less certain and uses the word 'pattern' to allow for the fact that strategies do not always follow a deliberately chosen and logical plan, but can emerge in more ad hoc ways. Sometimes strategies reflect a series of incremental decisions that only cohere into a recognisable pattern – or 'strategy' – after some time.

There are two advantages to our opening definition of strategy. First, the long-term direction of an organisation can include both deliberate, logical strategy and more incremental, emergent patterns of strategy. Second, long-term direction can include both strategies that emphasise difference and competition, and strategies that recognise the roles of cooperation and even imitation.

The three elements of this strategy definition – the long term, direction and organisation – can each be explored further. The strategy of Tesla Motors illustrates important points (see Illustration 1.1):

- *The long term.* Strategies are typically measured over years, for some organisations a decade or more. The importance of a long-term perspective on strategy is emphasised by the 'three horizons' framework shown in Figure 1.2. **The three-horizons framework suggests organisations should think of their businesses or activities in terms of different 'horizons', defined by time.** *Horizon 1* businesses are basically the current core activities. In the case of Tesla Motors, Horizon 1 includes the original Tesla Roadster car and subsequent models. Horizon 1 businesses need defending and extending but the expectation is that in the long term they risk becoming flat or declining in terms of profits (or whatever else the organisation values). *Horizon 2* businesses are emerging activities that should provide new future sources of profit. For Tesla, that might include the new mega-battery business. Finally, there are *Horizon 3* possibilities, which are more open and for which outcomes are even more uncertain. These are typically risky research and development projects, start-up ventures, test-market pilots or similar: at Tesla, these might

Illustration 1.1 Tesla Motors: the future is electric!

Are there enough Teslas in the world?

Source: Jim West/Alamy Stock Photo

The Tesla Roadster is a staggeringly quick car with a difference. There's no wheel-spin, no traction control stutter, no driveline shutter. Stamp on the throttle and the driver gets 686 lbs of torque immediately, rocketing the car from 0–60 mph in 3.2 seconds and with negligible noise – the car is electric.

The Tesla Roadster is the main product of Tesla Motors. Its charismatic chairman and main funder is PayPal cofounder, and SpaceX CEO, Elon Musk. Barely a decade old, Tesla Motors is already gigantic, $52bn market capitalisation, and adored. It's been called 'the world's most important automotive company' and the Tesla's Model S, 'the Most Loved Vehicle in America' – out-selling Mercedes S-class and BMW 7 series. And yet the last successful American car start-up was Ford, founded 111 years ago. How can Tesla Motors be so successful?

Tesla is the brain-child of three Silicon Valley engineers convinced by global warming arguments and looking for alternative fuel sources for cars. Co-founder Eberhard asked: 'How much of the energy that comes out of the ground makes your car go a mile?'[1] He observed 'hydrogen fuel cells are terrible – no more efficient than gas. Electric cars were superior to everything.'[1] He then discovered a bright yellow all-electric two-seater bullet car with zero emissions, 'tzero', built by AC propulsion. Inspired, Eberhard kept saying to potential recruits – 'try and touch the dashboard.'[1] He would then hit the accelerator – they couldn't! With Lamborghini-level acceleration, this demonstrated electric cars didn't have to be golf carts.

At the time industry logic said electric cars would never succeed, as GM had spent $1bn trying to develop one that was then scrapped and battery technology had not improved in a hundred years. However Eberhard realised lithium-ion batteries were different – improving 7 per cent per annum. So Tesla was positioned to ride the current of technological history.

The founders had no experience making cars, but realised car companies now outsourced everything, even styling. Manufacturing partners were ready to be connected; a 'fab-less' car company was possible.* Production began in 2008. The business

plan described the Roadster as 'disruptive' technology** – a high-end sports car with lower price and emissions than competitors – and a lower resource cost to the planet.

> ### Model S
>
> 0–60 mph < 2.5 seconds; 100mpg; world-class handling; Zero tailpipe emissions; +300 mile range; zero maintenance for 100,00 miles (other than tyres); 50 per cent price of the cheapest competitive sportscar.[1]

Tesla's strategy is 'to succeed in the high end of the market, where customers will pay a premium for a sports car without compromise, and then drive down market rapidly to higher unit volume and lower prices with each successive model. All free cash flow is ploughed back into R&D to drive down costs and bring follow-on products to market as fast as possible. Roadster customers are actually paying for development of the low-cost family car.'[2]

Tesla aims to provide zero emission electric power generation from their 'giga' battery factory in line with their overarching purpose to move from mine-and-burn hydrocarbons towards a sustainable solar electric economy.[2] Tesla Energy now sells batteries for home and business use and aims to offer an energy system for the world.

However, things continue to be problematic as Tesla battles Model 3 production and distribution difficulties and will need to make further large capital investments. Despite axing 7 per cent of its workforce in January 2019,[3] improving production output and price reductions to counter a federal tax credit cut, Elon Musk's previous outbursts, dismissing analysts' 'boring bonehead questions', an aborted attempt to take the company private and worries that his other business interests are distracting him, are causing analysts such as Goldman Sachs to predict that Tesla shares will fall 30 per cent in months with the rise of luxury marque competitor products. But when your mission is to save the earth, maybe Elon Musk's outspokenness is not surprising.[4]

Notes
* A car company without a factory.
** A phrase from Harvard professor Clayton Christensen.

Sources: (1) E. Musk, 'The Secret Tesla Motors Master Plan (just between you and me)', 2 August 2006; (2) D. Baer, 'The making of Tesla: invention, betrayal, and the birth of the Roadster', *Business Insider*, 11 November 2014; (3) Sainato, 'How do they expect to run without us', theguardian. com, 30 January 2019; (4) R. Water and P. Campbell, 'Tesla: Reality begins to collide with the Elon Musk's vision', *Financial Times,* 15 June 2018.

Questions

1 How does Tesla Motor's strategy fit with the various strategy definitions in Figure 1.1?

2 What seems to account for Tesla's success and current difficulties?

Figure 1.2 Three horizons for strategy

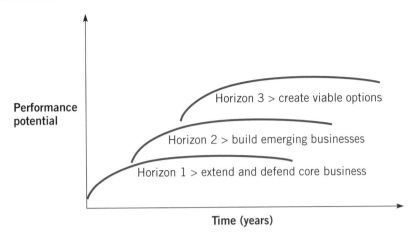

Source: Adapted from M. Baghai, S. Coley and D. White, *The Alchemy of Growth*, Texere Publishers, 2000. Figure 1.1, p. 5.

be further solar electric initiatives, rockets and space transportation. For a fast-moving organisation like Tesla, *Horizon 3* might generate profits a few years from the present time. In a pharmaceutical company, where the R&D and regulatory processes for a new drug take many years, *Horizon 3* might be a decade ahead. While timescales might differ, as industries and types of firm can move at different rates, the basic point about the 'three horizons' framework is that managers need to avoid focusing on the short-term issues of their existing activities. Strategy involves pushing out Horizon 1 as far as possible, at the same time as looking to Horizons 2 and 3.

- *Strategic direction.* Over the years, strategies follow some kind of long-term direction or trajectory. The strategic direction of Tesla Motors is from the original electric car to a diversified set of solar power offerings. Sometimes a strategic direction only emerges as a coherent pattern over time. Typically, however, managers and entrepreneurs try to set the direction of their strategy according to long-term *objectives.* In private-sector businesses, the objective guiding strategic direction is usually maximising profits for shareholders. However, profits do not always set strategic direction. First, public-sector and charity organisations may set their strategic direction according to other objectives: for example, a sports club's objective may be to move up from one league to a higher one. Second, even in the private sector profit is not always the sole criterion for strategy. Thus family businesses may sometimes sacrifice the maximisation of profits for family objectives, for example passing down the management of the business to the next generation. The objectives behind strategic direction always need close scrutiny.

- *Organisation.* Organisations typically have many internal and external *stakeholders*, in other words, people and groups that depend on the organisation and upon which the organisation itself depends. Internally, organisations are filled with people, typically with diverse, competing and more or less reasonable views of what should be done. At Tesla, co-founder and original CEO Eberhard was fired by new Chairman Elon Musk. In strategy, therefore, it is always important to look *inside* organisations and to consider the people involved and their different interests and views. Externally, organisations are surrounded by important relationships, for example with suppliers, customers, alliance partners, regulators and investors. For Tesla, relationships with investors and advertisers are crucial. Strategy, therefore, is also vitally concerned with an organisation's external *boundaries*: in other words, questions about what to include within the organisation and how to manage important relationships with what is kept outside.

1.2.2 The purpose of strategy: mission, vision, values and objectives

What is a strategy for? The core of a strategist's job[3] is defining and expressing a clear and motivating purpose for the organisation. Even for private-sector organisations this is generally more than simple profit-maximisation as long-term prosperity and employee motivation usually require expressions of purpose that go beyond just profits. The stated purpose of the organisation should address two related questions: *how* does the organisation make a difference; and *for whom* does the organisation make that difference? If the stakeholders of an organisation can relate to such a purpose it can be highly motivating. Indeed, research by Jim Collins and Jerry Porras suggests that the long-run success of many US corporations – such as Disney, General Electric or 3M – can be attributed (at least in part) to the clear guidance and motivation offered by such statements of purpose.[4]

There are four ways in which organisations typically define their purpose:

- **A mission statement aims to provide employees and stakeholders with clarity about what the organisation is fundamentally there to do.** This is often expressed in the apparently simple but challenging question: 'What business are we in?' Two linked questions that can clarify an organisation's 'business' are: 'What would be lost if the organisation did not exist?'; and 'How do we make a difference?' Though they do not use the term 'mission statement', Collins and Porras[5] suggest that understanding the fundamental mission can be done by starting with a descriptive statement of what the organisation actually does, then repeatedly delving deeper into the organisation's purpose by asking 'why do we do this?' They use the example of managers in a gravel and asphalt company arriving at the conclusion that its mission is to make people's lives better by improving the quality of built structures. At the University of Utrecht the mission includes educating students, training the next generation of researchers and addressing social issues.

- **A vision statement is concerned with the future the organisation seeks to create.** The vision typically expresses an aspiration that will enthuse, gain commitment and stretch performance. So here the question is: 'What do we want to achieve?' Porras and Collins suggest managers can identify this by asking: 'If we were sitting here in twenty years what do we want to have created or achieved?' They cite the example of Henry Ford's original vision in the very early days of automobile production that the ownership of a car should be within the reach of everyone. For the Swedish music site Spotify, the vision is to become 'the Operating System of music', a universal platform for listening just as Microsoft is for office software.

- **Statements of corporate values communicate the underlying and enduring core 'principles' that guide an organisation's strategy and define the way that the organisation should operate.** For example, Alphabet (previously Google), famously includes in its values 'you can be serious without a suit', 'fast is better than slow' and 'don't be evil'. It is important that these values are enduring, so a question to ask is: 'Would these values change with circumstances?' And if the answer is 'yes' then they are not 'core' and not 'enduring'. An example is the importance of leading-edge research in some universities. Whatever the constraints on funding, such universities hold to the enduring centrality of research. On the other hand, as Alphabet has grown and diversified, some critics wonder whether the company still abides by its principle of 'don't be evil'.

- **Objectives are statements of specific outcomes that are to be achieved.** These are often expressed in precise financial terms, for instance the level of sales, profits or share valuation in one, two or three years' time.[6] Organisations may also have quantifiable market-based objectives, such as market share, customer service, repeat business and so on. Sometimes objectives focus on the basis of competitive advantage: for example, low-cost airlines such as Ryanair set objectives on turnaround time for their aircraft because this is at the core of their distinctive low-cost advantage. Increasingly organisations are also setting objectives referred to as 'the triple bottom line', by which is meant not only economic objectives such as those above, but also environmental and social objectives to do with their corporate responsibility to wider society (see Section 5.4).

Although visions, missions and values may be liable to become bland and too wide-ranging,[7] they can offer more enduring sources of direction and motivation than the concrete nature of objectives. It is therefore crucial that vision, mission and values are meaningful when included in strategy statements.

1.2.3 Strategy statements

David Collis and Michael Rukstad[8] at the Harvard Business School argue that all entrepreneurs and managers should be able to summarise their organisation's strategy with a 'strategy statement'. **Strategy statements should have three main themes: the fundamental *goals* (mission, vision or objectives) that the organisation seeks; the *scope* or domain of the organisation's activities; and the particular *advantages* or capabilities it has to deliver all of these.**

Mission, vision and objectives have been described above in Section 1.2.2 so here we concentrate on the other two main themes, scope and advantage, with examples of all three given in Illustration 1.2:

- *Scope.* An organisation's scope or domain refers to three dimensions: customers or clients; geographical location; and extent of internal activities ('vertical integration'). For a university, scope questions are twofold: first, which academic departments to have (a business school, an engineering department and so on); second, which activities to do internally themselves (vertically integrate) and which to externalise to subcontractors (for example, whether to manage campus restaurants in-house or to subcontract them).

- *Advantage.* This part of a strategy statement describes how the organisation will achieve the objectives it has set for itself in its chosen domain. In competitive environments, this refers to the *competitive* advantage: for example, how a particular company or sports club will achieve goals in the face of competition from other companies or clubs. The organisation needs to be better than others at achieving its particular goal. In the public sector, advantage might refer simply to the organisation's capability in general. But even public-sector organisations frequently need to show that their capabilities are not only adequate, but superior to other rival departments or perhaps to private-sector contractors.

Collis and Rukstad suggest that strategy statements covering goals, scope and advantage should be no more than 35 words long. *The three themes are deliberately made highly concise.* Brevity keeps such statements focused on the essentials and makes them easy to remember and communicate. Thus for Tesla, a strategy statement might be: 'To accelerate the advent of

Illustration 1.2 Strategy statements

Both Samsung Electronics, the Korean telecommunications, computing and TV giant, and York University, a leading British university, publish a good deal about their strategies.

Samsung Electronics

At Samsung, we follow a simple business philosophy: to devote our talent and technology to creating superior products and services that contribute to a better global society.

Every day, our people bring this philosophy to life. Our leaders search for the brightest talent from around the world, and give them the resources they need to be the best at what they do. The result is that all of our products – from memory chips that help businesses store vital knowledge to mobile phones that connect people across continents – have the power to enrich lives. And that's what making a better global society is all about.

According to Samsung's new motto it intends to give the world inspiration to create the future of electronics. This new vision reflects Samsung Electronics' commitment to inspiring its communities by leveraging Samsung's three key strengths: 'New Technology', 'Innovative Products', and 'Creative Solutions'. As part of this vision, Samsung has mapped out a specific plan of reaching $400bn in revenue and becoming one of the world's top five brands by 2020. To this end, Samsung has also established three strategic approaches in its management: 'Creativity', 'Partnership', and 'Talent'.

As we build on our previous accomplishments, we look forward to exploring new territories, including health, medicine, and biotechnology. Samsung is committed to being a creative leader in new markets, becoming No. 1 business in the Global IT industry and in the Global top 5.

York University Strategy 2014–2020

York is a University with strong values. In all our activities, we are unconditionally committed to excellence, as measured by the highest national and international standards. We see ourselves as operating in a global environment, with important local and national responsibilities and aim to be among the best universities in the world. We encourage creativity, independence, enterprise and initiative. We support academic freedom and autonomy and we promote open academic debate and discussion. We will be inclusive and provide equal opportunities for all. We apply the highest ethical standards to all our activities and want to make a positive contribution to the development of a fairer and sustainable world.

We aim to provide an environment that attracts the very best staff and students from all over the world, encourages and facilitates academic endeavour, and provides a supportive atmosphere for the development and sharing of knowledge. We want to be a University in which every member of staff and every student feels valued as an individual. Even as we grow, we want to retain a genuine sense of belonging and community in our departments, colleges, clubs and societies. We particularly value our colleges' support for the cultural, social, academic and personal development of our students. We will play an active role in the City of York, which is central to our identity, and are committed to a mutually supportive relationship with the City and the region.

Guided by these values, we aim to build a University that distinguishes itself in three ways:

Key objective 1: to be a world leader in research, by being sufficiently large to be excellent, resilient and financially sustainable.

Key objective 2: to offer outstanding teaching and learning, by being organised in the most efficient and effective way.

Key objective 3: to offer all our students an outstanding and valuable experience, by working effectively with other organisations and stakeholders.

Sources: Edited extracts from www.samsung.com and the University of York Strategy, www.york.ac.uk

Questions

1 Construct short strategy statements covering the goals, scope and advantage of Samsung and the York University. How much do the different private and public sector contexts matter?

2 Construct a strategy statement for your own organisation (university, sports club or employer). What implications might this statement have for your particular course or department?

a sustainable solar economy by developing and incorporating superior battery-based technologies into compelling mass market electric products and bringing them to market as soon as possible.' The IKEA business idea is a little more specific: 'To create a better everyday life for the many people [by offering] a wide range of well-designed, functional home furnishing products at prices so low that as many people as possible will be able to afford them.' Of course, such strategy statements are not always fulfilled. Circumstances may change in unexpected ways. In the meantime, however, they can provide a useful guide both to managers in their decision-making and to employees and others who need to understand the direction in which the organisation is going. The ability to give a clear strategy statement is a good test of managerial competence in an organisation.

As such, strategy statements are relevant to a wide range of organisations. For example, a small entrepreneurial start-up can use a strategy statement to persuade investors and lenders of its viability. Public-sector organisations need strategy statements not only for themselves, but to reassure clients, funders and regulators that their priorities are the right ones. Voluntary organisations need persuasive strategy statements in order to inspire volunteers and donors. Thus organisations of all kinds frequently publish materials relevant to such strategy statements on their websites or annual reports. Illustration 1.2 provides published materials on the strategies of two very different organisations: the technology giant Samsung from the private sector and York University in the UK from the public sector.

1.2.4 Levels of strategy

So far we have considered an organisation as a whole, but inside an organisation, strategies can exist at three main levels.

- **Corporate-level strategy is concerned with the overall scope of an organisation and how value is added to the constituent businesses of the organisational whole.** Corporate-level strategy issues include geographical scope, diversity of products or services, acquisitions of new businesses, and how resources are allocated between the different elements of the organisation. For Tesla, moving from car manufacture to battery production for homes and businesses is a corporate-level strategy. Being clear about corporate-level strategy is important: determining the range of businesses to include is the basis of other strategic decisions, such as acquisitions and alliances.

- **Business-level strategy is about how the individual businesses should compete in their particular markets** (this is often called 'competitive strategy'). These might be stand-alone businesses, for instance entrepreneurial start-ups, or 'business units' within a larger corporation. Business-level strategy typically concerns issues such as innovation, appropriate scale and response to competitors' moves. For Tesla this means rolling out a lower-cost electric car to build volume and capture market share in advance of potential competitor entry. In the public sector, the equivalent of business-level strategy is decisions about how units (such as individual hospitals or schools) should provide best-value services. Where the businesses are units within a larger organisation, business-level strategies should clearly fit with corporate-level strategy.

- **Functional strategies are concerned with how the components of an organisation deliver effectively the corporate- and business-level strategies in terms of resources, processes and people.** For example, Tesla continues to raise external finance to fund its rapid growth: its functional strategy is partly geared to meeting investment needs. In most businesses, successful business strategies depend to a large extent on decisions that are taken, or activities that occur, at the functional level. Functional decisions need therefore to be closely linked to business-level strategy. They are vital to successful strategy implementation.

This need to link the corporate, business and functional levels underlines the importance of *integration* in strategy. Each level needs to be aligned with the others. The demands of integrating levels define an important characteristic of strategy: strategy is typically *complex*, requiring careful and sensitive management. Strategy is rarely simple.

1.3 The *Exploring Strategy* Framework

This book provides a three-part framework that emphasises the interconnected nature of strategic issues. **The *Exploring Strategy* Framework includes understanding *the strategic position* of an organisation; assessing *strategic choices* for the future; and managing *strategy in action.*** Figure 1.3 shows these elements and defines the broad coverage of this book. Together, the three elements provide you with a practical template for studying strategic situations. The following sections of this chapter will introduce the strategic issues that arise under each of these elements of the *Exploring Strategy* Framework. But first it is important to understand why the framework is drawn in this particular way.

Figure 1.3 could have shown the framework's three elements in a linear sequence – first understanding the strategic position, then making strategic choices and finally turning

Figure 1.3 The *Exploring Strategy* Framework

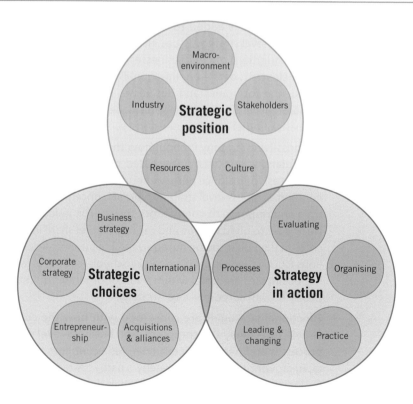

strategy into action. Indeed, this logical sequence is implicit in the definition of strategy given by Alfred Chandler (Figure 1.1) and many other textbooks on strategy. However, as Henry Mintzberg recognises, in practice the elements of strategy do not always follow this linear sequence. Choices often have to be made before the position is fully understood. Sometimes too a proper understanding of the strategic position can only be built from the experience of trying a strategy out in action. The real-world feedback from launching a new product is often far better at uncovering the true strategic position than remote analysis carried out in a strategic planning department at head office.

The interconnected circles of Figure 1.3 are designed to emphasise this potentially non-linear nature of strategy. Position, choices and action should be seen as closely related, and in practice none has priority over another. Although the book divides its subject matter into three sections in sequence, this does not mean that the process of strategy must follow a logical series of distinct steps. The three circles are overlapping and interdependent. The evidence provided in later chapters will suggest that strategy rarely occurs in tidy ways and that it is better not to expect it to do so.

However, the *Exploring Strategy* Framework does provide you with a comprehensive and integrated framework for analysing an organisation's *position*. It allows you to consider the *choices* it has and how strategies might be put into *action*. You can use each of the chapters to help you ask fundamental strategy questions and to select essential concepts and techniques that will help you answer them. Working systematically through questions and answers will provide you with the basis for persuasive strategy recommendations.

1.3.1 Strategic position

The strategic position is concerned with the impact on strategy of the external environment, the organisation's strategic resources and capabilities, the organisation's goals and the organisation's culture. Understanding these four factors is central for evaluating future strategy. These issues, and the fundamental questions associated with them, are covered in the first five chapters of this book:

- *Strategic purpose.* Most organisations claim for themselves a particular purpose, as encapsulated in their *vision, mission, values* and *objectives*. These may be captured in a key strategy tool, the *Strategy Statement*. But often an organisation's purpose is unclear, contested or unrealistic. Chapter 1 explains the components of a strategy statement and allows you to analyse an organisation's strategic purpose and ask 'what does it seek to achieve?' The *three-horizons* framework will also allow you to assess the sustainability of an organisation's strategy.

- *Macro-environment.* Organisations operate in complex multi-level environments. At the macro level organisations are influenced by political, economic, social, technological, ecological and legal forces. These may present both *opportunities* and *threats* for organisations. Chapter 2 contains key frameworks such as PESTLE, forecasting approaches and scenarios to help you assess key drivers of change in the macro context that may affect organisations and their industries.

- *Industry and sector.* At the industry level competitors, customers and suppliers also present challenges. These environments vary widely in terms of their competitive pressures and overall attractiveness and may present further *opportunities* and *threats* to the organisation. Key frameworks such as Porter's Five Forces, industry life cycle and strategic groups are all reviewed in detail with supporting examples in Chapter 3 to help you focus your analysis on priority issues in the face of contextual complexity and dynamism.

- *Resources and capabilities.* Each organisation has its own strategic *resources* (e.g. machines and buildings) and *capabilities* (e.g. technical and managerial skills) that support its position in a market. The fundamental question on capability regards the organisation's *strengths* and *weaknesses* (for example, where is it at a competitive advantage or disadvantage?). Are the organisation's capabilities adequate to the challenges of its environment and the demands of its goals? The key frameworks of VRIO, value chain and SWOT are all described in detail with examples in Chapter 4 to enable you to analyse such resources and capabilities.

- *Stakeholders and culture.* The wishes of key stakeholders should define the purpose of an organisation. Here the issue of *corporate governance* is important: how to ensure that managers stick to the agreed purpose. Questions of purpose and accountability raise issues of *corporate social responsibility* and *ethics*: is the purpose of an organisation an appropriate one and are managers sticking to it? Purpose and ethics will in turn be closely associated with organisational culture, implying the importance of cultural fit with desired strategy. Techniques that enable you to identify stakeholders, assess their relative importance through the use of a power/attention matrix, identify the corporate governance chain and analyse organisational culture with the cultural web, are described in Chapter 5.

The *Exploring Strategy* Framework (Illustration 1.1) points to the following positioning issues for Tesla Motors. What is the future of the company given the growing social, economic and political demands for businesses to be environmentally sustainable? Are its distinctive capabilities really valued sufficiently by consumers to provide a financial return to investors and to allow sustained investment in further innovative products? How will Tesla cope with rising competition from car industry giants that are now selling electric and hybrid cars?

1.3.2 Strategic choices

Strategic choices involve the options for strategy in terms of both the *directions* in which strategy might move and the *methods* by which strategy might be pursued. For instance, an organisation might have a range of strategic directions open to it: the organisation could diversify into new products; it could enter new international markets; or it could transform its existing products and markets through radical innovation. These various directions could be pursued by different methods: the organisation could acquire a business already active in the product or market area; it could form alliances with relevant organisations that might help its new strategy; or it could try to pursue its strategies on its own. Typical strategic choices, and the related fundamental questions, are covered in the next three chapters of this book:

- *Business strategy and models.* There are strategic choices in terms of how the organisation seeks to compete at the individual business level. For example, a business unit could choose to be the lowest cost competitor in a market, or the highest quality. The fundamental question here, then, is what strategy, and what business model, should a company use to compete? To help you decide, Chapter 6 explains the classic generic competitive strategies framework, a key business model components framework and common business models.

- *Corporate strategy.* The highest level of an organisation is typically concerned with issues of corporate scope; in other words, which businesses to include in the portfolio. This relates to the appropriate degree of *diversification,* with regard to products offered and markets served. Corporate-level strategy is also concerned both with internal relationships, both between business units and with the corporate head office. Chapter 7 provides you with the Ansoff matrix, which will allow you to consider alternative corporate strategy directions for development, and the BCG model which will help you assess appropriate portfolio configurations. In addition, the global integration and local responsiveness grid will help you identify alternative international expansion strategies.

- *Entrepreneurship and innovation.* Most existing organisations have to innovate constantly simply to survive. Entrepreneurship, the creation of a new enterprise, is an act of innovation too. A fundamental question, therefore, is whether the organisation is innovating appropriately. Chapter 8 helps you make choices about entrepreneurship and innovation. It shows how to make those choices based on an entrepreneurial opportunity recognition model, steps in the entrepreneurial process framework, evaluating entrepreneurial growth stages, the diffusion S-curve and the disruptive innovation model.

Again, issues of strategic choice are live in the case of Tesla Motors (Illustration 1.1). The *Exploring Strategy* Framework asks the following kinds of questions here. Should Tesla continue to produce new higher volume cheaper cars or remain specialised? How far should it widen the scope of its businesses: is producing batteries for homes really helping or detracting from car production? Where should Tesla innovate next?

1.3.3 Strategy in action

Managing strategy in action is about how strategies are formed and how they are implemented. The emphasis is on the practicalities of managing. Chapter 9 covers four issues for strategy in action:

- *Structuring* an organisation to support successful performance. A key question here is how centralised or structured should the organisational structure be. Structure matters for who is in charge and who is accountable.
- *Systems* to control the way in which strategy is implemented. Planning and performance systems are important to getting things done. The issue here is how to ensure that strategies are implemented according to plan.
- *Leadership* as the process for influencing an organisation's efforts towards achieving its aim or goal. Leaders have to get the right systems and structures in place and also influence organisational members to work within them.
- *Strategic change* to align an organisation in the pursuit of its strategy. How should change be led? Here key questions include the speed and comprehensiveness of change.

With regard to strategy-in-action, the *Exploring Strategy* Framework raises the following kinds of questions for Tesla. What kind of structure does Tesla need in order to organise its various activities and continue to grow in the future? Are Tesla's systems adequate to allow its strategies to be implemented effectively? As Tesla grows, what sort of leadership is appropriate and how should any organisational changes that may be necessary be managed?

Thus the *Exploring Strategy* Framework offers you a comprehensive way for analysing an organisation's position, considering alternative choices, and selecting and implementing strategies. This review of the main elements of the framework now allows us to refine and extend our earlier broad definition of strategy in Section 1.1 to state that **'Strategy is the long term direction of an organisation, formed by choices and actions about its resources and scope, in order to create advantageous positions relative to competitors and peers in changing environmental and stakeholder contexts'.** For more in-depth coverage of strategic planning and practice, see the authors' *Exploring Strategy*, 12th edition.

1.4 Strategy development processes

The previous section introduced strategic position, strategic choices and strategy in action. However, strategies do not always develop in a logical sequence of analysis, choice and action. There are two broad accounts of strategy development:

- The *rational-analytic view* of strategy development is the conventional account. Here strategies are developed through rational and analytical processes, led typically by top managers. These processes result in a strategic plan, typically containing the kind of elements outlined in Table 1.1. There is a linear sequence. The typical plan begins with statements of the overall strategy and mission, vision and objectives. Then there are macro-environmental and industry analyses followed by capability analysis. Next, a range of strategic options will be evaluated, with one proposed ahead of the others. The final elements of a strategic plan are putting the resources in place and addressing the key change processes. Each of these elements is covered in chapters in this book. The basis assumption in this rational-analytic view is that strategies are typically *intended*, in other words the product of deliberate choices. This rational-analytical view is associated with theorists such as Alfred Chandler and Michael Porter, in Figure 1.1.

- The *emergent strategy* view is the alternative broad explanation of how strategies develop. In this view, strategies often do not simply develop as intended or planned, but tend to emerge in organisations over time as a result of ad hoc, incremental or even accidental actions. Good ideas and opportunities often come from practical experience at the bottom of the organisation, not just from management at the top. Even the best-laid plans may need to be abandoned as new opportunities arise or the organisation learns from the marketplace. Learning from experience can be as valuable as planning in advance. This emergent view is particularly associated with Henry Mintzberg, referenced in Figure 1.1. The non-linear nature of the *Exploring Strategy* Model (Figure 1.3) reflects the possible role of emergent strategy.

The rational-analytic and emergent views of strategy development are not mutually exclusive. Intended strategies can often succeed, especially in stable markets where there are few surprises. Moreover, an organisation's key stakeholders – employees, owners, customers, regulators and so on – will typically want to see evidence of deliberate strategy-making: it is rarely acceptable to say that everything is simply emergent. The tools and concepts throughout the book are particularly helpful in this deliberate strategy-making. But still it is wise to be open as well to the possibilities of emergence. Inflexible plans can hinder learning and prevent the seizing of opportunities. Moreover, strategic choices do not always come about as a result of simple rational analysis: cultural and political processes in organisations can also drive changes in strategy (see Chapter 5).

Table 1.1   Key elements in a strategic plan[9]

The strategy statement (Chapter 1)
Mission, vision and objectives (Chapter 1)
Macro-environment analysis (Chapter 2)
Industry and sector analysis (Chapter 3)
Resources and capability analysis (Chapter 4)
Strategic options and proposed strategies (Chapters 5–8)
Key actions (Chapter 9)

Source: A practical introduction to strategic planning is V. Evans, FT Essential Guide to Developing a Business Strategy: How to Use Strategic Planning to Start Up or Grow Your Business, FT Publishing International, 2013.

This book allows for both the rational-analytical view and the emergent view. It is generally sensible for managers to start with a rational-analytical approach, and this is what many of the tools and concepts in this book are designed to help with. However, it is also sensible to allow for emergence and learning in action, and the roles of culture and politics in organisations should not be overlooked. Emergence is likely to have played a bigger role in Tesla, for instance, than is first apparent (Illustration 1.1).

Summary

- The basic definition of strategy is that it is *the long-term direction* of an organisation.
- The work of strategy is to define and express the purpose of an organisation through its *mission, vision, values* and *objectives*.
- A *strategy statement* should include an organisation's *goals*, *scope* of activities and the *advantages* or *capabilities* it brings to these goals and activities.
- *Corporate-level strategy* is concerned with an organisation's overall scope; *business-level strategy* is concerned with how to compete; and *functional strategy* is concerned with how corporate- and business-level strategies are actually delivered.
- The *Exploring Strategy* Framework has three major elements: understanding the *strategic position*, making *strategic choices* for the future and managing *strategy-in-action*.
- Strategy develops through *rational-analytic* and *emergent* processes.

Recommended key readings

It is always useful to read around a topic. As well as the specific references below, we particularly highlight:

- For an engaging review of the recent evolution of strategy, read R. Whittington, *Opening Strategy: Professional Strategists and Practice Change 1960 to today*, Oxford University Press, 2019.
- Two stimulating overviews of strategic thinking in general, aimed particularly at practising managers, are C. Montgomery, *The Strategist: Be the Leader your Business Needs*, Harper Business, 2012; and R. Rumelt, *Good Strategy/Bad Strategy: The Difference and Why it Matters*, Crown Business, 2011.

- For contemporary developments in strategy practice, see business newspapers such as the *Caixin* and *China Daily* (China), *Financial Times* (UK), *Handelsblatt* (Germany), *Les Echos* (France), *Nihon Keizai Shimbun* (Japan), *The Economic Times* (India) and the *Wall Street Journal* (US), and business magazines such as *Business Week*, *The Economist*, *L'Expansion* and *Manager-Magazin*. Several of these have well-informed Asian editions. See also the websites of the leading strategy consulting firms: www.mckinsey. com; www.bcg.com; www.bain.com.

References

1. The question 'What is strategy?' is discussed in R. Whittington, *What Is Strategy – and Does it Matter?*, International Thomson, 1993/2000 and M.E. Porter, 'What is strategy?', *Harvard Business Review*, November–December 1996, pp. 61–78.
2. T. Zenger, 'What is the theory of your firm', *Harvard Business Review,* June, 2013, pp. 72–80.
3. Cynthia A. Montgomery, 'Putting leadership back into strategy', *Harvard Business Review*, January 2008, pp. 54–60.
4. See J. Collins and J. Porras, *Built to Last: Successful Habits of Visionary Companies*, Harper Business, 2002.
5. J. Collins and J. Porras, 'Building your company's vision', *Harvard Business Review,* September–October, 1996, pp. 65–77.
6. See Sayan Chatterjee, 'Core objectives: clarity in designing strategy', *California Management Review*, vol. 47, no. 2, 2005, pp. 33–49. For some advantages of ambiguity, see J. Sillince, P. Jarzabkowski and D. Shaw, 'Shaping strategic action through the

rhetorical construction and exploitation of ambiguity', *Organization Science,* vol. 22, no. 2 (2011), pp. 1–21.

7. For example, see B. Bartkus, M. Glassman and B. McAfee, 'Mission statements: are they smoke and mirrors?', *Business Horizons*, vol. 43, no. 6 (2000), pp. 23–28.

8. D. Collis and M. Rukstad, 'Can you say what your strategy is?,' *Harvard Business Review*, April 2008, pp. 63–73.

9. A practical introduction to strategic planning is V. Evans, *FT Essential Guide to Developing a Business Strategy: How to Use Strategic Planning to Start Up or Grow Your Business*, FT Publishing International, 2013.

Case example
The rise of a unicorn: Airbnb

Duncan Angwin

Source: AlesiaKan/Shutterstock

A unicorn is a mythical animal that is very rare, difficult to tame, and often referred to by the US venture capital industry to describe a start-up company whose valuation exceeds $1bn dollars. For instance, Airbnb, founded in 2007, and valued at $38bn in 2018, is the most valuable 'unicorn', and a symbol of the sharing economy.[1] How could this start-up become so successful, so fast, and is it sustainable?

Origins

The founders of Airbnb, Joe Gebbia and Brian Chesky, first met at Rhode Island School of Design. Five years later, both aged 27, they were struggling to pay their rent when a design conference came to San Francisco. All the hotels were fully booked, so they set up a simple website with pictures of their loft-turned-lodging space – complete with three air mattresses on the floor and the promise of a home-cooked breakfast in the morning. This site got them their first three paying guests at $80 each. They realised it could be the start of something big. Both wanted to be entrepreneurs and Brian already had some experience with designing a product and website.[2] They created a website: airbedandbreakfast.com.

Targeting conferences and festivals across America they got local people to list their rooms on the website. When, in 2008, Barack Obama was to speak in Denver at the Democratic Party National Convention where 80,000 people were expected to attend, Joe and Brian thought there would be a hotel room shortage. They recorded 800 listings in one week. However it did not make any money. To survive they had to make use of their entrepreneurial skills, buying cereal in bulk and designing packaging such as 'Obama's O's' and 'Cap'n McCain' cereal, jokey references to the two Presidential candidates of the year. However, adding a payment facility to their website allowed them to charge up to 15 per cent of the booking (host pays 3 per cent; traveller 6–12 per cent). By April 2009 they were breaking even.

Growth

Attracting funding for their start-up was not easy. Investors saw them as designers, which did not fit the traditional start-up profile and they thought there would be little demand for listings mostly advertising sleeping on airbeds.

Nonetheless, in 2009 Airbnb received its first funding of $20,000 from angel investor, Harminder Graham, co-founder of Y Combinator (a start-up mentoring programme) who was impressed with their inventiveness and tenacity. The company was renamed Airbnb and it provided an app and website that connects people seeking lodging with renters who have listed their personal houses, apartments, guest rooms on either platform. Further funding followed, allowing the company to expand to 8,000 cities worldwide, increase the number of employees to 500 and to move out of the founders' flat – where staff had been making sales calls from the bathroom and holding conferences in the kitchen – to offices in the design district of San Francisco.

In 2010 Airbnb was experiencing sluggish listings in New York and Joe and Brian flew out to try to understand the problem. They realised hosts were presenting their properties poorly so they rented a $5,000 camera and took as many photos of New York apartments as possible. Listings in the city suddenly doubled. From there on hosts could automatically schedule a professional photographer. This was an immediate hit and by 2012 there were 20,000 freelance photographers being employed by Airbnb around the world. The photos also built trust for guests as they verified addresses. The company also introduced Airbnb Social Connections, which leverages users' social graphs via Facebook Connect. This shows whether friends have stayed with or are friends with the host and allows guests to search for hosts based on

Figure 1 Airbnb early growth story

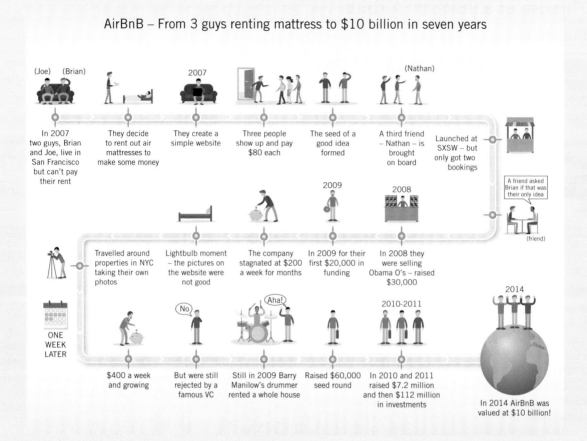

AirBnB – From 3 guys renting mattress to $10 billion in seven years

Airbnb proved attractive to guests and hosts as its listings were far superior to others available at the time, such as Craigslist. They were more personal, with better descriptions and nicer photos. The rooms were cheaper than equivalent ones at hotels and had more of a personal flavour. For instance in a recent stay in Paris a user noted the host had left a selection of food in the refrigerator, a bottle of wine on the counter for her guests and a welcoming note suggesting good places nearby to eat out and convenience shops. Staying in another person's apartment makes the visitor feel far more at home than an anonymous hotel room. For many young guests and hosts, Airbnb fitted into the contemporary sharing culture exemplified by Easy car club, where users can rent their car to others, and Girl Meets Dress, that allows girls to borrow and lend their dresses for special occasions. For hosts, rents provide a source of income to help pay for soaring accommodation costs in many major cities.

other characteristics, like alma mater. Again this reassured potential guests.

With further venture funding in 2011 Airbnb expanded through acquisitions acquiring their largest UK-based competitor Crashpadder just before the 2012 Summer Olympics in London. Offices were opened in Paris, Barcelona and Milan. Airbnb's growth was explosive with a higher valuation than Hyatt and Wyndham hotel groups by 2014 and more guest nights booked than Hilton Hotels (see Figure 2). By 2016 Airbnb was valued at $25bn – more than any other hotel group. The company justified its valuation by claiming that, when its price ($25bn) to sales ratio of 27.8 (based on estimated sales of $900 m for 2015) is divided by its high growth rate of 113 per cent per year, the resulting value for the group is broadly in line with the sector.[3] Airbnb forecasts $10bn of revenues by 2020, with $3bn of profits before tax.

Figure 2 Guest arrivals

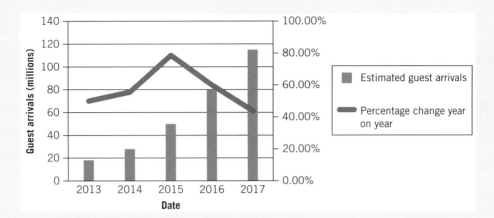

Managing growth

CEO Brian Cesky penned a memo in 2013 to his top management team, as follows:[4]

> **Hey team,**
>
> **Our next team meeting is dedicated to Core Values, which are essential to building our culture. It occurred to me that before this meeting, I should write you a short letter on why culture is so important to [co-founders] Joe, Nate, and me.**
>
> **. . . In 2012, we invited Peter Thiel [a major investor] to our office. This was late last year, and we were in the Berlin room showing him various metrics. Midway through the conversation, I asked him what was the single most important piece of advice he had for us.**
>
> **He replied, 'Don't f*** up the culture.'**
>
> **This wasn't what we were expecting from someone who just gave us $150m. I asked him to elaborate on this. He said one of the reasons he invested in us was our culture. But he had a somewhat cynical view that it was practically inevitable once a company gets to a certain size to 'f*** it up.**

Source: Founder and CEO Brian Cesky penned a memo in 2013

Accordingly, the company began to manage its culture more deliberately. For example, Joe had become concerned that as the company grew, it had become less open to dialogue. To encourage more discussion, he invented the notion of 'elephants, dead fish and vomit'. As he explains: 'Elephants are the big things in the room that nobody is talking about, dead fish are the things that happened a few years ago that people can't get over, and vomit is that sometimes people just need to get something off their mind and

you need someone to just sit there and listen.'[5] All three need to be aired. Airbnb also established a series of annual meetings called One Airbnb, bringing together employees (called 'Airfam') from all around the world to the San Francisco base for four-day conferences at which everyone can meet the founders, discuss strategy and also talk about both their work roles and their hobbies. The company has 'ground control' staff in every office in the world dedicated to making the company culture 'come alive', organising pop-up birthday celebrations, anniversary parties or baby showers. The company is rigorous in its recruitment policy, committed to hiring 'missionaries, not mercenaries'.

At the same time, the founders had begun to ask themselves again: 'What is our mission? What is the big idea that truly defines Airbnb?' As they recalled in their own words: 'It turns out the answer was right in front of us. For so long, people thought Airbnb was about renting houses. But really, we're about home. You see, a house is just a space, but a home is where you belong. And what makes this global community so special is that for the very first time, you can belong anywhere. That is the idea at the core of our company.'[6]

Airbnb in 2018

In 2018, Airbnb had an estimated 5.3 million listings in 81,000 cities in 191 countries, with an estimated 115 million guest arrivals in 2017 (see Figure 2). Anyone anywhere in the world can list spare space from a room to a tree house, from a castle to an island in Fiji, with prices ranging from $50 to $2000 per night. The headquarters' walls were covered with world maps dotted with hundreds of coloured pins, charting world domination. Airbnb was so popular that one of their rooms was booked every two seconds.[7]

The company was now focused on the whole travel trip with an emphasis on delivering local experiences. This focus on hospitality was not just about where you stay, but what you do – and whom you do it with – while you're there. To this end they introduced Airbnb Neighbourhoods and local lounges, partnering with local coffee shops that can offer free wifi, a comfortable setting and local guidebooks. They also acquired a small start-up that connects guests with locals who can answer their questions. They also offer cleaning services.

Airbnb was providing a strong challenge to hotels with prices 30–80 per cent lower than local operators. San Francisco hotels were having to slash prices to protect their occupancy rates. Incumbents in the industry fought back by arguing Airbnb rooms were dangerous and unsafe as they were unregulated. Although one must have a permit to rent for under 30 days, San Francisco residents were still illegally listing personal homes and apartments. Similar problems were being experienced in New York where an 'illegal hotel law' was passed preventing people from subletting apartments for less than 29 days and other cities across the world including Barcelona and Amsterdam and Japan imposed stringent regulations. In the EU Airbnb has been given an ultimatum about the lack of price transparency and in the background there are question marks over hosts not paying tax on earnings.

During 2016, Airbnb redesigned its website and apps with subtle animations and flashier imagery to make a transition from a hotel service to a lifestyle brand. Airbnb wanted their logo to be seen on a variety of products, houses and businesses, so people understood that owners supported their ideal and their brand. Airbnb's focus was now firmly on 'belonging'. This rebranding may not have been before time, as competition was brewing in the US from vacation rental site HomeAway Inc. (owned by Expedia), Roomorama, HouseTrip, Flipkey and Travel Advisor holiday rentals. Indeed websites have sprung up such as www.airbnbhell.com that list a string of internet accommodation providers. Nonetheless, at the time of writing Airbnb was rumoured to be the hottest IPO (an initial public offering of its stock to investors) tip for 2020.

References
1. Forbes.com (2018) 'As a rare profitable unicorn, Airbnb appears to be worth at least $38 Billion', Trefis team, 11 May.
2. Salter, J. (2012) 'Airbnb: The story behind the $1.3bn room-letting website', *The Telegraph,* 7 September; Lee A. (2013) 'Welcome To The Unicorn Club: Learning From Billion-Dollar Startups', *Techcrunch,* 2 November, https://techcrunch.com/2013/11/02/welcome-to-the-unicorn-club/.
3. A ratio of price/sales to revenue growth rate gives Airbnb a figure of 24.6 against Marriott at 19.2, Wyndham at 34.1 and Expedia at 12.2. (Guest post, 'Why that crazy-high AirBnB valuation is fair', www.valuewalk.com, 1 January 2016).
4. https://medium.com/@bchesky/dont-fuck-up-the-culture-597cde9ee9d4\#.5wd5kwtdm.
5. B. Clune, 'How Airbnb is building its culture through belonging', *Culture Zine.*
6. http://blog.airbnb.com/belong-anywhere/.
7. Zacks.com (2015) 'Investing in resting: is Airbnb a top 2016 IPO candidate?' 11 December 2015.

Questions

1 Sticking to the 35-word limit suggested by Collis and Rukstad in Section 1.2.3, what strategy statement would you propose for Airbnb?

2 Carry out a 'three-horizons' analysis (Section 1.2.1) of Airbnb, in terms of both existing activities and possible future ones. How might this analysis affect its future strategic direction?

3 Using the headings of environment, strategic capability, strategic purpose and culture seen in Section 1.3.1, identify key positioning issues for Airbnb and consider their relative importance.

4 Following on from the previous questions and making use of Section 1.3.2, what alternative strategies do you see for Airbnb?

5 Converting good strategic thinking into action can be a challenge: examine how Airbnb has achieved this by considering the elements seen in Section 1.3.3.

Chapter 2
Macro-environment analysis

Key terms

Learning outcomes

After reading this chapter, you should be able to:

- Analyse the broad macro-environment of organisations in terms of *political, economic, social, technological, ecological* and *legal* factors *(PESTEL)*.

- Evaluate different approaches to environmental *forecasting*.

- Construct alternative *scenarios* in order to address possible environmental changes.

2.1 Introduction

Organisations depend upon their environments for their survival. Here environments are being understood in their widest sense – to include political, economic, social, technological and legal factors as well as ecological ones. These environmental factors supply both opportunities and threats. Legal quarantines imposed during the 2020 covid-19 crisis hurt traditional cinemas and theatres, but boosted streaming services such as Netflix. The social clustering of millennials in high-rent cities has prompted the emergence of new co-living businesses, such as Roomi and Bedly, offering cheap and flexible accommodation. Drone technologies are creating opportunities ranging from audit for accounting firms such as Deloitte and Ernst & Young to wildlife protection in Africa. It is clearly important that entrepreneurs and managers analyse their environments as carefully as they can in order to anticipate and – if possible – take advantage of such environmental changes.

Environments can be considered in terms of a series of 'layers', as summarised in Figure 2.1. This chapter focuses on organisations' *macro-environments*, the outermost layer. **The macro-environment consists of broad environmental factors that impact to a greater or lesser extent many organisations, industries and sectors.** For example, the effects of macro-environmental factors such as the internet, economic growth rates, climate change and aging populations go far beyond one industry or sector, impacting a wide range of activities from tourism to agriculture. The *industry*, or *sector*, makes up the next layer within this broad macro-environment. This layer consists of organisations producing the same sorts of products or services, for example the automobile industry or the healthcare sector. The third layer is that of specific *competitors and markets* immediately surrounding organisations. For a car company like Nissan, this layer would include competitors such as Ford and Volkswagen; for a hospital, competitors would include other hospitals and markets would be types of patients. Whereas this chapter focuses on the macro-environment, Chapter 3 will analyse industries and sectors and competitors and markets. Chapters 4 and 5 examine the individual organisations at the heart of Figure 2.1.

Figure 2.1 Layers of the business environment

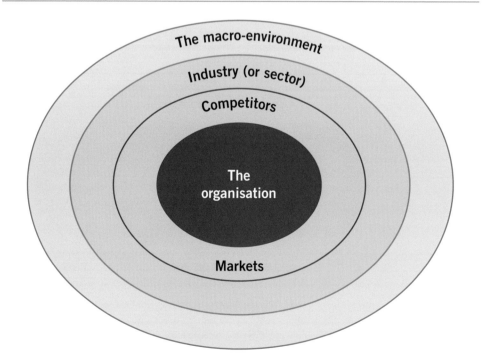

The chapter is organised in three main sections:

- *PESTEL* factors examine macro-environmental factors according to six key types: political, economic, social, technological, ecological and legal.
- *Forecasting*, which aims to predict the future environment, with varying degrees of precision or certainty. Macro-environmental forecasting draws on PESTEL analysis and often makes use of three conceptual tools: *megatrends, inflexion points* and *weak signals.*
- *Scenario analysis* – a technique that develops plausible alternative views of how the environment might develop in the future. Scenario analysis differs from forecasting because it avoids predictions about the future; it is more about *learning* different possibilities for environmental change.

2.2 PESTEL analysis

PESTEL analysis highlights six environmental factors in particular: political, economic, social, technological, ecological and legal. This list underlines that the environment includes not only the economics of markets, but also *nonmarket* factors, such as interactions with non-government organisations (NGOs), politicians, regulators, campaign groups and the media.

The following sections consider each of the PESTEL elements in turn, providing key analytical concepts and frameworks for each. Meanwhile, Illustration 2.1 on the so-called FANGs provides examples of various PESTEL factors, showing how in practice they often interrelate.

2.2.1 Politics

The political element of PESTEL highlights the role of the state and other political factors in the macro-environment. For every organisation it is helpful to identify systematically:

- The role of the *state*: in many countries and sectors the state is often important as a direct economic actor, for instance as a customer, supplier, owner or regulator of businesses.
- Exposure to *civil society* organisations: civil society comprises a whole range of organisations that are liable to raise political issues, including political lobbyists, campaign groups, social media or traditional media.

Where the state is important or exposure to civil society organisations is high, then political factors should be important in any PESTEL analysis.

Figure 2.2 describes industries according to the two dimensions of the role of the state and exposure to civil society organisations. To take one example from Figure 2.2, the defence industry faces a highly politicised environment. Defence companies typically have high direct state involvement: national armed services are of course key customers, while states are often owners of their national defence companies. At the same time, defence companies are often highly exposed to groups from civil society, for instance campaigners against the international arms trade. By contrast, food companies face less direct state involvement: most food companies are privately owned and operate in private-sector markets. However, the political environment is still important for food companies, as they are typically exposed to pressures from civil society in the form of fair trade campaigners, labour rights organisations and health lobbying groups. Canals are often state-owned, for instance in France, but nowadays are not highly exposed to political pressures from civil society organisations because of their declining importance. Industries can rapidly change positions: thus revelations about internet monitoring by national security agencies has placed companies such as Amazon and Facebook much more under scrutiny by governments, civil liberties groups and consumers (see Illustration 2.1).

Illustration 2.1 A PESTEL for the FANGs

In 2018, US technology giants were facing a toughening macro-environment.

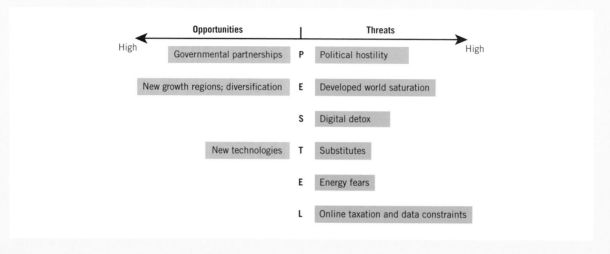

During mid-2018, the so-called FANG+ stock market index (including Facebook, Amazon, Netflix and Alphabet/Google) fell by more than 10 per cent. A PESTEL analysis helps to explain why.

PESTEL analyses can be done using published sources (e.g. company annual reports, media articles and consultants' reports) or more extensively by direct discussion with managers, customers, suppliers, consultants, academics, government officials and financial analysts. It is important not to rely just on an organisation's managers, who may have limited views. A PESTEL analysis of the four main FANG companies based on published sources shows a growing preponderance of macro-environmental threats over opportunities (specific industry analysis will be dealt with in Chapter 3). In the figure above, the scale of Opportunities and Threats on each of the PESTEL dimensions is indicated by the relative extent of the bars. Just taking some issues for illustration, the figure shows more and longer bars on the Threats side than the Opportunities side. Thus:

- *Political*: FANG companies face increasing political hostility. India has banned Facebook's Free Basics, a free but restricted internet service. The United Kingdom is planning specific taxes for online retailers such as Amazon.
- *Economic*: FANG companies are now facing market saturation in developed markets. In 2018, Netflix missed its subscriber growth targets by 1 million, and in the USA, the costs required to acquire each new subscriber have doubled from $60 to $120 (€105; £90.00). Netflix is spending big now on producing new content specifically for international markets. Facebook, facing declining usage in Europe, is diversifying into new activities such as digital dating.

- *Social*: growing awareness of internet addiction has increased consumer willingness to undertake digital detoxes. In 2018, Google launched a 'Digital Wellbeing' app, with user-friendly dashboards giving a detailed view on how users spend their time.
- *Technological*: autonomous planes and balloons are being developed by Facebook and Alphabet to deliver internet access to large populations in the developing world. New technologies may provide substitutes, as Telegram and Signal provide encrypted alternatives to Facebook Messenger.
- *Ecological*: the FANGs are big energy consumers, with cloud computing accounting for 2 per cent of energy consumption in the USA, and Google using as much power as San Francisco.
- *Legal*: Amazon alone accounts for nearly half of US retail spending, and 80 million Americans are part of its Prime membership programme. Both in the US and Europe, there is an increasing threat of legal regulation to curb the market power of Amazon and other FANG companies.

Questions

1 Taking one of the FANG companies, what do you think is its greatest macro-environmental threat, and what is its greatest macro-environmental opportunity?

2 Have the opportunities and threats changed since 2018? How would you update this analysis?

Figure 2.2 The political environment

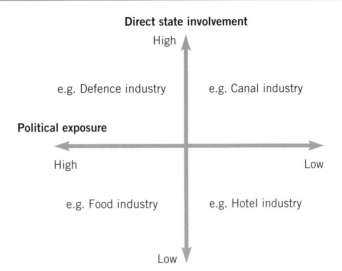

2.2.2 Economics

The macro-environment is also influenced by macro-economic factors such as currency exchange rates, interest rates and fluctuating economic growth rates around the world. It is important for an organisation to understand how its markets are affected by the prosperity of the economy as a whole. Managers should have a view on how changing exchange rates may affect viability in export markets and vulnerability to imports. They should keep an eye on changing interest rates, especially if they have to borrow to fund strategic investments. They should understand how economic growth rates rise or fall over time. There are many public sources of economic forecasts that can help in predicting the movement of key economic indicators, though these are often prone to error because of unexpected economic shocks (consider the covid-19 shock of 2020).[1]

A key concept for analysing macro-economic trends is the *economic cycle*. Despite the possibility of unexpected shocks, economic growth rates have an underlying tendency to rise and fall in cycles: several years of good growth are likely to be followed by a couple of years or so of lower or even negative growth. These cycles link to other important economic variables (Figure 2.3). For example, rises in interest rates are likely to decrease economic growth rates as consumers cut back on credit cards and businesses borrow less for investment. Awareness of cycles reinforces an important pattern in the macro-environment: good economic times do not last forever, while bad economic times lead eventually to recovery. The key is to identify cyclical turning points. It is very unwise to borrow money to invest in extra capacity at the top of a cyclical upswing.

Some industries are particularly vulnerable to economic cycles, for example:

- *Discretionary spend* industries: where purchasers can easily put off their spending for a year or so, there tend to be strong cyclical effects. Thus demand for furniture, restaurants and cars tends be highly cyclical because people can easily delay or curtail spending on these for a while. After a period of reduced spending, there is liable to be a strong upturn as pent-up demand is finally released into the market.

- *High fixed cost* industries: industries such as airlines, hotels and steel suffer from economic downturns because high fixed costs in plant, equipment or labour tend to encourage competitive price-cutting to ensure maximum capacity utilisation when demand is low. For example, an airline might try to fill its seats in the face of falling demand simply by offering cheap tickets. If its competitors do the same, the resulting price-war will result in low profits for all the airlines.

Figure 2.3 Economic cycles and strategic investments

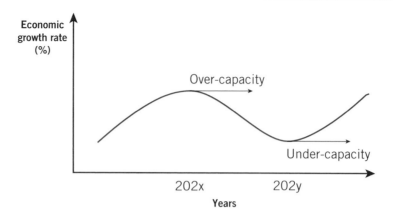

2.2.3 Social

The *social* elements of the macro-environment have at least two impacts upon organisations. First, they can influence the specific nature of demand and supply, within the overall economic growth rate. Second, they can shape the innovativeness, power and effectiveness of organisations.

In the first place, there are a number of key aspects of the social environment that can shape demand and supply. These can be analysed under the following four headings:

- *Demographics.* For example, the ageing populations in many Western societies create opportunities and threats for both private and public sectors. There is increasing demand for services for the elderly, but diminishing supplies of young labour to look after them.

- *Distribution.* Changes in wealth distribution influence the relative sizes of markets. Thus the concentration of wealth in the hands of elites over the last 20 years has constrained some categories of 'middle-class' consumption, while enlarging markets for certain luxury goods.

- *Geography.* Industries and markets can be concentrated in particular locations. In the United Kingdom, economic growth has in recent decades been much faster in the London area than in the rest of the country. Similarly, industries often form 'clusters' in particular locations: thus there are high concentrations of scientists and engineers in California's Silicon Valley.[2]

- *Culture.* Changing cultural attitudes can also raise strategic challenges. For example, new ethical attitudes are challenging profit-maximising investment strategies in the financial services industry. Changing cultural attitudes can be linked to changing demographics. Thus the rise of 'digital natives' (generations born after the 1980s, and thus from childhood immersed in digital technologies) is changing expectations about media, consumption and education.

A second important social aspect of the macro-environment is organisational *networks*, often reliant on social as well as economic linkages (see Figure 2.4). For a new hi-technology enterprise, important network connections might be research links to leading universities, friendships with leaders in other innovative firms, or longstanding relationships with respected venture capitalists. It is important to understand an organisation's position in its networks because of their implications for effectiveness, innovativeness and power. Three factors are significant here:

Figure 2.4 Sociogram of networks within an organisational field

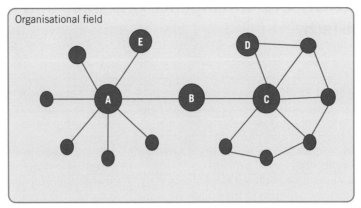

C's immediate network is denser than A's; B is a broker; A is a more central hub than C.

- *Network density* typically increases network effectiveness. Density refers to the number of interconnections between members in the network map. Effectiveness is increased by density because the more interconnections there are, the better the sharing of new ideas between network members. Everybody is talking to each other, and nobody with potentially useful information is isolated. It is easier to mobilise the whole network in support of new initiatives. Being part of a dense network is a source of potential advantage.

- *Broker positions*, which connect otherwise separate groups of organisations, are often associated with innovativeness. Brokers can link valuable information from one group of organisations with valuable information from the other group. Because they provide the connection between the two groups, they are able to exploit this combination of information before anybody else. Being a broker therefore increases the capacity to innovate.

- *Central hub positions* typically provide power within networks. A central hub connects many organisations. Hubs have power because network members rely on them for interconnection with other members. Hubs are also potentially innovative because they can collect ideas from the whole network, and they hear about what is going on in one part of the network before most other parts. Being a hub is therefore another source of advantage.

Environmental analysis therefore should identify key networks in which organisations participate, assess the density of these networks and consider the extent to which an organisation is a hub or broker. See Illustration 2.2 for an exploration of hubs and brokers in the Israeli Hi-Tech sector.

2.2.4 Technology

Further important elements within the macro-environment are *technologies* such as the internet, nanotechnology or new composite materials, whose impacts can spread far beyond single industries. As in the case of internet streaming, new technologies can open up opportunities for some organisations (e.g. Spotify and YouTube), while challenging others (traditional music and broadcasting companies).

It is useful to construct technology roadmaps for their sectors going forward.[3] *Technology roadmaps* project into the future various product or service demands, identify technology alternatives to meet these demands, select the most promising alternatives and

Illustration 2.2 Intelligence Unit 8200 and the Small World of Israeli Hi-Tech

Israel, a nation of just 8 million people, exports more than $6bn worth of cybersecurity products a year, accounting for about 10 per cent of the global cybersecurity market. At the heart of this success is Unit 8200, the largest unit of the Israeli Defence Forces and the equivalent of America's National Security Agency.

Unit 8200's alumni have produced more hi-tech start-ups per capita than the University of Stanford. Some of the successful companies originating with Unit 8200 include Check Point, with 2,900 employees and a pioneer in Virtual Private Networks; NICE Systems, with 2,700 employees and a pioneer in telephone recording technology; and Palo Alto Networks, with 3,000 employees and a pioneer in computer firewall technology. Unit 8200 recruits are drawn from young Israelis doing their national military service. Recruitment into Unit 8200 is highly selective (in the Israeli Defence Force, only pilot training is harder to enter) and favours skilled computer science students and linguists. Recruits come disproportionately from the richer and more highly educated Tel Aviv area of Israel, and from elite schools such as Leyada, the semi-private Hebrew University High School in Jerusalem (where the founder of Check Point was a student). Alumni of Unit 8200 go not only into hi-tech business; many pursue successful careers in politics, the judiciary, the media and academia. For example, the former CEO of NICE Systems became director general of the Israeli Ministry of Finance.

Unit 8200's young recruits are intensively trained and work long hours in small groups applying the latest technology to security matters that might involve life and death. To maximise security, Unit 8200's technology systems – from analytics to data mining, intercept and intelligence management – are designed and built in-house. This experience prepares Unit 8200 alumni well for futures in hi-tech business. Avi Hasson, Chief Scientist at the Israeli Economy Ministry and himself an alumnus of Unit 8200, describes the working environment: 'When it comes to managing a startup, Unit 8200 is a fantastic school. . . .

The unit encourages independent thought. It's something that was adopted later by many companies, a little like the culture in Google, in which good ideas can come from anywhere.'

Because recruitment in hi-tech tends to favour a 'buddy-system', alumni are often sought out for employment by other alumni. Experience of this intense, elitist organisation in the formative years of youth creates strong social bonds. The 8200 alumni association has more than 15,000 members, and hosts networking events and community outreach programmes, including start-up accelerators.

By 2020, Unit 8200 is due to move adjacent to the Advanced Technology Park at Be'er Sheva in southern Israel's Negev Desert. In 2013, Israel's President Benjamin Netanyahu had declared that Be'er Sheva would become the 'cybercenter of the Western hemisphere'. Be'er Sheva already had the advantage of the local Ben-Gurion University and its Cyber Security Research Centre. The National Cyber Bureau, a newly created agency advising the government on cyber policies, moved to Be'er Sheva in 2015. Companies already with operations in the Advanced Technology Park included many leading foreign firms such as Deutsche Telecom, IBM, Lockheed Martin, Oracle, PayPal and EMC. Venture capital firm JVP, with more than $1bn funding available, was also running a local 'cyberincubator' for start-ups. One of its first ventures was sold to PayPal.

Sources: Haaretz, 18 April and 24 April 2015; *Financial Times*, 10 July 2015; TechCrunch, 18 March 2015

Questions

1 Identify at least one important hub and one important broker in the Unit 8200 network.

2 If you were a foreign cybersecurity company, what would you do to access Israel's expertise?

Figure 2.5 Technology roadmap for the Internet of Things

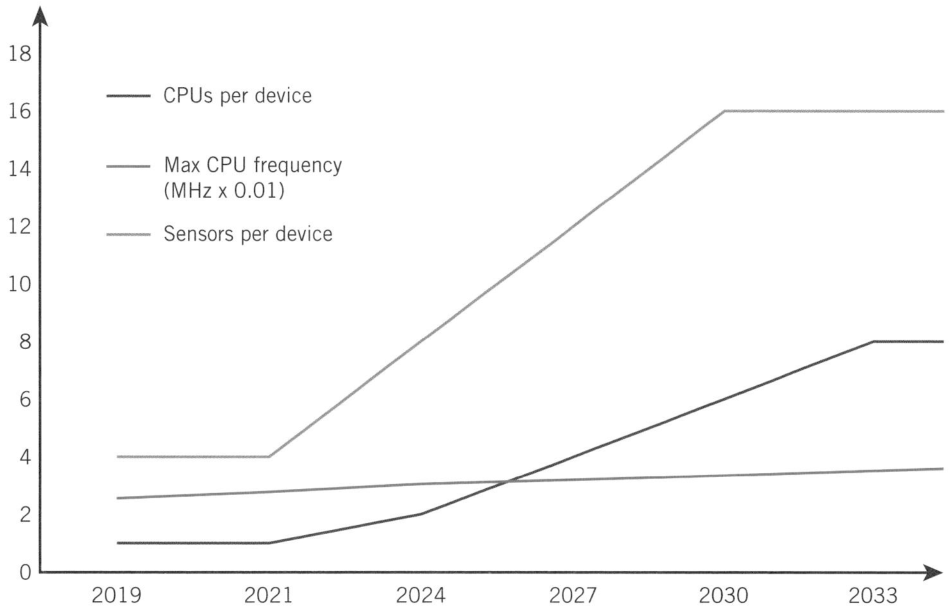

Source: Drawn from data extracted from the International Roadmap for Devices and Systems, 2018 edition, Institute for Electronics and Electrical Engineers.

then offer a timeline for their development. Thus they provide good indicators of future technological developments. Figure 2.5 provides a simplified technology roadmap for the Internet of Things, providing connectivity for devices from fridges to heart monitors: in the period to 2033, this roadmap forecasts rapid progress in the number of Central Processing Units (CPUs) and sensors per device, but less progress in CPU frequency, a measure of processing speed. This kind of roadmap has implications for product design strategies in industries far beyond the electronics industry, for instance architecture, domestic appliances and healthcare.

2.2.5 Ecological

Within the PESTEL framework, *ecological* stands specifically for 'green' macro-environmental issues, such as pollution, waste and climate change. Environmental regulations can impose additional costs, for example pollution controls, but they can also be a source of opportunity, for example the new businesses that emerged around mobile phone recycling.

When considering ecological issues in the macro-environment, there are three sorts of challenges that organisations may need to meet:[4]

- *Direct pollution* obligations are an obvious challenge, and nowadays typically involve not just cleaning up 'at the end of the pipe' (for example, disposing of waste by-products safely), but also minimising the production of pollutants in the first place. Having clean processes for supply, production and distribution is generally better than managing the consequences of polluting after the fact.

- *Product stewardship* refers to managing ecological issues through both the organisation's entire value chain and the whole life cycle of the firm's products. Stewardship here might involve responsibility for the ecological impact of external suppliers or final end-users. It will also involve responsibility for what happens to products at 'end of life', in other words how they are disposed of when consumers have no more use for them. Thus car manufacturers are increasingly responsible for the recycling and safe disposal of old cars.

- *Sustainable development* is a criterion of increasing importance and refers not simply to reducing environmental damage, but to whether the product or service can be produced indefinitely into the future. This sustainability criterion sets constraints on the over-exploitation of particular sources of raw materials, for instance in developing countries, and often raises issues regarding the economic and social well-being of local communities.

2.2.6 Legal

The final element in a PESTEL analysis of the macro-environment refers to *legal* aspects. These can cover a wide range of topics: for example, labour, environmental and consumer regulation; taxation and reporting requirements; and rules on ownership, competition and corporate governance. In recent years, the relaxation of legal constraints through deregulation has created many new business opportunities, for example for low cost airlines and public sector subcontracting in various countries. However, regulations can also handicap organisations: Illustration 2.3 shows how the e-cigarette company Juul ran into important legal issues as it entered new markets and regulators struggled to keep up with the new technology.

Legal issues form an important part of the *institutional environment* of organisations, by which is meant the formal and informal 'rules of the game'.[5] This concept of institutional environment suggests that it can be useful in a PESTEL analysis to consider not only formal laws and regulations but also more informal norms: the 'L' can be stretched to cover all types of rule, formal and informal. Informal rules are patterns of expected ('normal') behaviour that are hard to ignore. Thus, regardless of the law, there are fairly explicit norms regarding proper respect for the ecological environment. Organisations ignoring these norms would risk outrage among consumers or employees, whatever the legal situation.

The legal environment varies widely between sectors and countries. The charitable sector, for example, has different informal norms to the private sector. In some countries, both the formal and informal rules are stricter with regard to debt, for example. Within the United States, there is both legal and normative variation between states with regard to guns. When entering any market, it is important to appraise the legal environment in the widest sense and analyse the direction in which it is going.

As can be imagined, analysing these six PESTEL factors, together with their interrelationships, can produce long and complex lists of issues. Rather than getting overwhelmed by a multitude of details, it is necessary to step back to identify the *key drivers for change* in a particular context.[6] **Key drivers for change are the environmental factors likely to have a high impact on industries and sectors, and the success or failure of strategies within them.** Identifying key drivers for change in an industry or sector helps managers to focus on the PESTEL factors that are most important and which must be addressed most urgently. Without a clear sense of the key drivers for change, managers will not be able to take the strategic decisions that allow for effective responses. To return to Illustration 2.1 on the FANGs, it might be determined that political and technological issues are most significant, while ecological issues by and large are less pressing. Prioritising issues is an important final step in PESTEL analysis.

Illustration 2.3 Juul duels with the rules

The fashionable e-cigarette company addresses regulatory environments internationally.

Adam Bowen and James Monsees launched their distinctive Juul e-cigarette in 2015. The product's sleek style led to the Juul becoming known as the 'iPhone of e-cigarettes'. Juul became the most popular e-cigarette in the United States by the end of 2017, and by the end of 2018 commanded a market share of over 70 per cent. In November 2018, the Altria Group (a traditional tobacco company) bought one third of the company for $12.8bn, making the two founders billionaires.

Bowen and Monsees dreamt up their colourful e-cigarettes while pursuing their master's degrees at Stanford University. They were smokers themselves, wanting to free themselves of a dirty and dangerous habit. The Juul design uses a patented form of nicotine salts, at 5 per cent strength, to deliver the quick nicotine peak associated with traditional cigarettes. The website for their company declares its mission as to 'improve the lives of the world's one billion adult smokers by eliminating cigarettes'. Juul claims that it has converted one million adult smokers to Juul products, allegedly a safer product.

Traditional tobacco companies typically rely on television advertising, but Juul initially focused on powerful social marketing campaigns featuring attractive young models and singers on Instagram, Twitter and YouTube. Campaigns went viral, with celebrities such as Bella Hadid posting about Juul. The result was a surge of use among teenagers, attracted also by Juul's sweet flavours and by the fact that its small size and low odours help concealment. In 2018, it was estimated that 3.6 million American schoolchildren were using e-cigarettes, presumptively mostly Juuls.

However, Juul faced increasing criticism from the media, health professionals and regulators over its marketing. Nicotine addiction can cause substantial damage to the developing brain, including lasting impairment to memory and attention span, and increased psychiatric conditions such as depression and anxiety. Four lawsuits were filed in 2018 in the United Sates against Juul by parents, underage users and others, attacking its marketing strategy and safety claims.

Monsees declared: 'Any underage consumers using this product are absolutely a negative for our business. We don't want them. We will never market to them. We never have.' The company launched a new marketing and social media code underlining that its products were not appropriate for young people, switched to using only models aged over 35, restricted the availability of sweet flavours, and made increasing use of traditional television rather than social media channels. At the same time, it began exploring markets overseas.

Juul's first overseas market was Israel, which it entered early in 2018. At the time, Israel had no regulations on e-cigarettes. However, the Israeli government responded within two months, banning Juul on the grounds that its 5 per cent nicotine concentration was two and a half times the level required by the European Union, a norm that Israel freely adopted. Juul next launched in the United Kingdom, still in the European Union, using a formulation with less than 2 per cent nicotine. In late 2018, Juul launched in Canada, where a relaxed legal regime allowed it to offer both 3 and 5 per cent formulations plus a range of flavours larger than the recently restricted ones in the US.

At the same time, Juul was revealed to be considering expansion into Asia. Indonesia was one potential target market, given its fast-growing population of nearly 270 million. Indonesia is also one of a handful of countries which has not signed the World Health Organization's global treaty on tobacco control: two thirds of Indonesian men smoke tobacco daily. Other markets Juul was reportedly considering were Malaysia, Singapore, India, South Korea and the Philippines.

Main sources: *Fast Company*, December/January 2018/19; Reuters Business News, 18 November 2018; Forbes, 16 November 2018; www.juul.com.

Questions

1 Assess the relative importance of formal laws and informal norms for the development of Juul's strategy in the United States.

2 How do you think the different institutional environments internationally have influenced Juul's overseas strategy so far and what kinds of countries do you think it should prioritise?

2.3 Forecasting

In a sense, all strategic decisions involve forecasts about future conditions and outcomes. Thus a manager may decide to invest in new capacity because of a forecast of growing demand (condition), with the expectation that the investment will help capture increased sales (outcome). PESTEL factors will feed into these forecasts, for example in tracking economic cycles or mapping future technologies. However, accurate forecasting is notoriously difficult. Consequently, **forecasting takes three fundamental approaches to the future based on varying degrees of certainty: single-point, range and multiple-futures forecasting.** This section explains these three approaches and also introduces some key concepts that help explore the direction of future change.

2.3.1 Forecast approaches

The three approaches to forecasting are explored in the following and illustrated in Figure 2.6:[7]

- *Single-point forecasting* is where organisations have such confidence about the future that they will provide just one forecast number (as in Figure 2.6 i). For instance, an organisation might predict that the population in a market will grow by 5 per cent in the next two years. This kind of single-point forecasting implies a great degree of certainty. Demographic trends (for instance the increase in the elderly within a particular population) lend themselves to these kinds of forecasting, at least in the short term.

- *Range forecasting* is where organisations have less certainty, suggesting a range of possible outcomes. These different outcomes may be expressed with different degrees of probability, with a central projection identified as the most probable (the darkest shaded area in Figure 2.6 ii), and then a range of more remote outcomes given decreasing degrees of likelihood (the more lightly shaded areas). These 'fan charts' are often used in economic forecasting, for example economic growth rates or inflation.

- *Alternative futures forecasting* typically involves even less certainty, focusing on a set of possible yet distinct futures. Instead of a continuously graduated range of likelihoods, alternative futures are discontinuous: they happen or they do not, with radically different outcomes (see Figure 2.6 iii). These alternatives might result from fundamental

Figure 2.6 Forecasting under conditions of uncertainty

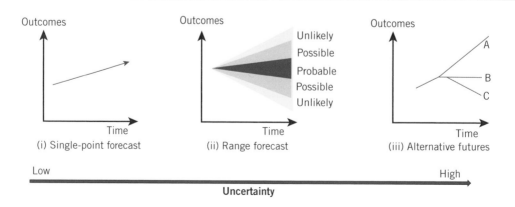

policy decisions. For example, for a country facing possible exit from a currency union (for instance the Euro), outcome A might reflect the consequences for growth or unemployment of staying in the union; outcome B might reflect the consequences of exiting the union; and outcome C would be a further alternative outcome, consequent on a decision that followed the initial decision pointing towards outcome B (for instance, to adopt trade barriers as well as to exit the currency union). It is sometimes helpful for decision-makers to put relative probabilities on the alternatives: for example, outcome A might have a 40 per cent probability of occurring.

2.3.2 Directions of change

It is helpful in forecasting to keep an eye on the fundamental directions of likely change. Managers need to check their forecasts are consistent with major trends and to be alert to possible turning points. Three concepts help focus both on major trends and on possible turning points that might invalidate existing forecasts:

- *Megatrends* are large-scale political, economic, social, technological, ecological or legal movements that are typically slow to form, but which influence many areas of activity, possibly over decades.[8] A megatrend typically sets the direction for other factors. Thus the social megatrend towards ageing populations in the West influences other trends in social care, retail spending and housing. It is important to identify major megatrends because they influence so many other things. Forecasts should be checked for consistency with such trends.

- *Inflexion points* are moments when trends shift in direction, for instance turning sharply upwards or downwards.[9] For example, after decades of stagnation and worse, in the early twenty-first century sub-Saharan Africa may have reached an inflexion point in its economic growth, with the promise of substantial gains in the coming decade or so. Inflexion points are likely to invalidate forecasts that extrapolate existing trends. Clearly it is valuable to grasp the inflexion point at the moment when trends just start to turn, in order either to take advantage of new opportunities early or to act against escalating decline as soon as possible.

- *Weak signals* are advanced signs of future trends and are particularly helpful in identifying inflexion points.[10] Typically these weak signals are unstructured and fragmented bits of information, often perceived by observers as 'weird'. An early weak signal foreshadowing the current success of Asian business schools was the first entry of the Hong Kong University of Science and Technology into the *Financial Times'* ranking of the top 50 international business schools in the early 2000s. The recent fashion for old technology such as vinyl records and 'dumb' phones may signal a revolt against intrusive forms of contemporary high tech. Not all weak signals predict new trends, but if they are repeated widely then they need to be considered seriously.

2.4 Scenario analysis

Scenarios offer plausible alternative views of how the macro-environment might develop in the future, typically in the long term. Scenario analysis is typically used in conditions of high uncertainty, for example where the environment could go in several highly distinct directions.[11] However, scenario analyses differs from alternative futures forecasting (Section 2.3.1), as scenario planners usually avoid presenting alternatives in terms of finely calculated probabilities. The point of scenarios is more to learn than to predict. Scenarios are used to explore the way in which environmental factors inter-relate and to help keep managers' minds open to alternatives possibilities in the future. A scenario with a very low likelihood may be valuable in deepening managers' understanding even if it never occurs.

Illustration 2.4 shows an example of scenario planning for the post-covid world of the early to mid-2020s published by Deloitte and Salesforce. The scenario process started with 24 medical, social, technological, economic, environmental (ecological) and political uncertainties. The next step was to take two of these uncertainties that were clearly differentiated in terms of having (i) high potential impact; (ii) high uncertainty; (iii) high independence from each other. Deloitte/Salesforce chose to focus on the medical severity of covid-19 and the social and political aspects of collaboration. These two factors yielded four highly divergent scenarios, with different implications for regions of the world and international trade and investment. Deloitte/Salesforce do not predict that one scenario will prevail over the others, nor do they allocate relative probabilities. Prediction would close managers' minds to alternatives, while probabilities would imply a spurious kind of accuracy at a time when so much was unknown.

While there are many ways to carry out scenario analyses, the process often follows five basic steps (as shown in Figure 2.7):[12]

- *Defining scenario scope* is an important first step in the process. Scope refers to the subject of the scenario analysis and the time span. For example, scenario analyses can be carried out for a whole industry globally, or for particular geographical regions and markets. Scenario time spans can be either a decade or so or perhaps just five years ahead (as in Illustration 2.4). The appropriate time span is determined partly by the expected life of investments. In the energy business, where oil fields might have a life span of several decades, scenarios often cover 20 years or more.

- *Identifying the key drivers for change* comes next. Here PESTEL analysis can be used to uncover issues, but the focus should be those likely to have a major *impact* upon the future of the industry, region or market; those with high *uncertainty*, in order to make different scenarios worthwhile (there's no point in developing alternative scenarios when only one outcome is likely); and those that are *mutually independent* (there's no point in considering factors individually if they lead to the same outcome anyway). In the oil industry, for example, political stability in the oil-producing regions is one major uncertainty; another is the development of new exploration technologies, enabling the quick and efficient identification of new oil fields. These could be selected as key drivers for scenario analysis because both are uncertain and important, while regional stability is independent of technological advances.

Figure 2.7 The scenario process

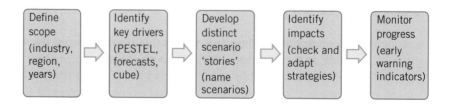

Illustration 2.4 Scenarios for the Next Normal

In April 2020, Deloitte Consulting and the software company Salesforce published together four scenarios for a post-covid world, looking three to five years ahead.

Source: The world remade by Covid-19: scenarios for resilient leaders', 06 April 2020, Deloitte.

In the first months of the covid-19 crisis, as businesses around the world were coping with sales collapses and emergency moves online, Deloitte and Salesforce used scenarios to explore how the pandemic could accelerate or redirect social and economic change over the next three to five years. They chose this period because organisations' immediate reactions were likely to impact their future opportunities in whatever the 'next normal' would be after the crisis.

First of all, the Deloitte/Salesforce team identified 24 key uncertainties regarding the future, under the headings of the medical nature of the disease itself, social impacts, technological aspects, the economy, the environment and politics. From these, they finally identified two fundamental but independent sources of uncertainty for the future: the overall severity of the pandemic and the level of collaboration within and between countries. The range of outcomes they considered for the disease itself ranged from a quick decline to a second-wave even fiercer than the first. For the level of collaboration, they contrasted coordinated responses, for example discipline on social distancing, with weak and divided responses, for example failure by governments to share information and resources.

The two dimensions of pandemic severity and level of collaboration yielded four distinct scenarios, each given an evocative title. As in the Figure below, the scenarios are:

- The passing storm, where the pandemic has relatively low impact and governments and societies coordinate well.
- Good company, where the pandemic is more prolonged and large companies provide the collaboration which governments neglect.
- Sunrise in the east, where the pandemic is severe, but East Asian nations are significantly more effective in managing the virus and become primary powers on the world stage.
- Lone wolves, where there are severe and repeated pandemics and weak policy responses by governments globally.

Each of these scenarios has different implications for the post-covid 'next normal', which Deloitte and Salesforce considered under the headings of society, technology, economy, environment and politics. The Passing storm and Lone wolves scenarios offer some strong contrasts. For example, politically the Passing storm scenario sees a rising importance for international institutions such as the World Health Organization, while the Lone wolves scenario implies a decline in international coordination, extending to the internet, student exchanges and climate change. Economically, the Lone wolves scenarios implies cuts in international supply chains and flows of investment, while the Passing storm impacts unevenly on generations and different kinds of business.

Deloitte/Salesforce did not ascribe probabilities to any of the scenarios. Instead they stated: 'At this moment, the question should be, what do we need to be ready for, even if we think it's improbable'.

Source: 'The world remade by Covid-19: scenarios for resilient leaders', Deloitte/Salesforce:. https://www2.deloitte.com/content/dam/Deloitte/global/Documents/About-Deloitte/COVID-19/Thrive-scenarios-for-resilient-leaders.pdf

Questions

1. What other 'uncertainties' might have been considered beyond the two finally considered here (use the headings of political, economic, social, technological, ecological and legal)?

2. What are the different implications of these scenarios for an international consulting firm such as Deloitte? Which scenario would it like best; which would it like least?

- *Developing scenario 'stories'.* As in films, scenarios are basically stories. Having selected opposing key drivers for change, it is necessary to knit together plausible stories that incorporate both key drivers and other factors into a coherent whole. These stories are often encapsulated with striking titles: for example, oil company Shell launched two opposing scenarios entitled simply 'Oceans' and 'Mountains', the first describing a more free-market world with solar power important, the second a more government-led world, with gas power important.[13] Striking titles help to communicate scenarios and embed them in strategic discussions (see also Illustration 2.4).

- *Identifying impacts* of alternative scenarios on organisations is the next key stage of scenario building. For example, in Illustration 2.4, a Lone wolf world would pose major challenges for international supply chains, with implications for many countries in South East Asia. It is important for an organisation to carry out *robustness checks* in the face of each plausible scenario and to adapt strategies that appear vulnerable and develop contingency plans in case they happen.

- *Monitor progress.* Once the various scenarios are drawn up, organisations should monitor progress over time, to alert themselves to whether and how developments actually fit scenario expectations. Here it is important to identify indicators that might give early warning about the final direction of environmental change, and at the same time set up systems to monitor these. In Illustration 2.4, the diminishing likelihood of a Passing storm scenario would raise alarm bells for many Western-dominated international organisations.

Summary

- Environmental influences can be thought of as layers around an organisation, with the outer layer making up the *macro-environment*, the middle layer making up the *industry or sector* and the inner layer *strategic groups* and *market segments*.

- The macro-environment can be analysed in terms of the *PESTEL factors* – political, economic, social, technological, ecological and legal.

- Macro-environmental trends can be *forecast* according to different levels of uncertainty, from single-point, through ranges to multiple-futures.

- A PESTEL analysis helps identify *key drivers of change*, which managers need to address in their strategic choices. Alternative *scenarios* about the future can be constructed according to how the key drivers develop.

Recommended key readings

- An overview of techniques for thinking ahead is given in P. Tetlock and D. Gardner, *Superforecasting: The art and science of prediction*, Crown, 2015. For approaches to how environments change, see K. van der Heijden, *Scenarios: The art of strategic conversation*, 2nd edition, Wiley, 2005 and R. Ramírez, J.W. Selsky and K. Van der Heijden (eds), *Business Planning for Turbulent Times: New methods for applying scenarios*, Taylor & Francis, 2010.

- A collection of academic articles on PEST, scenarios and similar is the special issue of *International Studies of Management and Organization*, vol. 36, no. 3 (2006), edited by Peter McKiernan.

References

1. Macroeconomic forecasts can be found at: www.oecd.org/eco/outlook/; www.imf.org/external/; www.worldbank.org/

2. M.E. Porter, 'Clusters and the new economics of competition', *Harvard Business Review*, vol. 76, no. 6 (1997), p. 7790.

3. J.H. Lee, H.I. Kim and R. Phaal, 'An analysis of factors improving technology roadmap credibility: a communications theory assessment of roadmapping processes', *Technological Forecasting and Social Change*, vol. 79, no. 2 (2012), pp. 263–80.

4. S.L. Hart and G. Dowell, 'A natural-resource-based view of the firm: Fifteen years after', *Journal of Management*, vol. 37, no. 5 (2010), pp. 1464–79.

5. J. Cantwell, J.H. Dunning and S.M. Lundan, 'An evolutionary approach to understanding international business activity: the co-evolution of MNEs and the institutional environment', *Journal of International Business Studies*, vol. 41, no. 4 (2010), pp. 567–86. See also M. Peng, H. Nguyen, J. Wang, M. Hasenhüttl and J. Shay, 'Bringing institutions into strategy teaching', *Academy of Management Learning & Education*, Vol. 17, No. 3 (2018), pp. 259–78.

6. R. Vecchiato, and C. Roveda, 'Strategic foresight in corporate organizations: handling the effect and response uncertainty of technology and social drivers of change', *Technological Forecasting and Social Change*, vol. 77, no. 9 (2010), pp. 1527–39.

7. U. Haran and D.A. Moore, 'A better way to forecast', *California Management Review*, vol. 57, no. (2014), pp. 5–15; H. Courtney, J. Kirkland and P. Viguerie, 'Strategy under uncertainty', *Harvard Business Review*, vol. 75, no. 6 (1997), pp. 67–79.

8. R.A. Slaughter, 'Looking for the real megatrends', *Futures*, October (1993), pp. 823–49.

9. A. Grove, *Only the Paranoid Survive*, Profile Books, 1998.

10. S. Mendonca, G. Caroso and J. Caraca, 'The strategic strength of weak signals', *Futures*, 44 (2012), pp. 218–28; and P. Schoemaker and G. Day, 'How to make sense of weak signals', *Sloan Management Review*, vol. 50, no. 3 (2009), pp. 81–9.

11. For a discussion of scenario planning in practice, see R. Ramirez, S. Churchhouse, A. Palermo and J. Hoffmann, 'Using scenario planning to reshape strategy', *MIT Sloan Management Review*, vol. 58, no. 4 (2017), pp. 31–37. For how scenario planning fits with other forms of environmental analysis such as PESTEL, see G. Burt, G. Wright, R. Bradfield and K. van der Heijden, 'The role of scenario planning in exploring the environment in view of the limitations of PEST and its derivatives', *International Studies of Management and Organization*, vol. 36, no. 3 (2006), pp. 50–76.

12. Based on P. Schoemaker, 'Scenario planning: a tool for strategic thinking', *Sloan Management Review*, vol. 36 (1995), pp. 25–34.

13. www.shell.com/global/future-energy/scenarios/new-lens-scenarios.html

Case example
Alibaba: the Yangtze River Crocodile
Richard Whittington

Jack Ma, founder of Alibaba.
Source: Eugenio Loreto/EPA-EFE/Shutterstock

In late 2018, Jack Ma, founder of China's largest e-commerce company Alibaba, announced shock news: in the coming year, he would step aside as company Chairman in favour of the Chief Executive, Daniel Zhang. Jack Ma had been Alibaba's charismatic leader for two decades. But Ma made it clear that he was not disappearing altogether: he remained a major shareholder and would be a permanent member of the 36-strong 'partnership' that nominated the majority of the company's board of directors. A senior banking analyst observed of Ma: 'He has been the spiritual leader of the company since he founded it, and everyone looks up to him. People call him Teacher Ma. That means people are not looking at him as manager or chief executive or chairman – they are looking to him for guidance.'

The new Chairman and Chief Executive Daniel Zhang was more of a professional manager than the entrepreneurial Ma. Educated in China, he had begun his career in the accounting firms Arthur Andersen and PwC before joining Alibaba in 2007. One of Zhang's great successes at Alibaba had been the idea of making Singles' Day in November a national festival of shopping, all served by Alibaba's online commerce businesses of course. Recently Zhang has rolled out Singles' Day internationally, backed by his experience in international firms. During a company-wide strategy session soon after becoming Chief Executive in 2015, he said: 'We must absolutely globalize. We will organize a global team and adopt global thinking to manage the business and achieve the goal of *global buy and global sell.*'

Jack Ma and colleagues had launched Alibaba in 1999 as China's first business-to-business portal connecting domestic manufacturers with overseas buyers. Since then, the Group has grown in many directions. 1688.com was founded for business-to-business trade within China. Alibaba's Taobao Marketplace serves small businesses and individuals. Tmall.com provides electronic shop fronts to help overseas companies such as Nike, Burberry and Decathlon to reach Chinese consumers. Juhuasuan offers daily deals on everything from toys to laptops. Behind all this are Alibaba's enormous server farms, which form the basis for another market-leading business, cloud computing. There is also Alipay, effectively under Ma's personal control but functioning as the Group's equivalent to PayPal, which processes most Group transactions. One way or another, it is possible for Alibaba's customers to trade almost anything: the American security services have even set up a sting operation on Alibaba to catch traders selling uranium to Iran. In 2018, Alibaba had approaching 58 per cent of the e-commerce market in China, the largest e-commerce market in the world. In 2015, Alibaba had invested in the Indian e-commerce business Snapdeal and the following year it bought a majority stake in the Singapore e-commerce business, Lazada. The company also had strong positions in Brazil and Russia. International e-commerce represented nearly 7 per cent of the company's sales in the last quarter of 2018 (about $1,247m out of total quarterly sales of $17,057m: see also Table 1).

Alibaba had always had an international bent. Jack Ma had started his career as an English language teacher in the city of Hangzhou, capital of the prosperous province of Zhejiang and not very far from Shanghai. Ma had discovered the internet on his trips to the United States in the mid-1990s. As early as 2000, Ma had persuaded both the leading American investment bank Goldman Sachs and the Japanese internet giant Softbank to invest. The then ascendant American internet company Yahoo had bought nearly a quarter of the Group in 2005. Even after Alibaba went public in 2015, SoftBank still held 32.4 per cent of the shares and Yahoo 15 per cent. The Alibaba Group board counted as members Yahoo's founder Jerry Yang, Softbank's founder Masayoshi Son and Michael Evans, former vice-chairman of Goldman Sachs. Even so, Jack Ma was ambivalent about Western investors: 'Let the Wall Street investors curse us if they wish!', Ma had

Table 1 Key statistics

	2010	2012	2014	2015	2016	2017	2018
Alibaba Group Sales Yuan bn	6.7	20.0	52.5	76.2	101.1	158.3	250.3
Chinese GDP Yuan Tr.	40.4	53.4	64.4	68.9	74.4	82.7	90.0
Chinese online retail sales Yuan Tr.	0.5	1.3	2.8	3.9	5.2	7.2	n.a.
Per cent of Chinese using Internet	34.3	41.0	46.0	50.3	52.2	55.8	n.a.

Sources: Statistical Report on Internet Development in China; InternetLiveStats.com; Statista.com. One Yuan = €0.13; $0.15; £0.11.

proclaimed at a staff rally. 'We will still follow the principle of customers first, employees second and investors third!'

Strictly, overseas investors do not directly own stakes in the Alibaba Group, instead owning shares in a shell company – a so-called variable interest entity (VIE) – that has a contractual claim on Alibaba's profits. This VIE structure is a common way for Western-listed Chinese firms to get around Beijing's foreign-ownership rules. But the Chinese government could close the loophole at any time, and it gives foreign shareholders limited recourse against abuses by Chinese companies' managers. Ironically, the most notorious VIE controversy so far involved Alibaba's Jack Ma, who in 2011 separated Alipay from the rest of the Group without board approval. Ma said new Chinese regulations forced him to make the move. Yahoo was only told about the spin-off five weeks after it had happened. A fundraising round for Alipay's new parent company valued Alipay at nearly $50bn.

Jack Ma cultivated important relationships within China as well as abroad. Early on he socialised with a group of businessmen known as the Zhejiang Gang, because of their common roots in the province whose capital was Ma's home city of Hangzhou. Prominent members of this group included some of China's most successful entrepreneurs: for example, Guo Guangchang of the huge diversified Fosun Group; Shen Guojun of China Yintai Holdings, a retail property developer; and Shi Yuzhu, of the online gaming company Giant Interactive.

Alibaba's relationship with the Chinese government is hard to read. Jack Ma insists that he has never taken loans or investment from the Chinese government or its banks: he had gone to overseas investors instead. However, given that a third of Chinese business activity is carried out within state-owned enterprises, the government is bound to be in close liaison with the dominant national player in e-commerce. Ma explained his philosophy as: 'Always try to stay in love with the government, but don't marry them.' The Alibaba Group has built up its political connections. Tung Chee-hwa, Hong Kong's first chief executive after its return to China, served on its board of directors.

Alibaba has also allied with several so-called 'princelings', children of important political leaders. Princeling investors include Winston Wen, son of a former Chinese premier; Alvin Jiang, grandson of a former Chinese President; He Jinlei, son of a former Politburo member and a senior manager of the state Chinese Development Bank; and Jeffrey Zang, son of a former vice premier and a senior manager at China's state sovereign wealth fund, Citic Capital.

Given Chinese President Xi Jinping's sweeping political and economic reform campaign, there are no guarantees of Alibaba's position domestically. In 2015, princeling investor He Jinlei's older brother was placed under house arrest because of accusations of corruption. 2015 had also seen the publication of an investigation by China's State Administration for Industry and Commerce into counterfeit goods and fake listings on the Group's Taobao site, leading to a 10 per cent fall in Alibaba's share price. Jack Ma commented on his relations with Chinese regulators: 'Over the past two years, not only was I a very controversial figure, but also these days, the disputes are bigger and bigger.' He continued, 'I, too, felt puzzled, sometimes wronged – how did things become this way?' Nonetheless, Ma promised to clean up the site. In 2018, in an apparent reproof, Chinese state media let out the news, previously withheld, that Jack Ma was a longstanding member of the Chinese Communist Party.

President Xi Jinping's reform campaigns were partly in response to changing economic conditions in China. After three decades of double-digit growth, China's growth rate has slowed to around 7 per cent a year more recently (see Table 1). Such growth is very respectable by world standards. Besides, faced with rising domestic concern about the environment, President Xi was happy to restrain the expansion of high polluting industries such as cement, coal and steel. At the same time, the Chinese government was promoting e-commerce as a key area for future economic growth. However, there were causes for concern. Many local authorities and firms had borrowed heavily on expectations of higher growth, and there were fears that financial institutions had over-lent. Some warned of a consequent crash. Moreover, it was hard to see China's growth rate picking up again, on account of an aging population and the drying up of the traditional supply of young labour from rural villages: the Chinese labour force participation rate has dropped from a high of 79 per cent in 1990 to 69 per cent by 2017. Although the government relaxed the famous one-child per family rule in 2013, Chinese parents are still reluctant to have more children because of the cost of housing and good education in the main urban centres. It is predicted that by the early 2030s, about a quarter of China's population will be over 65 (against 17 per cent in the United Kingdom). Slower economic growth in China overall is being matched by a slowing in the rate of growth of the Chinese e-commerce market (see Table 1).

At the same time, Alibaba faces greater competition in its home market. A decade ago, Alibaba had seen off an attack by American rival eBay in the Chinese market with a fierce price-war. Jack Ma had proclaimed: 'EBay is a shark in the ocean; we are a crocodile in the Yangtze River. If we fight in the ocean, we will lose, but if we fight in the river, we will win.' A combination of cultural, linguistic and government policy factors kept Western internet companies at arm's length in the Chinese market: Google has been reduced to a market share of about 1 per cent, while Amazon eventually chose to list on Alibaba's TMall site after a decade pushing its own venture in China.

But now Alibaba's home-market dominance is facing a local challenge from the aggressive JD.com. JD.Com's founder and chief executive Richard Liu has declared a goal of beating Alibaba to the top position: 'The competition makes the two companies stronger. I'm actually enjoying competing.' While Alibaba depended for a long time on China's unreliable postal service to get its goods to customers' doors, JD.com has been more like Amazon in investing heavily in its own distribution centres and delivery services. By 2018, JD.com had 16.3 per cent of China's e-commerce market. Tencent, China's largest social networking and online games company, has taken a 15 per cent stake in JD.com, giving the challenger access to more than 890 million users of its WeChat phone messaging app. WeChat allows users to scan product bar codes with their smartphone cameras to make instant purchases through JD.com. Mobile commerce is increasingly important in China, with 788 million people being mobile users, 98 per cent of the country's total user base in 2017. Mobile has been a challenge for Alibaba's traditional PC-based retail model, but the company has been catching up with about 80 per cent of its e-commerce business on mobile devices by 2017.

In a context of slower Chinese growth and increased domestic competition, the internationalisation strategy of Alibaba's new Chairman Daniel Zhang seemed to make sense. However, Zhang faced one major challenge: resistance in the world's second largest e-commerce market, the United States. In January 2017, the first month of the new American Presidency, Jack Ma had met Donald Trump in New York and promised that Alibaba's investment in the United States would bring one million new jobs to America. Alibaba invested in two large data centres for its expanding cloud computing business. However, the United States was the home of Amazon, Microsoft and Google, all with vast cloud businesses of their own. Besides, nationalist Donald Trump was imposing boycotts on Chinese technology companies and threatening tariffs. At the end of 2018, Alibaba announced the winding down of its cloud computing operations in the United States. For the Yangtze River crocodile, attacking the ocean sharks in their home seas may have been a step too far.

Main case sources: China Daily, 8 and 13 May 2015; *Financial Times*, 9 September 2014 and 14 September 2018; *South China Morning Post*, 12 February 2015; *Washington Post*, 23 November 2014; *Wall Street Journal*, 4 December 2018.

Questions

1 Carry out a PESTEL analysis of Alibaba at the time of the case. Evaluate the balance of opportunities and threats, using the same kind of figure as in Illustration 2.1.

2 Draw a basic sociogram of Alibaba's network (see Section 2.2.3 and Figure 2.4): some simplification may be necessary. Explain why Alibaba's network might be useful.

Chapter 3
Industry and sector analysis

Key terms

Learning outcomes

After reading this chapter, you should be able to:

- Define industries and use *Porter's competitive five forces* framework to analyse industries or sectors: rivalry, threat of entrants, substitute threats, customer's power and supplier power.

- On the basis of the five competitive forces define *industry attractiveness* and identify how the forces can be managed.

- Understand how industries develop and change in *industry life cycles* and how to make five force analyses dynamic through *comparative industry structure analysis*.

- Analyse strategic and competitor positions in terms of *strategic groups* and *market segments*.

- Use these various concepts and techniques together with those from Chapter 2 in order to recognise *threats* and *opportunities* in the industry and marketplace.

3.1 Introduction

In the last chapter we considered how the broad macro-environment influences opportunities and threats. The impact of these general factors tends to surface in the immediate environment of the specific industry or sector and this nearby environment is the focus of this chapter. For example, Samsung's strategy depends on the smartphone industry: here it must take account of competitors' strategies, customers' needs, and the supply of phone components, for example microchips. Similarly, a hospital needs to consider actors in the healthcare sector including clients, other healthcare providers and the supply of healthcare inputs such as pharmaceuticals. This suggests that it is crucial for managers to carefully examine the industry or sector and the actors these involve carefully in order to determine what strategy to pursue.

The focus here is thus on the middle 'industry' and 'sector' layer in Figure 2.1 (see the last chapter), which involves central actors that influence an organisation's long term survival and success including competitors, customers or clients, and suppliers. **An industry is a group of firms producing products and services that are essentially the same.**[1] Examples are the automobile industry and the airline industry. Industries are also often described as 'sectors', especially in public services (e.g. the health sector or the education sector). Industries and sectors are often made up of several specific markets or market segments. **A market is a group of customers for specific products or services that are essentially the same (e.g. a particular geographical market).** Thus, the automobile industry has markets in North America, Europe and Asia, for example.

This chapter examines three main topics and provides different frameworks and concepts for understanding the industry or sector:

- Industry analysis through the use of the *Competitive Five Forces Framework*, which examines five essential industry forces: competitors, customers, potential entrants, suppliers and substitutes. One additional factor is *complementors* and the related phenomenon *network effects*. Together these forces and factors provide an understanding of industry attractiveness and competitive strategy.

- Fundamental industry dynamics, which include examinations of how industries evolve through *industry life cycles*, which might influence changes in the five forces that can be examined with a *comparative five force analysis*.

- Competitor groups and segments including examinations of *strategic groups*, groups of organisations with similar strategies and of *market segments*, groups of customers with similar needs. This focus provides a more fine-grained understanding of competition within an industry or sector.

3.2 Industry analysis

Industries vary widely in terms of their long-term attractiveness, as measured by how easy it is for participating firms to earn high profits. A key determinant of profitability is the extent of competition and the strength of buyers and suppliers and this varies between industries. Where competition and buyer and supplier strengths are low, and there is little threat of new competitors, participating firms should normally expect good profits. Profitability between industries can thus vary considerably; for example, the pharmaceutical industry has performed very well historically while others, like the airline industry, have underperformed.[2]

Porter's Five Forces Framework assists industry analysis and helps to identify industry attractiveness in terms of five competitive forces: (i) extent of rivalry between competitors; (ii) threat of entry; (iii) threat of substitutes; (iv) power of buyers; and (v) power of suppliers. These five forces together determine an industry's 'structure' and its attractiveness (see Figure 3.1). Once this has been understood, the five forces can help set an agenda for action on various critical issues: for example, what specific strategy to pursue in order to control excessive rivalry in a particular industry? Managers should try to find positions where the organisation can best defend itself against strong competitive forces or where they can influence them in its favour. The rest of this section first discusses how to define the scope of an industry and then introduces each of the five forces in more detail and discusses the implications of these for strategy. Illustration 3.3 at the very end of this section summarises industry and sector analysis and provides an overview of its various steps.

Figure 3.1 The five forces framework

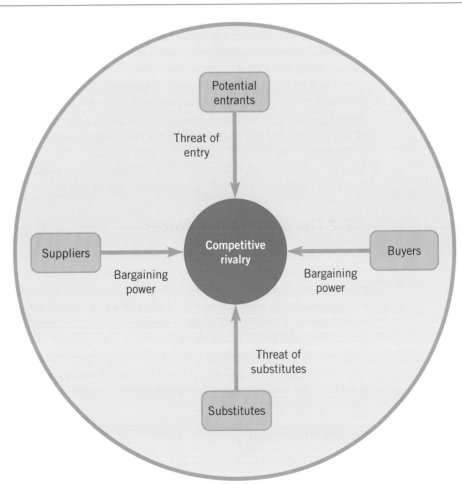

Source: Adapted from *Competitive Strategy: Techniques for Analyzing Industries and Competitors*, The Free Press by Michael E. Porter 1980.

3.2.1 Defining the industry

One of the primary issues for managers is to identify the arena of competition. The first step in an industry analysis is thus to define the industry. If defined incorrectly there is a risk that significant strategy aspects are overlooked. There are three fundamental issues to consider here. First, and most generally, the industry must not be defined too broadly or narrowly. For example, if an entrepreneur considers starting a taxi business in Stockholm and makes an industry analysis it would be much too broad to define the industry as 'the Swedish personal transportation industry' while 'the minicab industry in central Stockholm' would be too narrow. The first definition would include such a wide variety of actors that the analysis risk becoming meaningless, while the second risks excluding important competitors (e.g. taxi firms from the suburbs).

Secondly, the broader industry value chain needs to be considered. Different industries often operate in different parts of a value chain or value system and should be analysed separately (see Section 4.4.2 for a discussion of value systems). For example, the iron ore industry (including companies like Vale, Rio Tinto and BHP Billiton) delivers to the steel manufacturing industry (including companies like Mittal Steel and Tata Steel) that in turn delivers to a wide variety of industries such as automobiles and construction. These three stages in the broader value chain or system should be analysed separately.

Thirdly, most industries can be analysed at different levels, for example different geographies, markets and even different product or service segments within them (see Section 3.4.2 below). Thus, the airline industry has different geographical markets (Europe, China and so on) and it also has different service segments within each market (e.g. leisure, business and freight). The competitive forces are likely to be different for each of these markets and segments, with distinct buyers, suppliers and barriers, etc. Michael Porter has his own rule of thumb here and suggests that you are likely dealing with distinct industries if there are differences between them in more than one competitive force, or where differences in any force are large. In brief, it is important to consider both to what extent a market is national, regional or global and if product and service segments differ.

3.2.2 The competitive forces

Porter's main message is that where the competitive five forces are strong, industries are not attractive to compete in. Excessive competitive rivalry, powerful buyers and suppliers and the threat of substitutes or new entrants will all combine to squeeze profitability. Although initially developed with businesses in mind, the five forces framework is relevant to most organisations. It can provide a useful starting point for strategic analysis even where profit criteria may not apply. In the public sector, it is important to understand how powerful suppliers can push up costs; in the charity sector it is important to avoid excessive rivalry within the same sector and market. Not for profits may also want to consider how likely a grant provider for an organisation or member of a charity organisation would substitute for someone else providing similar services.

Competitive rivalry

At the centre of five forces analysis is the rivalry between the existing players – 'incumbents' – in an industry. The more competitive rivalry there is, the worse it is for incumbents. *Competitive rivals* are organisations aiming at the same customer groups and with similar products and services (i.e. not substitutes). In the European airline industry, Air France and British

Airways are rivals; high-speed trains are a 'substitute' (see below). Five factors tend to define the extent of rivalry in an industry or market:

- *Competitor concentration and balance.* Where competitors are numerous or of roughly equal size or power there is the danger of intensely rivalrous behaviour as competitors attempt to gain dominance over others, through aggressive price cuts for example. Conversely, less rivalrous industries tend to have one or two dominant organisations, with the smaller players reluctant to challenge the larger ones directly (e.g. by focusing on niches to avoid the 'attention' of the dominant companies).

- *Industry growth rate.* In situations of strong growth, an organisation can grow with the market, but in situations of low growth or decline, any growth is likely to be at the expense of a rival and meet with fierce resistance. Low-growth markets are therefore often associated with price competition and low profitability. The *industry life cycle* influences growth rates, and hence competitive conditions: see Section 3.3.2.

- *High fixed costs.* Industries with high fixed costs, perhaps because they require high investments in capital equipment or initial research, tend to be highly rivalrous. Companies will seek to spread their fixed costs (i.e. reduce unit costs) by increasing their volumes: to do so, they typically cut their prices, prompting competitors to do the same and thereby triggering price wars in which all competitors in the industry suffers. Similarly, if extra capacity can only be added in large increments (as in many manufacturing sectors, for example a chemical or glass factory), the competitor making such an addition is likely to create short-term *overcapacity* in the industry, leading to increased competition to use capacity.

- *High exit barriers.* The existence of high barriers to exit – in other words, high closure or disinvestment costs – tends to increase rivalry, especially in declining industries. Excess capacity persists and consequently incumbents fight to maintain market share. Exit barriers might be high for a variety of reasons: for example, high redundancy costs or high investment in specific assets such as plant and equipment which others would not buy.

- *Low differentiation.* In a commodity market, where products or services are poorly differentiated, rivalry is increased because there is little to stop customers switching between competitors and the only way to compete is on price. Petrol is a commodity market, for instance.

The threat of entry

How easy it is to enter the industry influences the degree of competition. The greater the threat of entry, the worse it is for incumbents in an industry. An attractive industry has high barriers to entry that reduce the threat of new competitors. *Barriers to entry* are the factors that need to be overcome by new entrants if they are to compete in an industry. Illustration 3.1 describes the entry barriers into the banking industry and the obstacles they provide for new entrants. Five important entry barriers are:

- *Scale and experience.* In some industries, *economies of scale* are extremely important: for example in pharmaceuticals where there are extremely high fixed costs for extensive R&D and marketing that must be spread over high levels of output (see Chapter 6 for further details on economies of scale). Once incumbents have reached a large scale, it will be very expensive for new entrants to match them and until they reach a similar volume they will have higher unit costs. Barriers to entry also come from *experience curve* effects that give incumbents a cost advantage because they have learned how to do things more efficiently than an inexperienced new entrant could possibly do (see Section 6.2.1). Until the new entrant has built up equivalent experience over time, it will tend to produce at higher cost.

Illustration 3.1 Busted banking barriers?

The barriers to entry into the retail banking industry have traditionally been very high, but there are signs they could possibly be tumbling.

The high barriers to entry in financial services include structural barriers due to basic industry conditions like economies of scale, network effects and regulation. The latter is significant in this particular industry; to protect the safety and stability of the financial system there are high regulatory walls. While incumbents may complain as authorities introduce new regulations, they often promote them once they adapted to them as regulations raise barriers for new entrants. Hence, they tend to exploit and lobby for structural regulation barriers to their own advantage to keep competitors out.

In the UK regulative and other barriers have resulted in the 'Big Five' domination: HSBC, Barclays, Royal Bank of Scotland, Lloyds and Santander. Other markets are very similar with a 'Big Five' in Canada, 'Big Three' in Spain and the Netherlands and a 'Big Four' in Sweden. In the aftermath of the 2008 financial crisis regulations have increased further. The dilemma for regulators is that they have two partly conflicting objectives. First, to secure the stability of the financial system they need to have capital requirements and other strict regulations for banks. The second aim is to deliver more efficiency and more services for customers through increased competition. To act on this second objective regulators have started to encourage more entrants and assist them to find cracks in the barriers without totally breaking them. For example, the Managing Director Hannah Nixon of Britain's Payment Systems Regulator proposes: 'There needs to be a fundamental change in the industry to encourage new entrants to compete on service, price and innovation in an open and transparent way.'

UK's financial regulators have even launched a start-up unit to help new players to enter as Andrew Bailey, former CEO of the Prudential Regulation Authority explained:

'The New Bank Start-Up Unit builds on the work we have already done to reduce the barriers to entry for prospective banks, which has led to twelve new banks now authorised since April 2013.'

It remains to be seen if competition will increase, but adding to the regulators' efforts is a new breed of potent rivals that may prove more powerful. Helped by new IT technologies, software and mobile banking there are over a hundred so-called 'fintech' (finance and technology) start-ups as confirmed in a Deloitte report:

'New, agile and hitherto unregulated players are emerging and are disintermediating the traditional incumbents [reducing the use of intermediaries between banks and consumers].'

Even if incumbent banks also try to jump on this fintech bandwagon they may not be able to dominate it. In contrast to the flourishing fintech start-ups they are often bound by current regulations as the report continued:

'Regulation is making it harder to innovate and grow, whilst legacy strategy, infrastructure and thinking, are preventing the existing players from responding aggressively from this threat.'

Sources: E. Robinson, *Bloomberg Business*, 16 February 2016; H. Jones, *Reuters*, 25 February 2016; *Financial Conduct Authority*, 20 January 2016; J. Cumbo, *Financial Times*, 6 December 2015.

Questions

1 Evaluate the strengths of the banking industry's entry barriers according to Porter's criteria.

2 How would you evaluate the behaviour of banks trying to keep competition out from an ethical point of view?

In addition to these supply-side economies of scale there are 'demand or buyer side' economies of scale or so called *network effects* in some industries as buyers value being in a 'network' of a large number of other customers (see Section 3.2.3 below for further details).

- *Access to supply or distribution channels.* In many industries incumbents have had control over supply and/or distribution channels. Sometimes this has been through direct ownership (vertical integration), sometimes just through customer or supplier loyalty. In some industries this barrier has been overcome by new entrants who have bypassed retail distributors and sold directly to consumers through e-commerce (e.g. Dell Computers and Amazon). Similarly, incumbents may have cost or quality advantages not available to entrants including access to proprietary technology (e.g. patents), geographical locations or brand identity (e.g. Coca Cola).

- *Capital requirements.* The level of financial resources needed to enter an industry can prevent entry. To enter the pharmaceutical industry, for example, huge research and development investments over many years are needed. While large corporations may have access to the capital needed it may limit the number of likely entrants.

- *Legislation or government action.* Legal restraints on new entry vary from patent protection (e.g. pharmaceuticals), to regulation of markets (e.g. pension selling), through to direct government action (e.g. tariffs). Of course, organisations are vulnerable to new entrants if governments remove such protection, as has happened with deregulation of the airline industry over the last couple of decades.

The threat of substitutes

Substitutes are products or services that offer the same or a similar function and benefit to an industry's own products or services, but have a different nature. For example, aluminium is a substitute for steel; a tablet computer is a substitute for a laptop; charities can be substitutes for public services. Managers often focus on their competitors in their own industry, and neglect the threat posed by substitutes. Substitutes can reduce demand for a particular type of product as customers switch to alternatives – even to the extent that this type of product or service becomes obsolete. However, there does not have to be much actual switching for the substitute threat to have an effect. The simple risk of substitution puts a cap on the prices that can be charged in an industry. Thus, although Eurostar trains has no direct competitors in terms of train services from Paris to London, the prices it can charge are ultimately limited by the cost of flights between the two cities.

There are two important points to bear in mind about substitutes:

- *Extra-industry effects* are the core of the substitution concept. Substitutes come from outside the incumbents' industry and should not be confused with competitors' threats from within the industry. The value of the substitution concept is to force managers to look outside their own industry to consider more distant threats and constraints. If the buyers' *switching costs* for the substitute are low the threat increases. The higher the threat, the less attractive the industry is likely to be.

- *The price/performance ratio* is critical to substitution threats. A substitute is still an effective threat even if more expensive, so long as it offers performance advantages that customers value. Thus, aluminium is more expensive than steel, but its relative lightness and its resistance to corrosion give it an advantage in some automobile manufacturing applications. It is the ratio of price to performance that matters, rather than simple price.

The power of buyers

Buyers are the organisation's immediate customers, not necessarily the ultimate consumers. If buyers are powerful, then they can demand low prices or costly product or service improvements.

Buyer power is likely to be high when some of the following four conditions prevail:

- *Concentrated buyers.* Where a few large customers account for the majority of sales, buyer power is increased. This is the case for items such as milk in the grocery sector in many European countries, where just a few retailers dominate the market. If a product or service accounts for a *high percentage of total purchases* of the buyer their power is also likely to increase as they are more likely to 'shop around' to get the best price and therefore 'squeeze' suppliers more than they would for more trivial purchases.

- *Low switching costs.* Where buyers can easily switch between one supplier and another, they have a strong negotiating position and can squeeze suppliers who are desperate for their business. Switching costs are typically low for *standardised and undifferentiated products* such as steel. They are also likely to be low when the buyers are *fully informed* about prices and product performance.

- *Buyer competition threat.* If the buyer has the capability to supply itself, or if it has the possibility of acquiring such a capability, it tends to be powerful. In negotiation with its suppliers, it can raise the threat of doing the suppliers' job themselves. This is called *backward vertical integration* (see Section 7.4), moving back to sources of supply, and might occur if satisfactory prices or quality from suppliers cannot be obtained. For example, some steel companies have gained power over their iron ore suppliers as they have acquired iron ore sources for themselves.

- *Low buyer profits and impact on quality.* For industrial or organisational buyers there are two additional factors that can make them price sensitive and thus increase their threat: first, if the buyer group is unprofitable and pressured to reduce purchasing costs and, second, if the quality of the buyer's product or services is little affected by the purchased product.

The power of suppliers

Suppliers are those who supply the organisation with what it needs to produce the product or service. As well as fuel, raw materials and equipment, this can include labour and sources of finance. The factors increasing supplier power are the converse to those for buyer power. Thus *supplier power* is likely to be high where there are:

- *Concentrated suppliers.* Where just a few producers dominate supply, suppliers have more power over buyers. The iron ore industry is now concentrated in the hands of three main producers, leaving the steel companies, still relatively fragmented, in a weak negotiating position for this essential raw material.

- *High switching costs.* If it is expensive or disruptive to move from one supplier to another, then the buyer becomes relatively dependent and correspondingly weak. Microsoft is a powerful supplier because of the high switching costs of moving from one operating system to another. Buyers are prepared to pay a premium to avoid the trouble, and Microsoft knows it.

- *Supplier competition threat.* Suppliers have increased power where they are able to enter the industry themselves or cut out buyers who are acting as intermediaries. Thus airlines have been able to negotiate tough contracts with travel agencies as the rise of online booking has allowed them to create a direct route to customers. This is called *forward vertical integration*, moving up closer to the ultimate customer.

- *Differentiated products.* When the products or services are highly differentiated suppliers will be more powerful. For example, although discount retailers like Walmart are extremely powerful, suppliers with strong brands, like P&G with Gillette, still have high negotiating power. Also, if there is no or few substitutes for the input the supplier group will be more powerful, like pilots' unions in the airline industry.

Most organisations have many suppliers, so it is necessary to concentrate the analysis on the most important ones or types. If their power is high, suppliers can capture all their buyers' own potential profits simply by raising their prices. Star football players have succeeded in raising their rewards to astronomical levels, while even the leading football clubs – their 'buyers' – struggle to make money. Similarly, Pilot's unions have significant power over airlines.

3.2.3 Complementors and network effects

Some industries may need the understanding of a sixth factor (or 'force'), organisations or companies that are complementors rather than simple competitors. **An organisation is your complementor if it enhances your business attractiveness to customers or suppliers.**[3] On the *demand side*, if customers value a product or service more when they also have the other organisation's product there is a complementarity with respect to customers. For example, app providers are complementors to Apple and other smartphone and tablet suppliers because customers value the iPhone and iPad more if there are a wide variety of appealing apps to download. This suggests that Apple and other actors in this industry need to take the app providers into consideration when forming their strategies. On the *supply side* another organisation is a complementor with respect to suppliers if it is more attractive for a supplier to deliver when it also supplies the other organisation. This suggests that competing airline companies, for example, can be complementary to each other in this respect because for a supplier like Boeing it is more attractive to invest in particular improvements for two customers rather than one. Complementarity implies a significant shift in perspective. While Porter's Five Forces sees organisations as battling against each other for share of industry value, complementors may *cooperate* to increase the total value available. Hence, this suggests that both value-creating cooperation as well as competition need to be considered in an industry analysis: this combination of competition and collaboration together is sometimes described as *co-opetition*.[4]

Customers may not only value a product more if they also have another product or service as discussed above, but if other customers use the same product or service. When this is the case the product or service shows network effects or network externalities. **There are network effects in an industry when one customer of a product or service has a positive effect on the value of that product for other customers.** This implies that the more customers that use the product, the better for everyone in the customer network.[5] For example, the value of the online auction site eBay increases for a customer as the network of other sellers and buyers grows on the site. The more goods that are offered on the site, the better for customers and this makes eBay's site and services more attractive to users than smaller competitors. Network effects are very important for Facebook too (see Illustration 3.2). Network effects can make an industry structurally attractive with high barriers to entry, low intensity of rivalry and power over buyers as entrants and rivals can't compete with other companies' larger networks and buyers become locked into them.

3.2.4 Implications of the competitive five forces

The Five Forces Framework provides several useful insights into the forces at work in the industry or market environment of an organisation. The objective is more than simply listing the strength of the forces and their underlying driving factors. It is rather to determine whether the industry is a good one to compete in or not and to conclude whether there are

Illustration 3.2 Facebook's network fears

Considering Facebook's dominance, they should have nothing to fear, but internet history is littered with fast rising and fast falling social networks.

Mark Zuckerberg, Facebook CEO .

Source: Robert Galbraith/Reuters/Alamy Stock Photo

With over 1.75bn users Facebook is not only the largest social network globally, but they control the second, third and seventh largest networks: WhatsApp (1.5bn), Facebook Messenger (1.3bn) and Instagram (1bn). It seems they are well ahead of everyone else in network effects and have created high switching costs for users to move to another social network. When users have built up a set-up of perhaps hundreds of friends and have archives of their whole life including photos they don't easily switch to another company and network just because it's something fresh.

Nevertheless, despite Facebook's clear lead, history shows it's far from obvious that any social network incumbent can stay relevant and dominate long term. Friendster pioneered the online community in 2002, three years before Facebook, and gained over three million users within a year; attracting tens of millions of users at its height. It was, however, soon overtaken by Myspace, which appealed to even more and younger users with their hip features including music and music videos. By 2008 it was the leading US social networking site with over 75m users and consistently ahead of Facebook in traffic. However, soon Facebook started to attract teenagers with their new features with corresponding losses for Myspace. This illustrates that social networks quickly can gain millions of users and huge valuations, but can just as quickly face slowing growth, users leaving in

millions and final collapse. Further back in internet history there are several other implosions of those with social network ambitions: BBS, CompuServe, AOL, etc.

Founder and CEO Mark Zuckerberg has, however, seen the threats and acted. Instagram was acquired in 2012 when they were becoming the biggest mobile photo-sharing service with many younger users posting content there rather than on Facebook's own web-based photo service. Next was the messaging service WhatsApp, it was bought in 2014 as users started to move their activities to mobile platforms. To fence off LinkedIn and Snapchat they launched 'Workplace' and 'Facebook Stories' respectively. Not even Google has managed to remove Facebook from the social networking throne. Google's first social networking effort Buzz was based on its Gmail service, but it never managed to attract enough users. Many Facebook users tried their next and even bigger bet, Google Plus, but soon discovered that not many of their friends followed so they returned to Facebook.

Facebook remains unbeaten and has perhaps learnt from social networking history. With their current valuation they can possibly continue to make defensive acquisitions when users get attracted to competing platforms, content and media. But how long will it last? Some question Facebooks staying power and claim it's quite possible they will be overtaken. Mark Zuckerberg, however, only sees this as inspiration to build Facebook even stronger:

> 'This is a perverse thing, personally, but I would rather be in the cycle where people are underestimating us. It gives us latitude to go out and make big bets that excite and amaze people.'

Sources: *Statista* 2018; R. Waters, *Financial Times*, 29 January 2016; J. Gapper, *Financial Times*, 12 April 2015; P. Economy, Inc.com, 26 March 2015; A. Liu, digitaltrends.com, 5 August 2014; R. Waters, *Financial Times*, 21 February 2014; J. Gapper, *Financial Times*, 3 October 2013.

Questions

1 Why is Facebook so powerful? Would you switch to another social network if it had better features even if it was considerably smaller?

2 What other social media networks and apps do you use that you think could beat Facebook? Why?

advantageous strategic positions where an organisation can defend itself against strong competitive forces, can exploit weak ones or can influence the forces in its favour. The aim of the five-force analysis is thus an assessment of the *attractiveness* of the industry and any possibilities to *manage strategies* in relation to the forces to promote long-term survival and competitive advantage. As Illustration 3.3 shows, these considerations make up the last three steps in an industry analysis together with an assessment of industry change, which is discussed in the next section. When each of the five forces has been evaluated, the next step is thus to understand the implications of these:

- *Which industries to enter (or leave)?* One important purpose of the five forces framework is to identify the relative attractiveness of different industries: industries are attractive when the forces are weak. In general, entrepreneurs and managers should invest in industries where the five forces work in their favour and avoid, or disinvest from, markets where they are strongly unfavourable. Entrepreneurs sometimes choose markets because entry barriers are low: unless barriers are likely to rise quickly, this is precisely the wrong reason to enter. Here it is important to note that just one significantly adverse force can be enough to undermine the attractiveness of the industry as a whole. For example, powerful buyers can extract all the potential profits of an otherwise attractive industry structure by forcing down prices. Chapters 6 and 7 further examines these *strategic choices* and *corporate strategy* and what to consider when to invest into or divest out of various industries.

- *How can the five forces be managed?* Industry structures are not necessarily fixed but can be influenced by deliberate managerial strategies. Managers should identify strategic positions where the organisation best can defend itself against strong competitive forces, can exploit weak ones or can influence them. As a general rule, managers should try to influence and exploit any weak forces to its advantage and neutralise any strong ones. For example, if barriers to entry are low, an organisation can raise them by increasing advertising spending to improve customer loyalty. Managers can buy up competitors to reduce rivalry and to increase power over suppliers or buyers. If buyers are very strong, an organisation can try to differentiate products or services for a specific customer group and thus increase their loyalty and switching costs. Managing and influencing industry structure involves many issues relating to *strategic choices* and *business strategy* and will be a major concern of Chapter 6.

- *How are competitors affected differently?* Not all competitors will be affected equally by changes in industry structure, deliberate or spontaneous. If barriers are rising because of increased R&D or advertising spending, smaller players in the industry may not be able to keep up with the larger players and be squeezed out. Similarly, growing buyer power is likely to hurt small competitors most. Strategic group analysis is helpful here (see Section 3.4.1).

Although originating in the private sector, five forces analysis can have important implications for organisations in the public and charity sectors too. For example, the forces can be used to adjust the service offer or focus on key issues. Thus, it might be worth switching focus from an arena with many crowded and overlapping services (e.g. social work, probation services and education) to one that is less rivalrous and where the organisation can do something more distinctive. Similarly, strategies could be launched to reduce dependence on particularly powerful and expensive suppliers, for example energy sources or high-shortage skills.

Illustration 3.3 Steps in an industry analysis

There are several important steps in an industry analysis before and after analysing the five forces.

Emily wants to start a coffee shop and perhaps even try to grow the business into several outlets. She needs to consider the following steps and questions:

1. **Define the industry clearly.** Do the actors in the industry face the same buyers, suppliers, entry barriers and substitutes?
   - Vertical scope: What stages of the industry value chain/ system?
   - Product or service scope: What products or services? Which ones are actually parts of other, separate industries? What segments?
   - Geographic scope: local, national, regional or global competition?

Emily should consider that many diverse businesses serve coffee. They include not only local cafés and coffee shop chains, but fast food chains, kiosks and restaurants. The definition also depends on whether Emily intends to start in an urban or rural area.

2. **Identify the actors of each of the five forces and, if relevant, define different groups within them and the basis for this.**
   Which are the. . .

   - competitors that face the same competitive forces? (compare point 1 above)
   - buyers and buyer groups (e.g. end customers vs. intermediaries, individual vs. organisational)?
   - suppliers and supplier groups (e.g. diverse supplier categories)?
   - potential entrants?
   - substitutes?

Given a clear industry definition the identification of the actors for each force should be rather straightforward for Emily, but groups within them need to be considered. On the supplier side, for example, they not only include inputs like coffee, but also the landlord of the premises and labour supply.

3. **Determine the underlying factors of and total strength of each force.**
   - Which are the main underlying factors for each force? Why?
   - Which competitive forces are strong? Which are weak? Why?

Not all underlying factors on the five force checklists will be equally relevant for Emily. With respect to buyers, for example, the products' degree of standardisation and prices matters most, while others are less important.

4. **Assess the overall industry structure and attractiveness.**
   - How attractive is the industry? Why?
   - Which are the most important competitive forces? Which control profitability?
   - Are more profitable competitors better positioned in relation to the five forces?

For Emily several of the forces are quite strong, but some are relatively more important for profitability. In addition, some competitors, like large coffee chains, are better positioned versus the five forces than others.

5. **Assess recent and expected future changes for each force.**
   - What are the potential positive/negative changes? How likely are they?
   - Are new entrants and/or competitors changing the industry structure in any way?

For example, Emily needs to consider the proliferation of coffee chains during the last few years and that pubs and bakeries have improved their coffee offerings lately. Maybe she can also spot possible changes in consumer trends and growth.

6. **Determine how to position your business in relation to the five forces.**
   Can you:

   - exploit any of the weak forces?
   - neutralise any of the strong forces?
   - exploit industry change in any way?
   - influence and change the industry structure to your advantage?

To cope with the forces Emily could possibly identify a concept that would attract a certain group of customers even if buyers have many choices in urban areas. This could neutralise threats from competition and entry somewhat and perhaps provide loyalty from some customers.

Sources: M.E. Porter, 'The five competitive forces that shape strategy', *Harvard Business Review*, vol. 86, no. 1, 2008, pp. 58–77; J. Magretta, *Understanding Michael Porter: The Essential Guide to Competition and Strategy*, Harvard Business Review Press, 2012.

Questions

1 Help Emily and go through each step above. Answer the questions and make a complete analysis. What is your assessment of the industry?

2 Based on your analysis: How should Emily handle the different forces? What strategic options should she consider?

3.3 Industry dynamics

The five forces framework is the most well-known strategy tool for industry analysis, but it has to be used carefully. Even though industry structures are typically fairly stable they do change, and some can be in flux for considerable periods of time. This suggests that industry dynamics in competitive forces need to be considered, which this section examines.

Industry structure analysis can easily become too static: after all, structure implies stability. However, industries are not always stable. To begin with industry borders can change over time and this needs to be considered when first defining an industry. For example, many industries, especially in high-tech arenas, are converging. Convergence is where previously separate industries begin to overlap or merge in terms of activities, technologies, products and customers.[6] Technological change has brought convergence between the telephone, photographic and the PC industries; for example, as mobile phones have become smartphones and include camera and video, e-mailing and document editing functions. Hence, companies that once were in separate industries, like Samsung in mobile phones, Sony in cameras and Apple in computers are now in the same smartphone industry. This section examines two approaches to understanding change in industry structure: the *industry life-cycle* concept and *comparative five forces analyses*.

3.3.1 The industry life cycle

The industry life-cycle concept proposes that industries start small in their development or introduction stage, then go through a period of rapid growth (the equivalent to 'adolescence' in the human life cycle), culminating in a period of 'shake-out'. The final two stages are first a period of slow or even zero growth ('maturity'), and then the final stage of decline ('old age'). The power of the five forces typically varies with the stages of the industry life cycle (see Figure 3.2).[7]

Figure 3.2 The industry life cycle

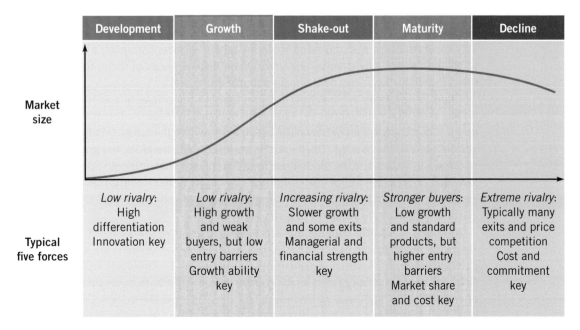

The *development stage* is an experimental one, typically with few players, little direct rivalry and highly differentiated products. The five forces are likely to be weak, therefore, though profits may actually be scarce because of high investment requirements. The next stage is one of *high growth*, with rivalry low as there is plenty of market opportunity for everybody. Low rivalry and keen buyers of the new product favour profits at this stage, but these are not certain. Barriers to entry may still be low in the growth stage, as existing competitors have not built up much scale, experience or customer loyalty. Suppliers can be powerful too if there is a shortage of components or materials that fast-growing businesses need for expansion. The *shake-out stage* begins as the market becomes increasingly saturated and cluttered with competitors. Profits are variable, as increased rivalry forces the weakest competitors out of the business. In the *maturity stage*, barriers to entry tend to increase, as control over distribution is established and economies of scale and experience curve benefits come into play. Products or services tend to standardise, with relative price becoming key. Buyers may become more powerful as they become less avid for the industry's products and more confident in switching between suppliers. Profitability at the maturity stage relies on high market share, providing leverage against buyers and competitive advantage in terms of cost. The *decline stage* can be a period of extreme rivalry, especially where there are high exit barriers, as falling sales force remaining competitors into dog-eat-dog competition. However, survivors in the decline stage may still be profitable if competitor exit leaves them in a monopolistic position. Figure 3.2 summarises some of the conditions that can be expected at different stages in the life cycle.

It is important to avoid putting too much faith in the inevitability of life-cycle stages. One stage does not follow predictably after another. First, industries vary widely in the length of their growth stages. Many internet-based industries have matured quickly and moved through the stages in less than a decade, for example online travel and dating services. Second, some industries can rapidly 'de-mature' through radical innovation. Thus, the telephony industry, based for nearly a century on fixed-line telephones, rejuvenated rapidly with the introduction of mobile and internet telephony.

3.3.2 Comparative industry structure analyses

The previous sub-section raised the issue of how competitive forces may change over time. The industry life cycle thus underlines the need to make industry structure analysis dynamic. This implies that we not only need to understand the current strength of the competitive forces, but how it may change over time. One effective means of doing this is to compare the competitive five forces over time in a simple 'radar plot'.

Figure 3.3 provides a framework for summarising the power of each of the five forces on five axes. Power diminishes as the axes go outwards. Where the forces are low, the total area enclosed by the lines between the axes is large; where the forces are high, the total area enclosed by the lines is small. The larger the enclosed area, therefore, the greater is the profit potential. In Figure 3.3, the industry at Time 0 (represented by the red lines) has relatively low rivalry (just a few competitors) and faces low substitution threats. The threat of entry is moderate, but both buyer power and supplier power are relatively high. Overall, this looks like only a moderately attractive industry to invest in.

However, given the dynamic nature of industries, managers need to look forward. Figure 3.3 represents five years forward by the green lines. Managers are predicting in this case some rise in the threat of substitutes (perhaps new technologies will be developed). On the other hand, they predict a falling entry threat, while both buyer power and supplier power will be easing. Rivalry will reduce still further. This looks like a classic case of an industry in which a few players emerge with overall dominance. The area enclosed by the green lines

Figure 3.3 Comparative industry structure analysis

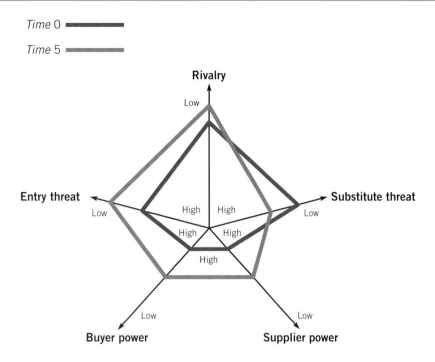

is large, suggesting a relatively attractive industry. For a firm confident of becoming one of the dominant players, this might be an industry well worth investing in.

Comparing the five forces over time on a radar plot thus helps to give industry structure analysis a dynamic aspect. The lines are only approximate, of course, because they aggregate the many individual elements that make up each of the forces into a simple composite measure. Such radar plots can nonetheless be both a useful device for initial analysis and an effective summary of a final, more refined and dynamic analysis.

3.4 Competitors and markets

An industry or sector may be too high a level to provide for a detailed understanding of competition. The five forces can impact differently on different kinds of players, requiring a more fine-grained understanding. For example, Hyundai and Porsche may be in the same broad industry (automobiles), but they are positioned differently: they are protected by different barriers to entry and competitive moves by one are unlikely to affect the other. It is often useful to disaggregate. Many industries contain a range of companies, each of which have different capabilities and compete on different bases. Some of these competitor differences are captured by the concept of *strategic groups*. Customers too can differ significantly, and these can be captured by distinguishing between different *market segments*. Thinking in terms of different strategic groups and market segments provides opportunities for organisations to develop highly distinctive positionings within broader industries. Besides disaggregating the analysis of industry competition these approaches may help in understanding how value is created differently by different competitors.

3.4.1 Strategic groups

Strategic groups are organisations within the same industry or sector with similar strategic characteristics, following similar strategies or competing on similar bases.[8] These characteristics are different from those in other strategic groups in the same industry or sector. For example, in the grocery retailing industry, supermarkets, convenience stores and corner shops each form different strategic groups. There are many different characteristics that distinguish between strategic groups and these can be grouped into two major categories of strategic dimensions (see Figure 3.4). First, the *scope* of an organisation's activities (such as product range, geographical coverage and range of distribution channels used). Second, the *resource commitment* (such as brands, marketing spend and extent of vertical integration). Which characteristics are relevant differs from industry to industry, but typically important are those characteristics that separate high performers from low performers. It helps to make a competitive force analysis first as it identifies different types of rivals.

Strategic groups can be mapped onto two-dimensional charts – for example, one axis might be the extent of product range and the other axis the size of marketing spend. One method for choosing key dimensions by which to map strategic groups is to identify top performers (by growth or profitability) in an industry and to compare them with low performers. Characteristics that are shared by top performers, but not by low performers, are likely to be particularly relevant for mapping strategic groups. For example, the most profitable firms in an industry might all be narrow in terms of product range, and lavish in terms of marketing spend, while the less profitable firms might be more widely spread in terms of products and restrained in their marketing. Here the two dimensions for mapping would be product range and marketing spend. A potential recommendation for the less profitable firms would be to cut back their product range and boost their marketing.

Figure 3.4 Some characteristics for identifying strategic groups

Strategic dimensions are based on the extent to which organisations differ in terms of **characteristics** such as:

Scope of activities

- Extent of product (or service) range
- Extent of geographical coverage (e.g. national, regional, global)
- Number of market segments served
- Distribution channels used

Resource commitment

- Extent (number) of **branding**
- **Marketing effort** (e.g. advertising spread, size of salesforce)
- Extent of **vertical integration**
- Product or service **quality**
- R&D spending and technological leadership (leader vs. follower)
- **Size** of organisation

The strategic group concept is useful in at least three ways. First, for *understanding competition*: managers can focus on their direct competitors within their particular strategic group, rather than the whole industry as rivalry often is strongest between these. Second, in *analysing strategic opportunities*: strategic group maps can identify the most attractive 'strategic spaces' within an industry. Finally, strategic groups are helpful when *analysing mobility barriers*. Of course, moving across the strategic group map to take advantage of opportunities is not costless. Often it will require difficult decisions and rare resources. Strategic groups are therefore characterised by 'mobility barriers', obstacles to movement from one strategic group to another. These are the equivalent to barriers to entry in five forces analysis, but between different strategic groups within the same industry.

3.4.2 Market segments

The concept of strategic groups discussed above helps with understanding the similarities and differences in terms of competitor characteristics. Industries can also be disaggregated into smaller and specific market sections known as segments. The concept of market segment focuses on differences in *customer* needs. A **market segment**[9] **is a group of customers who have similar needs that are different from customer needs in other parts of the market.** Where these customer groups are relatively small, such market segments are often called 'niches'. Dominance of a market segment or niche can be very valuable, for the same reasons that dominance of an industry can be valuable following five forces reasoning.

Segmentation should reflect an organisation's strategy[10] and strategies based on market segments must keep customer needs firmly in mind. Therefore, two issues are particularly important in market segment analysis:

- *Variation in customer needs.* Focusing on customer needs that are highly distinctive from those typical in the market is one means of building a long-term segment strategy. Customer needs vary for a whole variety of reasons – some of which are identified in Table 3.1.

Table 3.1   Some bases of market segmentation

Type of factor	Consumer markets	Industrial/organisational markets
Characteristics of people/organisations	Age, gender, ethnicity Income Family size Life-cycle stage Location Lifestyle	Industry Location Size Technology Profitability Management
Purchase/use situation	Size of purchase Brand loyalty Purpose of use Purchasing behaviour Importance of purchase Choice criteria	Application Importance of purchase Volume Frequency of purchase Purchasing procedure Choice criteria Distribution channel
Users' needs and preferences for product characteristics	Product similarity Price preference Brand preferences Desired features Quality	Performance requirements Assistance from suppliers Brand preferences Desired features Quality Service requirements

Theoretically, any of these factors could be used to identify distinct market segments. However, the crucial bases of segmentation vary according to market. In industrial markets, segmentation is often thought of in terms of industrial classification of buyers: steel producers might segment by automobile industry, packaging industry and construction industry, for example. On the other hand, segmentation by buyer behaviour (e.g. direct buying versus those users who buy through third parties such as contractors) or purchase value (e.g. high-value bulk purchasers versus frequent low-value purchasers) might be more appropriate. Being able to serve a highly distinctive segment that other organisations find difficult to serve is often the basis for a secure long-term strategy.

- *Specialisation* within a market segment can also be an important basis for a successful segmentation strategy. This is sometimes called a 'niche strategy'. Organisations that have built up most experience in servicing a particular market segment should not only have lower costs in so doing, but also have built relationships which may be difficult for others to break down. Experience and relationships are likely to protect a dominant position in a particular segment. However, precisely because customers value different things in different segments, specialised producers may find it very difficult to compete on a broader basis. For example, a small local brewery competing against the big brands on the basis of its ability to satisfy distinctive local tastes is unlikely to find it easy to serve other segments where tastes are different, scale requirements are larger and distribution channels are more complex.

3.5 Opportunities and threats

The concepts and frameworks discussed above and in Chapter 2 should be helpful in understanding the factors in the macro-, industry and competitor/market environments of an organisation. However, the critical issue is the *implications* that are drawn from this understanding in guiding strategic decisions and choices. The crucial next stage, therefore, is to draw from the environmental analysis specific strategic opportunities and threats for the organisation. Identifying these opportunities and threats is extremely valuable when thinking about strategic choices for the future (the subject of Chapter 6). Opportunities and threats form one half of the Strengths, Weaknesses, Opportunities and Threats (SWOT) analyses that shape many companies' strategy formulation (see Section 4.4.3). In responding strategically to the environment, the goal is to reduce identified threats and take advantage of the best opportunities.

The techniques and concepts in this and the previous chapter should help in identifying environmental threats and opportunities, for instance:

- *PESTEL analysis* of the macro-environment might reveal threats and opportunities presented by technological change, or shifts in market demographics or such like factors (see Chapter 2).

- Identification of *key drivers for change* can help generate different *scenarios* for managerial discussion, some more threatening and others more favourable.

- *Porter's five forces analysis* might, for example, identify a rise or fall in barriers to entry, or opportunities to reduce industry rivalry, perhaps by acquisition of competitors.

Summary

- The environment influence closest to an organisation includes the *industry or sector*.

- Industries and sectors can be analysed in terms of *Porter's five forces* – barriers to entry, substitutes, buyer power, supplier power and rivalry. Together with *complementors* these determine industry or sector attractiveness and possible ways of managing strategy.

- Industries and sectors are dynamic, and their changes can be analysed in terms of the *industry life cycle* and *comparative five forces radar plots*.

- Within industries *strategic group* analysis and *market segment* analysis can help identify strategic gaps or opportunities.

Recommended key readings

- The classic book on the analysis of industries is M.E. Porter, *Competitive Strategy*, Free Press, 1980. An update is available in M.E. Porter, 'The five competitive forces that shape strategy', *Harvard Business Review*, vol. 86, no. 1 (2008), pp. 58–77.

- For an in-depth discussion of how to apply Porter's Competitive Force Framework, see J. Magretta, *Understanding Michael Porter: The Essential Guide to Competition and Strategy*, Harvard Business Review Press, 2012.

References

1. See M.E. Porter, *Competitive Strategy: Techniques for Analyzing Industries and Competitors*, Free Press, 1980, p. 5.
2. See endnote 1 above and M. Porter, 'The five competitive forces that shape strategy', *Harvard Business Review*, vol. 86, no. 1 (2008), pp. 58–77.
3. A. Brandenburger and B. Nalebuff, 'The right game', *Harvard Business Review*, July–August 1995, pp. 57–64.
4. See A. Brandenburger and B. Nalebuff, *Co-opetition*, Doubleday, New York, 1996 and K. Walley, 'Coopetition: an introduction to the subject and an agenda for research', *International Studies of Management and Organization*, vol. 37, no. 2 (2007), pp. 11–31.
5. For an overview of recent empirical research of strategy and network effects see D.P. McIntyre and M. Subramaniam, 'Strategy in network industries: a review and research agenda', *Journal of Management* (2009), pp. 1–24.
6. See for example F. Hacklin, B. Battistini, and G. Von Krogh. 'Strategic choices in converging industries', *MIT Sloan Management Review* 55.1 (2013): 65–73.
7. A classic academic overview of the industry life cycle is S. Klepper, 'Industry life cycles', *Industrial and Corporate Change*, vol. 6, no. 1 (1996), pp. 119–43.
8. For examples of strategic group analysis, see G. Leask and D. Parker, 'Strategic groups, competitive groups and performance in the UK pharmaceutical industry', *Strategic Management Journal*, vol. 28, no. 7 (2007), pp. 723–45; and W. Desarbo, R. Grewal and R. Wang, 'Dynamic strategic groups: deriving spatial evolutionary paths', *Strategic Management Journal*, vol. 30, no. 8 (2009), pp. 1420–39.
9. A useful discussion of segmentation in relation to competitive strategy is provided in M.E. Porter, *Competitive Advantage*, Free Press, 1985, Chapter 7.
10. For a discussion of how market segmentation needs to be broadly related to an organisation's strategy and not only narrowly focused on the needs of advertising see D. Yankelovich and D. Meer, 'Rediscovering market segmentation', *Harvard Business Review*, February, 2006, pp. 73–80.

Case example

Game-changing forces and the global advertising industry

Peter Cardwell

This case is centred on the global advertising industry which faces significant strategic game-changing forces driven by technological innovation, the rise of consumer spending in developing economies, changes in consumer media consumption and pressures from major advertisers for results-based compensation.

In the second decade of the new millennium, advertising agencies faced a number of unanticipated challenges. Traditional markets and industry operating methods, developed largely in North America and Western Europe following the rise of consumer spending power in the twentieth century, were being radically reappraised.

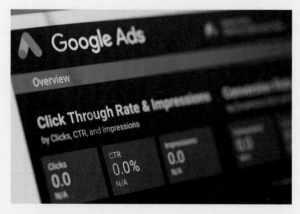

Source: PixieMe/Shutterstock

The industry was subject to game-changing forces from the so-called 'digital revolution' with the entry of search companies like Google, Facebook and Amazon as rivals for advertising budgets on mobile devices. Changing patterns in global consumer markets impacted on both industry dynamics and structure. Budgets being spent through traditional advertising agencies were being squeezed as industry rivalry intensified with the entry of specialist consultancies.

Overview

Traditionally, the business objective of advertising agencies is to target a specific audience on behalf of clients with a message that encourages them to try a product or service and ultimately purchase it. This is done largely through the concept of a brand being communicated via media channels. Brands allow consumers to differentiate between products and services and it is the job of the advertising agency to position the brand so that it is associated with functions and attributes which are valued by target consumers. These brands may be consumer brands (e.g. Procter & Gamble, Samsung, Nestle) or business-to-business (B2B) brands (e.g. IBM, Airbus Industrie and UPS). Some brands target both consumers and businesses (e.g. Microsoft and Apple).

As well as private-sector brand companies, governments spend heavily to advertise public-sector services such as healthcare and education or to influence individual behaviour (such as 'Don't drink and drive'). For example, the UK government had an advertising budget of £300m (€335m) in the late-2010s. Charities, political groups, religious groups and other not-for-profit organisations also use the advertising industry to attract funds into their organisation or to raise awareness of issues. Together these account for approximately 3 per cent of advertising spend.

Advertisements are usually placed in selected media (TV, press, radio, mobile and desktop internet, etc.) by an advertising agency acting on behalf of the client brand company; thus they are acting as 'agents'. The client company employs the advertising agency to use its knowledge, skills, creativity and experience to create advertising and marketing to drive consumption of the client's brands. Clients traditionally have been charged according to the time spent on creating the advertisements plus a commission based on the media and services bought on behalf of clients. However, in recent years, larger advertisers such as Coca-Cola, Procter & Gamble and Unilever have been moving away from this compensation model to a 'value' or results-based model based on a number of metrics, including growth in sales and market share.

Ad industry growth

Money spent on advertising has increased dramatically over the past two decades and in 2018 was over $205bn (€176bn, £158bn) in the USA and $583bn worldwide. While there might be a decline in recessionary years, it is predicted that spending on advertising will exceed $787bn globally by 2022.

The industry is shifting its focus as emerging markets drive revenues from geographic sectors that would not have been significant 5 to 10 years ago, such as the BRICS

Table 1 Global advertising expenditure by region (US$ million, at 2017 average rates)

	2014	2015	2016	2017	2018 *(estimate)*
N America	169,277	175,024	183,075	191,130	196,099
W Europe	111,300	114,712	119,531	124,790	128,035
Asia Pacific	122,000	130,711	137,639	145,695	149,483
C & E Europe	32,284	35,514	36,691	37,305	38,275
Latin America	34,082	36,836	38,530	39,226	42,315
Africa/ME/ROW	25,941	28,044	29,334	28,608	29,352
World	**494,884**	**520,841**	**544,800**	**568,771**	**583,911**

Source: Zenith Media, Statista, December 2018.

countries and the Middle East and North Africa. This shift has seen the emergence of agencies specialising in Islamic marketing, characterised by a strong ethical responsibility to consumers. Future trends indicate the strong emergence of consumer brands in areas of the world where sophisticated consumers with brand awareness are currently in the minority (see Table 1).

In terms of industry sectors, three of the top 10 global advertisers are car manufacturers. However, the two major fmcg (fast-moving consumer goods) producers Procter & Gamble and Nestlé are in the three top spots for global advertising spend. Healthcare and beauty (L'Oréal), consumer electronics (Samsung), fast food, beverage and confectionery manufacturers are all featured in the top 20 global advertisers. The top 100 advertisers account for nearly 50 per cent of the measured global advertising economy.

Despite the increase in worldwide advertising revenues, the holding companies that own the world's largest advertising groups: WPP, Publicis, Omnicom and Interpublic Group (see Table 2) are under intense pressure in a changing business environment to deliver shareholder value.

Intensifying competition

Advertising agencies come in all sizes and include everything from one- or two-person 'boutique' operations (which rely mostly on freelance outsourced talent to perform most functions), small- to medium-sized agencies, large independents to multinational, multi-agency conglomerates employing over 200,000 people. The industry has gone through a period of increasing concentration through acquisitions, thereby creating multi-agency

Table 2 Top five multi-agency conglomerates: 2017, by revenue, profit before interest and tax, number of employees and agency brands.

Group name	Revenue	PBIT	Employees	Advertising agency brands
1. WPP (UK)	£15.2bn	£2.16bn	200,000	GroupM, JWT, Grey, Ogilvy, Y&R
2. Omnicom (US)	$15.4bn	$2.059bn	76,000	BBDO, DDB, TBWA
3. Publicis Groupe (France)	€10.8bn	€1.51bn	79,000	Leo Burnett, Saatchi & Saatchi, Publicis, BBH
4. IPG (US)	$7.88bn	$973m	49,700	McCann Erickson, FCB, MullenLowe Group
5. Dentsu (Japan)	$7.2bn	$938m	47,324	Aegis, Carat, Denstu Media, iProspect, Isobar

Source: WPP, Omnicom, Publicis Groupe, IPG, Dentsu

conglomerates such as those listed in Table 2. While these conglomerates are headquartered in London, New York, Paris and Tokyo, they operate globally.

Large multi-agency conglomerates compete on the basis of the quality of their creative output (as indicated by industry awards), the ability to buy media more cost-effectively, market knowledge, global reach and increasingly range of digital services. Some agency groups have integrated vertically into higher-margin marketing services. Omnicom, through its Diversified Agency Services, has acquired printing services and telemarketing/customer care companies. Other agency groups have vertically integrated to lesser or greater degrees.

Mid-sized and smaller boutique advertising agencies compete by delivering value-added services through in-depth knowledge of specific market sectors, specialised services such as digital and by building a reputation for innovative and ground-breaking creative advertising/marketing campaigns. However, they might be more reliant on outsourced creative suppliers than larger agencies.

Many small specialist agencies are founded by former employees of large agencies. In turn, smaller specialist agencies are often acquired by the large multi-agency conglomerates in order to acquire specific capabilities to target new sectors or markets or provide additional services to existing clients.

With the development of the internet and online search advertising, a new breed of interactive digital media agencies. These agencies differentiate themselves by offering a mix of web design/development, search engine marketing, internet advertising/marketing, or e-business/e-commerce consulting. They are classified as 'agencies' because they create digital media campaigns and implement media purchases of ads on behalf of clients on social networking and community sites such as YouTube, Facebook, Instagram, Flickr and other digital media.

The rise of mobile and the digital duopoly

Search companies such as Google, Bing and Yahoo and social network Facebook, exploit their ability to interact with and gain information about millions of potential consumers of branded products. Facebook and Google have effectively become a 'digital duopoly' to the extent that they represent almost 60 per cent of the global digital mobile ad market, according to eMarketer, the research group.

Digital search and mobile advertising budgets are increasing faster than other traditional advertising media as search companies like Google and Facebook generate revenues from paid search as advertisers discover that targeted ads on mobile and desktop are highly effective (see Table 3). By 2017, Google had a 66 per cent market share of the $81.6bn spent on online search advertising globally, with Facebook also increasing its share.

Sir Martin Sorrell, the former CEO of WPP the world's largest multi-service agency group, pointed out that Google is a rival for the service relationships with WPP's clients. WPP group spent more than $6bn of its clients' ad budgets with Google in 2017 and $2.1bn with Facebook. Sorrell called Google a 'frenemy' – the combination of 'friend' and 'enemy'. Google is a 'friend' where it allows WPP to place targeted advertising based on Google

Table 3   Global advertising expenditure by medium (US$ million, at 2016 average rates)

	2013	2014	2015	2016	2017
Newspapers	93,019	92,300	91,908	90,070	88,268
Magazines	42,644	42,372	42,300	40,185	39,391
Television	191,198	202,380	213,878	210,670	210,459
Radio	32,580	33,815	35,054	34,457	34,130
Cinema	2,393	2,538	2,681	2,767	2,850
Outdoor	30,945	32,821	34,554	36,143	36,324
Internet – Mobile & Desktop	70,518	80,672	91,516	130,019	156,543
Total	**463,297**	**486,898**	**511,891**	**544,311**	**567,956**

Note: The totals in Table 3 are lower than in Table 1, since that table includes advertising expenditure for a few countries where it is not itemised by advertising medium.
Source: ZenithMedia, e-Marketer, Statista, February 2018.

Table 4 US mobile ad spending 2015–2019

	2015	2016	2017	2018 (estimate)	2019 (estimate)
Mobile ad spending (US$bn)	28.72	40.50	49.81	57.78	65.87
% change	50.00%	41.00%	23.00%	16.00%	14.00%
% of digital ad spending	49.00%	60.40%	66.60%	67.70%	72.20%
% of total media ad spending	15.30%	20.40%	23.90%	26.30%	28.60%

Source: US Mobile Ad Spending, In-App vs. Mobile Web, 2015-2019, eMarketer Inc.

analytics and an 'enemy' where it does not share these analytics with the agency and becomes a potential competitor for the customer insight and advertising traditionally created by WPP.

Mobile ad spending on sites such as YouTube, Pinterest, Twitter, continues to increase at the expense of desktop, taking a bigger share of marketers' budgets. The shift to mobile ad spending is being driven mainly by consumer demand and is predicted to be over 28 per cent of total media ad spending in the US which is why Google has made acquisitions in this sector (see Table 4).

Entry of 'big data' technology consultancies

The analysis of 'big data' is playing an increasingly important role in helping to create targeted and personalised advertising campaigns for the world's major marketers. Consultancies, such as Accenture Interactive and IBMiX, as well as the large accountancy firms PwC Digital Services and Deloitte Digital, all with global reach, are now competing for a share of the advertising market by acquiring creative agencies to add to their 'big data' digital services and have now entered the top 10 agencies ranked on the basis of turnover.

Their services include programmatic advertising and the use of artificial intelligence algorithms that analyse consumer behaviour allowing for real-time campaign optimisations towards an audience more likely to convert to the advertiser's product or service, which is a major innovation, the impact of which is still being assessed.

This has led some industry experts to observe that 'Madmen' now need to become 'Mathsmen', as data analytics and artificial intelligence are seen to be becoming more important than creativity which traditional advertising agencies have relied upon as a differentiator. This is enabling them to offer a range of services to the major marketing companies that compete directly with traditional advertising agencies.

The disruptive change in the advertising industry at the beginning of the twenty-first century started with the internet. The convergence of internet, TV, smart phones, tablets and laptop computers has had a major impact on the advertising industry.

Factors that have driven competitive advantage to date may not be relevant in the future. Traditionally the advertising industry has embodied the idea of creativity as the vital differentiator between the best and the mediocre – and individuals have often been at the heart of this creativity. The emergence of data analytics, programmatic advertising and the use of artificial intelligence algorithms are disruptive to 'business as usual' in the industry. A key question is whether creativity will be important in the future, in relation to breadth of services, global reach and data analysis.

Sources: Reprinted with permission from Peter Cardwell.

Questions

1 Carry out a five forces analysis of the advertising industry. What are the strengths of the five forces and what underlying factors drive them? What is the industry attractiveness?

2 What strategic group dimensions and strategic groups can you identify? What are the differences between them?

3 Which PESTEL factors are driving changes in the industry? Which factors are becoming more negative or positive for the major advertising agencies?

Chapter 4
Resources and capabilities analysis

Key terms

Learning outcomes

After reading this chapter, you should be able to:

- Identify organisational *resources* and *capabilities* and how these relate to the strategies of organisations.

- Analyse how resources and capabilities might provide sustainable competitive advantage on the basis of their *Value*, *Rarity*, *Inimitability* and *Organisational support (VRIO)*.

- Diagnose resources and capabilities by means of *VRIO analysis*, *value chain analysis* and *SWOT analysis*.

- Consider how resources and capabilities can be developed based on *dynamic capabilities*.

4.1 Introduction

Chapters 2 and 3 emphasised the importance of the external environment of an organisation and how it can create both strategic opportunities and threats. However, it is not only the external environment that matters for strategy; there are also differences between organisations that need to be considered. For example, manufacturers of saloon cars compete within the same industry and within the same technological environment, but with markedly different success. BMW has been consistently successful based on its engineering capabilities and brand. Chrysler has found it more difficult to maintain its competitive position and others, like SAAB cars in Sweden, have gone out of business. It is not so much the characteristics of the environment which explain these differences in performance, but differences in organisation-specific *resources and capabilities*. This puts the focus on variations between companies within the same environment and how they vary in their resources and capabilities arrangements. It is the strategic importance of organisations' resources and capabilities that is the focus of this chapter.

Two key notions underlie the analysis of resources and capabilities. The first is that organisations are not identical but have different resources and capabilities; they are 'heterogeneous' in this respect. The second is that it can be difficult for one organisation to obtain or imitate the resources and capabilities of another. The implication for managers is that they need to understand how their organisations are different from their rivals in ways that may form the basis of sustainable competitive advantage and superior performance. These concepts underlie what has become known as the **resource-based view** (RBV) of strategy pioneered by Jay Barney at the University of Utah: **that the competitive advantage and superior performance of an organisation are explained by the distinctiveness of its resources and capabilities.**[1]

The chapter has four further sections:

- Section 4.2 discusses the foundations of what *resources* and *capabilities* are. It also draws a distinction between *threshold* resources and capabilities required to compete in a market and *distinctive* resources and capabilities that may be a basis for achieving competitive advantage and superior performance.

- Section 4.3 explains the ways in which distinctive resources and capabilities can contribute to *sustained competitive advantage* (in a public-sector context the equivalent concern might be how some organisations sustain relative superior performance over time). In particular, the importance of the *Value, Rarity, Inimitability and Organisational support* (VRIO) of resources and capabilities is explained.

- Section 4.4 moves on to consider different ways resources and capabilities might be analysed. These include *VRIO analysis* and *value chain*. The section concludes by explaining the use of *SWOT* analysis as a basis for pulling together the insights from the analyses of the environment (explained in Chapters 2 and 3) and of resources and capabilities in this chapter.

- Finally, Section 4.5 discusses some of the key issues of *dynamic capabilities* and how resources and capabilities can be created, developed and managed.

4.2 Foundations of resources and capabilities

Given that different writers, managers and consultants use different terms and concepts, it is important to understand how concepts relating to resources and capabilities are used in this book. The **resources and capabilities** of an organisation contribute to its long-term

survival and potentially to competitive advantage. However, to understand and to manage resources and capabilities it is necessary to explain their components.[2]

4.2.1 Resources and capabilities

Resources are the assets that organisations have or can call upon and capabilities are the ways in which those assets are deployed. A shorthand way of thinking of this distinction is that resources are 'what we *have*' (nouns) and capabilities are 'what we *do*' (verbs).[3] Other terms are sometimes used; for example 'capabilities' and 'competences' are often used interchangeably (earlier editions of this text used the term 'competences' for capabilities).[4]

Resources and capabilities are typically related, as Table 4.1 shows. Resources are certainly important, but how an organisation employs and deploys its resources in the form of capabilities matters at least as much for long-term survival. There would be no point in having state-of-the-art equipment if it were not used effectively. The efficiency and effectiveness of physical or financial resources, or the people in an organisation, depend not just on their existence, but on the systems and processes by which they are managed. These can, for example, involve the relationships and cooperation between people, their adaptability, their innovative capacity, the relationship with customers and suppliers, and the experience and learning about what works well and what does not. Illustration 4.1 shows examples of how executives explain the importance of the resources and capabilities of their different organisations.

4.2.2 Threshold and distinctive resources and capabilities

A distinction needs to be made between resources and capabilities that are at a threshold level and those that might help the organisation achieve competitive advantage and superior performance. **Threshold resources and capabilities are those needed for an organisation to meet the necessary requirements to compete at all in a given market and achieve parity with competitors in that market.** Without these the organisation could not survive over time. For example, start-up businesses may simply not have or cannot obtain the resources or capabilities needed to compete with established competitors. Identifying threshold requirements is, however, also important for established businesses. There could be changing *threshold resources* required to meet minimum customer requirements: for example, the increasing demands by modern multiple retailers of their suppliers mean that those suppliers must possess a quite sophisticated IT and digital infrastructure simply to stand a chance of meeting retailer requirements. Or there could be *threshold capabilities* required to deploy resources to meet customers' requirements and support particular strategies. Retailers do not simply expect suppliers to have the required digital infrastructure, but to be able to use it effectively so as to guarantee the required level of service.

Table 4.1   Resources and capabilities

Resources: what we have (nouns), e.g.		Capabilities: what we do (verbs), e.g.
Machines, buildings, raw materials, patents, databases, computer systems	Physical	Ways of achieving utilisation of plant, efficiency, productivity, flexibility, marketing
Balance sheet, cash flow, suppliers of funds	Financial	Ability to raise funds and manage cash flows, debtors, creditors, etc.
Managers, employees, partners, suppliers, customers	Human	How people gain and use experience, skills, knowledge, build relationships, motivate others and innovate

Illustration 4.1 Resources and capabilities

Executives emphasise the importance of resources and capabilities in different organisations.

The Australian Red Cross

To achieve the vision of improving the lives of vulnerable people the Australian Red Cross emphasises the crucial role of capabilities in its strategic plan. 'Capabilities are integral to our overriding strategy to create one Red Cross,' writes CEO Robert Tickner. The Australian Red Cross distinguishes between technical competency and behavioural capability. The former refers to specialist skills and may include such competencies as project management, financial management, community development, social work, administrative or in information technology. Capabilities at the Red Cross refer to the behaviours they expect its people to demonstrate in order to be successful in achieving objectives. The organisation aims to increasingly invest in the capabilities and skills of Red Cross people and supporters including members, branches and units, volunteers, aid workers, staff and donors. For example, this involves investing in a diverse workforce and supporter base, with strong engagement of 'young people, Aboriginal and Torres Strait Islander people, and other culturally and linguistically diverse people'. The emphasis is on people who are engaged, dynamic, innovative, entrepreneurial and motivated to realise the vision and goals.[1]

AstraZeneca

For AstraZeneca, a leading global pharmaceutical company, both resources and capabilities feature prominently when they describe their strategy: 'R&D resources: We have approximately 8,400 employees in our R&D organisation, working in various sites around the world. We have three strategic R&D centres: Gaithersburg, MD, US; Gothenburg, Sweden; and Cambridge, UK'; 'We are using our distinctive scientific capabilities, as well as investing in key programmes and focused business development, to deliver life-changing medicines'; '[Our] Distinctive R&D capabilities: Small molecules, oligonucleotides and other emerging drug platforms, as well as biologic medicines, including immunotherapies, and innovative delivery devices'; 'Co-location near bioscience clusters at three strategic centres. . . helps to leverage our capabilities and foster collaboration with leading scientists and research organisations'; 'Operations 2020 was launched in 2015 to enhance supply capabilities in order to respond better to patient and market needs'; 'We will also harness our internal capabilities to develop robust strategies on data and analytics, software engineering and cloud technology – all of which will support the business and its various transformation programmes.'[2]

Infosys

The Indian company Infosys is a global leader in information technology, outsourcing, system integration services and IT consulting. It is listed as one of the world's most reputable companies with close to 150,000 employees worldwide. The company's 'Infosys 3.0 strategy' is taking a further step to provide more advanced IT products and services, which requires investments in new resources and capabilities. Infosys CEO S.D. Shibulal: 'We continue to make focused investments in our organisational capabilities.'

The strategy emphasises innovation and focuses on higher-value software. Innovation abilities are central for this, as stated on the website: 'The foundation of our innovation capability is our core lab network – Infosys Labs – and the new thinking that our team of over 600 researchers brings to the table.' The strategy thus requires human resource and training capabilities including the ability to attract, employ, educate and retain new high-quality engineers. As Srikantan Moorthy, Senior Vice President and Group Head explains: 'We are currently hiring and developing talent in the areas of cloud, mobility, sustainability, and product development. In addition, a key focus is consultative skills. All of these are in line with our Infosys 3.0 strategy. We place significant value on continuous learning and knowledge sharing.'[3]

Sources: (1) Australian Red Cross Capability Framework 2015, (2) AstraZeneca Annual Report 2017, pp 4–32, (3) *Financial Times*, 13 August 2012; *Financial Times*, 11 September 2012; http://www.infosys.com © Infosys; http://www.skillingindia.com/.

Questions

1 Categorise the range of resources and capabilities highlighted by the executives above in terms of Section 4.2 and Table 4.1.

2 To what extent and why might these resources and capabilities be the basis of *sustained* competitive advantage?

3 Imagine you are the general manager of an organisation of your choice and undertake the same exercise as in questions 1 and 2 above.

Identifying and managing threshold resources and capabilities raises a significant challenge because threshold levels will change as critical success factors change or through the activities of competitors and new entrants. To continue the example above, suppliers to major retailers did not require the same level of IT, digital and logistics support a decade ago. But the retailers' drive to reduce costs, improve efficiency and ensure availability of merchandise to their customers means that their expectations of their suppliers have increased markedly in that time and continue to do so. So, there is a need for those suppliers continuously to review and improve their digital and logistics resource and capability base just to stay in business.

While threshold resources and capabilities are important, they do not of themselves create competitive advantage or the basis of superior performance. They can be thought of as 'qualifiers' to be able to compete at all with competitors while distinctive resources and capabilities are 'winners' required to triumph over competitors. **Distinctive resources and capabilities are required to achieve competitive advantage.** These are dependent on an organisation having a distinctiveness or uniqueness that is of value to customers and which competitors find difficult to imitate. This could be because the organisation has *distinctive resources* that critically underpin competitive advantage and that others cannot imitate or obtain – a long-established brand, for example. Or it could be that an organisation achieves competitive advantage because it has *distinctive capabilities* – ways of doing things that are unique to that organisation and effectively utilised so as to be valuable to customers and difficult for competitors to obtain or imitate. For example, Apple has distinctive resources in smartphone technologies and in its powerful brand together with distinctive capabilities in design and in understanding consumer behaviour.

Section 4.3 that follows discusses in more depth the role played by distinctive resources and capabilities in contributing to long-term, sustainable competitive advantage. Section 4.3.3 explores further the importance of linkages.

4.3 Distinctive resources and capabilities as a basis of competitive advantage

As explained above, distinctive resources and capabilities are necessary for sustainable competitive advantage and superior economic performance. In the public-sector and not-for-profit context the equivalent concern is how to sustain relative superior performance and set the organisation apart from others that have a similar purpose. This section considers four key criteria by which resources and capabilities can be assessed in terms of them providing a basis for achieving such competitive advantage: **V**alue, **R**arity, **I**nimitability and **O**rganisational support – or **VRIO**.[5] Figure 4.1 illustrates these four fundamental criteria and the questions they address.

4.3.1 V – value of resources and capabilities

Resources and capabilities are valuable when they create a product or a service that is of value to customers and enables the organisation to respond to environmental opportunities or threats. There are three components to consider here:

- *Value to customers*: it may seem an obvious point to make that resources and capabilities need to be of value to customers, but in practice it is often ignored or poorly understood. For example, managers may seek to build on resources and capabilities that *they* may see as valuable, but which do not meet customers' critical success factors. Or they may see a distinctive capability as of value simply because it is unique, although it may not be valued

Figure 4.1 VRIO

V	**Value:** Do resources and capabilities exist that are valued by customers and enable the organisation to respond to environmental opportunities or threats?
R	**Rarity:** Do resources and capabilities exist that no (or few) competitors possess?
I	**Inimitability:** Are resources and capabilities difficult and costly for competitors to obtain and imitate?
O	**Organisational support:** Is the organisation appropriately organised to exploit the resources and capabilities?

Source: The VRIO criteria were introduced by Jay Barney in J.B. Barney, *Gaining and sustaining competitive advantage*, Addison-Wesley, 1997.

by customers. Having resources and capabilities that are different from other organisations' is not, of itself, a basis of competitive advantage. Or a resource and capability may historically have been of value to customers but may no longer be.

- *Taking advantage of opportunities and neutralising threats*: the most fundamental point is that to be valuable resources and capabilities need to address opportunities and threats that arise in an organisation's environment. This points to an important complementarity with the external environment of an organisation (Chapters 2 and 3). An external opportunity is addressed when a resource or capability increases the value for customers either through lowering the price or by increasing the attractiveness of a product or service. For example, IKEA has valuable resources in its cost-conscious culture and size and related capabilities that lower its costs compared to competitors and this addresses opportunities of low-priced designed furniture for customers that competitors do not attend to. Using a resource and capability that fails to exploit opportunities or neutralise threats risks not creating value and even decreasing revenues and increasing costs.

- *Cost*: the product or service needs to be provided at a cost that still allows the organisation to make the returns expected of it. The danger is that the cost of developing or acquiring the resources and/or capabilities to deliver what customers especially value is such that products or services are not profitable.

4.3.2 R – rarity

Resources and capabilities that are valuable but common among competitors are unlikely to be a source of competitive advantage. If competitors have the same or similar resources and capabilities, they can respond quickly to the strategic initiative of a rival. This has happened in competition between car manufacturers as they have sought to add more accessories and gadgets to cars. As soon as it becomes evident that these are valued by customers, they are introduced widely by competitors that typically have access to the same technology. **Rare resources and capabilities**, on the other hand, **are those possessed uniquely by one organisation or by a few others**. Here competitive advantage is longer-lasting. For example, a company can have patented products or services that give it advantage. Some libraries have unique collections of books unavailable elsewhere; a company can have a powerful brand; or retail stores can have prime locations. In terms of capabilities, organisations can have unique skills or business processes developed over time or make use of special relationships with customers or suppliers not widely possessed by competitors. However, it can be dangerous to assume that rarity will simply endure. It may therefore be necessary to consider other bases of sustainability in competitive advantage.

4.3.3 I – inimitability

It should be clear by now that the search for resources and capabilities that provides sustainable competitive advantage is not straightforward. Having resources and capabilities that are valuable to customers and relatively rare is important, but this may not be enough. Sustainable competitive advantage also involves identifying **inimitable resources and capabilities** – **those that competitors find difficult and costly to imitate or obtain or substitute**. If an organisation has a competitive advantage because of its particular marketing and sales skills it can only sustain this if competitors cannot imitate, obtain or substitute for them or if the costs to do so would eliminate any gains made. Often the barriers to imitation lie deeply in the organisation in linkages between activities, skills and people.

At the risk of over-generalisation, it is unusual for competitive advantage to be explainable by differences in the tangible resources of organisations, since over time these can usually be acquired or imitated (key geographic locations, certain raw material resources and intangible resources like brands, etc., can, however, be exceptions). Advantage is more likely to be determined by the way in which resources are deployed and managed in terms of an organisation's activities; in other words on the basis of capabilities.[6] For example, as indicated above, it is unlikely that an IT system will improve an organisation's competitive standing in itself, not least because competitors can probably buy something very similar on the open market. On the other hand, the capabilities to manage, develop and deploy such a system to the benefit of customers may be much more difficult and costly to imitate. Compared to physical assets, capabilities tend to involve more intangible imitation barriers. In particular, they often include *linkages* that integrate activities, skills, knowledge and people both inside and outside the organisation in distinct and mutually compatible ways. These linkages can make capabilities particularly difficult for competitors to imitate and there are three primary reasons why this may be so. These are summarised in Figure 4.2 and are now briefly reviewed.

Figure 4.2 Criteria for the inimitability of resources and capabilities

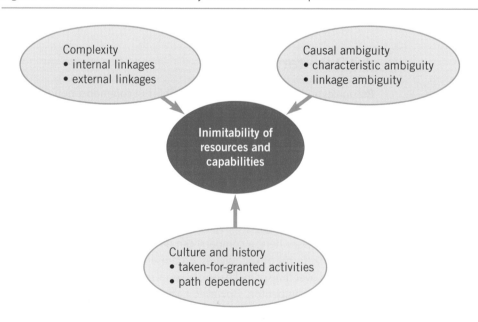

Complexity

The resources and capabilities of an organisation can be difficult to imitate because they are complex and involve interlinkages. This may be for two main reasons:

- *Internal linkages.* There may be linked activities and processes that, together, deliver customer value. This represents a complexity because of the numerous interactions between tightly knit activities and decisions.[7] This is not only because of the complexity itself but because, very likely, it has developed on the basis of custom and practice built up over years and is specific to the organisation concerned. For example, companies like IKEA and Ryanair still enjoy competitive advantages despite the availability of countless case studies, articles and reports on their successes.

- *External interconnectedness.* Organisations can make it difficult for others to imitate or obtain their bases of competitive advantage by developing activities together with customers or partners such that they become dependent on them. Apple, for example, has many intricate linkages with various app developers, partners and music labels that others may find difficult to imitate.

Causal ambiguity

Another reason why resources and capabilities might be difficult and costly to imitate is that competitors find it difficult to discern the causes and effects underpinning an organisation's advantage. This is called *causal ambiguity* and it may exist in two different forms:[8]

- *Characteristic ambiguity.* Where the significance of the characteristic itself is difficult to discern or comprehend, perhaps because it is rooted in the organisation's culture or based on tacit knowledge. For example, the know-how of the buyers in a successful fashion retailer may be evident in the sales achieved for the ranges they buy year after year. But this may involve subtleties like spotting new trends and picking up feedback from pioneering customers that may be very difficult for competitors to comprehend so they will find it difficult to imitate.

- *Linkage ambiguity.* Where competitors cannot discern which activities and processes are dependent on which others to form linkages that create distinctiveness. The expertise of the fashion buyers is unlikely to be lodged in one individual or even one function. It is likely that there will be multiple and complex links to a network of suppliers, fashion experts, style bloggers and designers to understand the market. Indeed, in some organisations the managers themselves admit that they do not fully comprehend the linkages throughout the organisation that deliver customer value. If this is so it would certainly be difficult for competitors to understand them.

Culture and history

Resources and capabilities that involve complex social interactions and interpersonal relations within an organisation can be difficult and costly for competitors to imitate. For example, capabilities can become embedded in an organisation's culture. Coordination between various activities occurs 'naturally' because people know their part in the wider picture or it is simply 'taken for granted' that activities are done in particular ways. We see this in high-performing sports teams and in groups of people that work together to combine specialist skills as in hospital operating theatres. Linked to this cultural embeddedness is the likelihood that such capabilities have developed over time and in a particular way. The origins and history by which capabilities and resources have developed over time are referred to as *path dependency*.[9] This history is specific to the organisation and cannot be imitated.

Illustration 4.2 Groupon and the sincerest form of flattery

When a firm identifies a new market niche it must also make sure its resources and capabilities are valuable, rare, inimitable and supported by the organisation.

Chicago-based Groupon was launched in 2008 by Andrew Mason with the idea to email subscribers daily deals of heavily discounted coupons for local restaurants, theatres, spas, etc. Via the emails or by visiting the Groupon website customers purchase these substantially discounted deals in the form of electronic coupons which can be redeemed at the local merchant. Groupon brings exposure and more customers to the merchants and charges them commissions for the same. The venture rapidly grew into a daily deal giant and became the fastest-growing internet business ever to reach a $1bn valuation milestone and, thus, became a 'unicorn' (name for start-ups with valuations over $1bn). In 2010 Groupon rejected a $6bn (€4.5bn) takeover bid by Google and instead went public at $10bn in 2011.

While Groupon's daily deals were valued by customers – the company quickly spread to over 40 countries – they also attracted thousands of copycats worldwide. Investors questioned Groupon's business and to what extent it had rare and inimitable resources and capabilities. CEO Andrew Mason denied in *Wall Street Journal* (*WSJ*) that the model was too easy to replicate:

'There's proof. There are over 2000 direct clones of the Groupon business model. However, there's an equal amount of proof that the barriers to success are enormous. In spite of all those competitors, only a handful is remotely relevant.'

This, however, did not calm investors and Groupon shares fell by 80 per cent at its all-time low in 2012. One rare asset Groupon had was its customer base of more than 50 million customers, which could possibly be difficult to imitate. The more customers, the better deals and this would make customers come to Groupon rather than the competitors and the cost for competitors to acquire customers would go up. Further defending Groupon's competitiveness, the CEO emphasised in *WSJ* that it is not as simple as providing daily deals, but that a whole series of things have to work together, and competitors would have to replicate everything in its 'operational complexity':

'People overlook the operational complexity. We have 10,000 employees across 46 countries. We have thousands of salespeople talking to tens of thousands of merchants every single day. It's not an easy thing to build.'

Mason also emphasised Groupon's advanced technology platform that allowed the company to 'provide better targeting to customers and give them deals that are more relevant to them'. Part of this platform, however, was built via acquisitions – a route competitors possibly also could take.

If imitation is the highest form of flattery Groupon has been highly complimented, but investors have not been flattered. Consequently, Andrew Mason was forced out in 2013, succeeded by the chairman Eric Lefkofsky. Even though Amazon and other copycats left the daily-deals business he struggled to explain how Groupon would fight off imitators. The company was forced to exit over 30 international markets. Lefkofsky later returned to his chairman role and was followed by Rich Williams 2015. He managed to turn Groupon profitable for the first time ever in 2017, but still did not regain investors' confidence with the share still below $4, far from the $20 IPO price. Williams, however, was optimistic:

'[Groupon] is one of the first unicorns. It got a lot of praise and attention it didn't deserve at the beginning. We've not recovered from that. Over time, the numbers will speak for themselves.'

Sources: Crains Chicago Business, 9 March 2018 (John Pletz: 'What's this? Groupon is now profitable') Groupon Shares Crumble After Company Names New CEO, 3 November 2015, *Forbes*; Groupon Names Rich Williams CEO, 3 November 2015, *Wall Street Journal*; All Things Digital, 2 November 2012, *Wall Street Journal*; *Financial Times*, 2 March 2013; *Wall Street Journal*, 31 January 2012.

Questions

1 Assess the bases of Groupon's resources and capabilities using the VRIO criteria (Figure 4.2 and Table 4.2).

2 Andrew Mason admits that Groupon has thousands of copycats, yet his assessment is that imitating Groupon is difficult. Why do you think that investors disagreed?

3 If you were the new Groupon CEO what resources and capabilities would you build on to give the company a sustainable competitive advantage?

4.3.4 O – organisational support

Providing value to customers and possessing capabilities that are rare and difficult to imitate provides a potential for competitive advantage. However, the organisation must also be suitably organised to support these capabilities including appropriate organisational processes and systems. This implies that to fully take advantage of the resources and capabilities an organisation's structure and formal and informal management control systems need to support and facilitate their exploitation. The question of organisational support works as an adjustment factor. Some of the potential competitive advantage can be lost if the organisation is not organised in a way that it can fully take advantage of valuable, rare and inimitable resources and capabilities. For example, if an organisation has a unique patent underlying a product that customers value it may still not be able to convert this into a competitive advantage if it does not have the appropriate sales force to sell the product. Supporting capabilities have been labelled *complementary capabilities* as, by themselves, they are often not enough to provide for competitive advantage, but they are useful in the exploitation of other capabilities that can provide for competitive advantage.[10] In brief, even though an organisation has valuable, rare and inimitable capabilities some of its potential competitive advantage may not be realised if it lacks the organisational arrangements to fully exploit these.

In summary and from a resource-based view of organisations, managers need to consider whether their organisation has resources and capabilities to achieve and sustain competitive advantage. To do so they need to consider how and to what extent it has capabilities which are (i) valuable, (ii) rare, (iii) inimitable and (iv) supported by the organisation. Illustration 4.2 gives an example of the tough challenges in meeting these criteria in the context of the fastest-growing internet business ever, Groupon.

4.4 Analysing resources and capabilities

So far, this chapter has been concerned with explaining concepts associated with the strategic significance of organisations' resources and capabilities. This section now provides some ways in which they can be understood and diagnosed. It can be quite difficult to discern where the basis of competitive advantage lies. Hence, if managers are to manage the resources and capabilities of their organisation, the sort of analysis explained here, the VRIO analysis tool, the value chain and SWOT, are centrally important. If resources and capabilities are not understood at these levels, there are dangers that managers can take the wrong course of action.

4.4.1 VRIO analysis

One lesson that emerges from an understanding of the strategic importance of resources and capabilities is that it can be difficult to discern where the basis of competitive advantage lies. The strict criteria of the VRIO framework discussed above (see Section 4.3) can conveniently be used as a strategic tool to analyse whether an organisation has resources and capabilities to achieve and sustain competitive advantage. **A VRIO analysis thus helps to evaluate if, how and to what extent an organization or company has resources and capabilities that are (i) valuable, (ii) rare, (iii) inimitable and (iv) supported by the organisation**. Table 4.2 summarises the VRIO analysis of capabilities and shows that there is an additive effect. Resources and capabilities provide sustainable bases of competitive advantage the more they meet all four criteria. This analysis can be done for different functions in an organisation (technology, manufacturing, purchasing, marketing and sales, etc.) or more fine-grained for individual resources and capabilities (see Table 4.1). Another approach is to evaluate different sections of the value chain with this tool (see Section 4.4.2 below).

Table 4.2   The VRIO framework

			Is the capability . . .	
Valuable?	**Rare?**	**Inimitable?**	**supported by the Organisation?**	**Competitive implications**
No	–	–	No	Competitive disadvantage
Yes	No	–	↑	Competitive parity
Yes	Yes	No	↓	Temporary competitive advantage
Yes	Yes	Yes	Yes	Sustained competitive advantage

Source: Adapted with the permission of J.B. Barney and W.S. Hesterly, *Strategic Management and Competitive Advantage*, Pearson, 2012.

Sometimes it may be challenging to establish the exact competitive implication, for example when a resource or capability is on the border between sustained or temporary competitive advantage (Illustration 4.2 demonstrates this). However, for managers it is most important to distinguish between sustained or temporary competitive advantage vs. competitive parity or competitive disadvantage (see Table 4.2). If it is difficult to discern whether a function or resource or capability provides for sustained competitive advantage, it may help to divide it into subparts. For example, manufacturing in itself may not provide for competitive advantage, but perhaps product engineering or design do. And even if machines and equipment generally do not provide for competitive advantage there may be a particular type of equipment that do.

4.4.2 The value chain

If organisations are to achieve competitive advantage by delivering value to customers, managers need to understand which activities their organisation undertakes that are especially important in creating that value and which are not. **The value chain describes the categories of activities within an organisation which, together, create a product or service.** This can then be used to model the value generation of an organisation. The important point is that the concept of the value chain invites the strategist to think of an organisation in terms of sets of activities. There are different frameworks for considering these categories: Figure 4.3 is a representation of a value chain as developed by Michael Porter.[11]

Primary activities are directly concerned with the creation or delivery of a product or service. For example, for a manufacturing business:

- *Inbound logistics* are activities concerned with receiving, storing and distributing inputs to the product or service including materials handling, stock control, transport, etc.
- *Operations* transform these inputs into the final product or service: machining, packaging, assembly, testing, etc.
- *Outbound logistics* collect, store and distribute the product or service to customers; for example, warehousing, materials handling, distribution, etc.
- *Marketing and sales* provide the means whereby consumers or users are made aware of the product or service and are able to purchase it. This includes sales administration, advertising and selling.
- *Service* includes those activities that enhance or maintain the value of a product or service, such as installation, repair, training and spares.

Figure 4.3 The value chain within an organisation

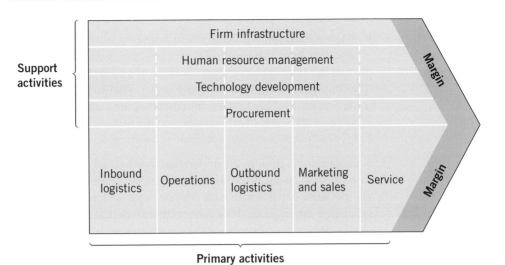

Source: Adapted from *Competitive Advantage: Creating and Sustaining Superior Performance* by Michael E. Porter. The Free Press, a Division of Simon & Schuster, Inc.

Each of these groups of primary activities is linked to *support activities* which help to improve the effectiveness or efficiency of primary activities:

- *Procurement.* Processes that occur in many parts of the organisation for acquiring the various resource inputs to the primary activities. These can be vitally important in achieving scale advantages. So, for example, many large consumer goods companies with multiple businesses none the less procure advertising centrally.

- *Technology development.* All value activities have a 'technology', even if it is just know-how. Technologies may be concerned directly with a product (e.g. R&D, product design) or with processes (e.g. process development) or with a particular resource (e.g. raw materials improvements).

- *Human resource management.* This transcends all primary activities and is concerned with recruiting, managing, training, developing and rewarding people within the organisation.

- *Infrastructure.* The formal systems of planning, finance, quality control, information management and the structure of an organisation.

The value chain can be used to understand the strategic position of an organisation and analyse resources and capabilities in three ways:

- As a *generic description of activities*. Figure 4.3 might be appropriate as a general framework here or a value chain more specific to an organisation can be developed. The important thing is to ask (i) which separate categories of activities best describe the operations of the organisation and (ii) which of these are most significant in delivering the strategy and achieving advantage over competitors?

- In analysing the competitive position of the organisation by using the *VRIO analysis* for individual value chain activities and functions (see Section 4.4.1 above).

- To *analyse the value and cost of activities* of an organisation. This could involve the following two steps:

  - *Identifying sets of value activities.* Which activities add most value to the final product or service (and in turn to the customer) and which do not? For example, it is likely that in a branded pharmaceutical company research and development and marketing activities will be crucially important. It can also be important to establish which sets of activities are linked to or are dependent on others and which, in effect, are self-standing.

- *Relative importance of activity costs internally.* In which activities and how can costs be reduced? Does the significance of costs align with the significance of activities? Can costs be reduced in some areas without affecting the value created for customers? For example, organisations that have undertaken such analyses often find that central services have grown to the extent that they are a disproportionate cost and do not add value to other sets of activities or to the customer. Can some activities be outsourced, for example those that are relatively free-standing and do not add value significantly?

- A single organisation rarely undertakes in-house all of the value activities from design through to the delivery of the final product or service to the final consumer. There is usually specialisation of activities so, any one organisation is part of a wider *value system*, the set of inter-organisational links and relationships that are necessary to create a product or service. Here, the 'make or buy' or outsourcing decision for a particular activity is critical, the question is thus which activities most need to be part of the internal value chain because they are central to achieving competitive advantage and which can be outsourced.

4.4.3 SWOT[12]

It can be helpful to summarise the key issues arising from an analysis of resources and capabilities discussed in this chapter and the analysis of the business environment discussed in Chapter 3 to gain an overall picture of an organisation's strategic position. **SWOT provides a general summary of the Strengths and Weaknesses explored in an analysis of resources and capabilities** (Chapter 4) **and the Opportunities and Threats explored in an analysis of the environment** (Chapters 2 and 3). This analysis can also be useful as a basis for generating strategic options and assessing future courses of action.

The aim is to identify the extent to which strengths and weaknesses are relevant to, or capable of dealing with, the changes taking place in the business environment. Illustration 4.3 takes the example of a pharmaceuticals firm (Pharmcare).[13] It assumes that key environmental impacts have been identified from analyses explained in Chapters 2 and 3 and that major strengths and weaknesses have been identified using the analytic tools explained in this chapter. A scoring mechanism (plus 5 to minus 5) is used as a means of getting managers to assess the interrelationship between the environmental impacts and the strengths and weaknesses of the firm. A positive (+) denotes that the strength of the company would help it take advantage of, or counteract, a problem arising from an environmental change or that a weakness would be offset by that change. A negative (–) score denotes that the strength would be reduced or that a weakness would prevent the organisation from overcoming problems associated with that change.

Pharmcare's share price has been declining because investors were concerned that its strong market position was under threat. This had not been improved by a merger that was proving problematic. The pharmaceutical market was changing with new ways of doing business, driven by new technology, the quest to provide medicines at lower cost and politicians seeking ways to cope with soaring healthcare costs and an ever more informed patient. But was Pharmcare keeping pace? The strategic review of the firm's position (Illustration 4.3a) confirmed its strengths of a flexible sales force, well-known brand name and new healthcare department. However, there were major weaknesses, namely relative failure on low-cost drugs, competence in information and communication technology (ICT) and a failure to get to grips with increasingly well-informed users.

Illustration 4.3 SWOT analysis of Pharmcare

A SWOT analysis explores the relationship between the environmental influences and the resources and capabilities of an organisation compared with its competitors.

(a) SWOT analysis for Pharmcare

	Environmental change (opportunities and threats)					
	Healthcare rationing	Complex and changing buying structures	Increased integration of healthcare	Informed patients	+	–
Strengths						
Flexible sales force	+3	+5	+2	+2	12	0
Economies of scale	0	0	+3	+3	+6	0
Strong brand name	+1	+3	0	–1	4	–1
Healthcare education department	+3	+3	+4	+5	15	0
Weaknesses						
Limited capabilities in biotechnology and genetics	–1	0	–4	–3	0	–8
Ever lower R&D productivity	–3	–2	–1	–2	0	–8
Weak ICT capabilities	–3	–2	–5	–5	0	–15
Over-reliance on leading product	–2	–1	–3	–1	0	–7
Environmental impact scores	+7	+11	+9	+10		
	–9	–5	–13	–12		

(b) Competitor SWOT analyses

	Environmental change (opportunities and threats)				
	Healthcare rationing	Complex and changing buying structures	Increased integration of healthcare	Informed and passionate patients	Overall impact
Pharmcare	–2	+6	–4	–2	–2
	Big global player suffering fall in share price, low research productivity and post-mega-merger bureaucracy	Struggling to prove cost-effectiveness of new drugs to new regulators of healthcare rationing	Well-known brand, a flexible sales force combined with a new healthcare education department creates positive synergy	Weak ICT and lack of integration following mergers means sales, research and admin. are all underperforming	Have yet to get into the groove of patient power fuelled by the internet	Declining performance over time worsened after merger

(b) Competitor SWOT analyses (continued)

	Environmental change (opportunities and threats)				
	Healthcare rationing	**Complex and changing buying structures**	**Increased integration of healthcare**	**Informed and passionate patients**	**Overall impact**
Company W	−4	−4	+0	+4	−4
Big pharma with patchy response to change, losing ground in new areas of competition	Focus is on old-style promotional selling rather than helping doctors control costs through drugs	Traditional sales force not helped by marketing which can be unaccommodating of national differences	Alliances with equipment manufacturers but little work done across alliance to show dual use of drugs and new surgical techniques	New recruits in the ICT department have worked cross-functionally to involve patients like never before	Needs to modernise across the whole company
Organisation X	+3	+2	+2	+3	+10
Partnership between a charity managed by people with venture capital experience and top hospital geneticists	Potentially able to deliver rapid advances in genetics-based illnesses	Able possibly to bypass these with innovative cost-effective drug(s)	Innovative drugs can help integrate healthcare through enabling patients to stay at home	Patients will fight for advances in treatment areas where little recent progress has been made	Could be the basis of a new business model for drug discovery – but all to prove as yet
Company Y	+3	0	+2	+1	+6
Only develops drugs for less common diseases	Partnering with big pharma allows the development of drugs discovered by big pharma but not economical for them to develop	Focus on small market segments so not as vulnerable to overall market structure, but innovative approach might be risky	Innovative use of web to show why products still worthwhile developing even for less common illnesses	Freephone call centres for sufferers of less common illnesses Company, like patients, is passionate about its mission	Novel approach can be considered either risky or a winner, or both!

Questions

1 What does the SWOT analysis tell us about the competitive position of Pharmcare within the industry as a whole?

2 How readily do you think executives of Pharmcare identify the strengths and weaknesses of competitors?

3 Identify the benefits and dangers (other than those identified in the text) of a SWOT analysis such as that in the illustration.

Source: Prepared by Jill Shepherd, Segal Graduate School of Business, Simon Fraser University, Vancouver, Canada.

However, in the context of this chapter, if this analysis is to be useful, it must be remembered that the exercise is not absolute but relative to its competitors. So SWOT analysis is most useful when it is comparative – if it examines strengths, weaknesses, opportunities and threats in relation to competitors. When the impact of environmental forces on competitors was analysed (Illustration 4.3b), it showed that Pharmcare was still outperforming its traditional competitor (Company W), but potentially vulnerable to changing dynamics in the general industry structure courtesy of niche players (X and Y).

There are two main dangers in a SWOT exercise:

- *Listing.* A SWOT exercise can generate very long lists of apparent strengths, weaknesses, opportunities and threats, whereas what matters is to be clear about what is really important and what is less important. So prioritisation of issues matters. Three brief rules can be helpful here. First, as indicated above, focus on strengths and weaknesses that differ in *relative* terms compared to competitors or comparable organisations and leave out areas where the organisation is at par with others. Second, focus on opportunities and threats that are directly *relevant* for the specific organisation and industry and leave out general and broad factors. Third, summarise the *results* and draw concrete conclusions based on the analysis (the TOWS matrix below can be of help here).

- A summary, *not a substitute*. SWOT analysis is an engaging and fairly simple tool. It is also useful in summarising and consolidating other analysis that has been explained in Chapters 2, 3 and 4. It is *not*, however, a substitute for that analysis. There are two dangers if it is used on its own. The first is that, in the absence of more thorough analysis, managers rely on preconceived, often inherited and biased views. The second is again the danger of a lack of specificity. Identifying very general strengths, for example, does not explain the underlying reasons for those strengths.

SWOT can also help focus discussion on future choices and the extent to which an organisation is capable of supporting these strategies. A useful way of doing this is to use a TOWS matrix[14] as shown in Figure 4.4. This builds directly on the information in a SWOT exercise. Each box of the TOWS matrix can be used to identify options that address a different combination of the internal factors (strengths and weaknesses) and the external factors (opportunities and threats). For example, the top left-hand box prompts a consideration of options that use the strengths of the organisation to take advantage of opportunities in the business environment. An example for Pharmcare might be the re-training of the sales force to deal with changes in pharmaceuticals buying. The bottom right-hand box prompts options that

Figure 4.4 The TOWS matrix

		Internal factors	
		Strengths (S)	**Weaknesses (W)**
External factors	**Opportunities (O)**	**SO Strategic options** Generate options here that use strengths to take advantage of opportunities	**WO Strategic options** Generate options here that take advantage of opportunities by overcoming weaknesses
	Threats (T)	**ST Strategic options** Generate options here that use strengths to avoid threats	**WT Strategic options** Generate options here that minimise weaknesses and avoid threats

minimise weaknesses and also avoid threats; for Pharmcare this might include the need to develop its ICT systems to better service more informed patients. Quite likely this would also help take advantage of opportunities arising from changes in the buying structure of the industry (top right). The bottom left box suggests the need to use strengths to avoid threats, perhaps by building on the success of the healthcare education department to also better service informed patients.

4.5 Dynamic capabilities

The previous section was concerned with analysing resources and capabilities. This section considers what managers can do to manage and improve resources and capabilities. If resources and capabilities for competitive advantage do not exist, then managers need to consider if they can be developed. Also, if they are to provide a basis for long-term success, resources and capabilities cannot be static; they need to change. University of Berkeley economist David Teece has introduced the concept of **dynamic capabilities**, by which he means **an organisation's ability to renew and recreate its resources and capabilities to meet the needs of changing environments.** He argues that the resources and capabilities that are necessary for efficient operations, like owning certain tangible assets, controlling costs, maintaining quality, optimising inventories, etc., are unlikely to be sufficient for sustaining superior performance long term.[15]

In other words, there is a danger that capabilities and resources that were the basis of competitive success can over time be imitated by competitors, become common practice in an industry or become redundant as its environment changes. So, the important lesson is that if resources and capabilities are to be effective over time they need to change; they cannot be static. Dynamic capabilities are directed towards that strategic change. They are dynamic in the sense that they can create, extend or modify an organisation's existing capabilities. New product development is a typical example of a dynamic capability and strategic analysis is another. Dynamic capabilities may also take the form of relatively formal organisational systems, such as reorganisation, recruitment and management development processes and cooperating with others through alliances or acquisitions, by which new skills are learned and developed.[16]

Teece suggests the following three generic types of dynamic capabilities:

- *Sensing*. Sensing implies that organisations must constantly scan, search and explore opportunities across various markets and technologies. Research and development and investigating customer needs are typical sensing activities. For example, companies in the PC operating systems industry, like Microsoft, sensed the threats from and opportunities in tablets and cloud computing services and applications.

- *Seizing*. Once an opportunity is sensed it must be seized and addressed through new products or services, processes, activities etc. Microsoft, for example, seized opportunities by launching their own tablet devices and cloud computing services.

- *Reconfiguring*. To seize an opportunity may require renewal and reconfiguration of organisational capabilities and investments in new technologies, manufacturing, markets, etc. For example, Microsoft's inroad into tablets and cloud computing and related software and apps required major changes in its existing PC and game console resources and capabilities. The company needed to discard some of its old capabilities, acquire and build new ones and recombine them.

Summary

- To be able to compete at all in a market an organisation needs *threshold* resources and capabilities, but to achieve sustained competitive advantage they also need to be unique and *distinctive*.
- To be distinctive and provide for sustainable competitive advantage resources and capabilities need to fulfil the *VRIO* criteria of being *Valuable, Rare, Inimitable* and *supported by the Organisation*.
- Ways of diagnosing organisational resources and capabilities include:
  - *VRIO analysis* of resources and capabilities as a tool to evaluate if they contribute to competitive advantage.
  - Analysing an organisation's *value chain* as a basis for understanding how value to a customer is created and can be developed.
  - *SWOT analysis* as a way of drawing together an understanding of the strengths, weaknesses, opportunities and threats an organisation faces.
- Managers need to adapt and change resources and capabilities if the environment changes and/or competitors catch up and this can be done based on *dynamic capabilities*: *sensing*, *seizing* and *reconfiguring* new or modified resources and capabilities.

Recommended key readings

- For an understanding of the resource-based view of the firm, an early and much cited paper is by Jay Barney: 'Firm resources and sustained competitive advantage', *Journal of Management*, vol. 17 (1991), pp. 99–120.

- For a discussion of dynamic capabilities see D.J. Teece, 'The foundations of enterprise performance: Dynamic and ordinary capabilities in an (economic) theory of firms', The *Academy of Management Perspectives* vol. 28, no. 4, 2014, pp. 328–352.

References

1. The seminal and most cited paper is by Jay Barney, 'Firm resources and sustained competitive advantage', *Journal of Management*, vol. 17, no. 1 (1991), pp. 99–120.
2. The literature most commonly differentiates between 'resources' and 'capabilities'. See, for example, an early article by R. Amit. and P.J.H. Schoemaker, 'Strategic assets and organizational rent', *Strategic Management Journal*, vol. 14 (1993), pp. 33–46.
3. In earlier editions of this book capabilities were specified as 'what we do *well*', but an organisation's capabilities need not necessarily be carried out well or in a superior way compared to others. Instead, 'what we do' can be categorised into 'threshold' or 'distinctive capabilities' where the latter signify those capabilities that we perform particularly well in comparison to others.
4. We use the terms 'resources' and 'capabilities' as most contemporary strategy texts do, and the latter corresponds to what we in earlier editions referred to as 'competences'. 'Capabilities' is commonly used in both research and in practice-oriented writings and in discussions within organisations.
5. The VRIO criteria were introduced by Jay Barney in J.B. Barney, *Gaining and sustaining competitive advantage*, Addison-Wesley, 1997.
6. This is borne out in a meta-study of research on RBV by S.L. Newbert, 'Empirical research on the Resource Based View of the firm: an assessment and suggestions for future research', *Strategic Management Journal*, vol. 28 (2007), pp. 121–46.
7. For an explanation of how complex capabilities and strategies contribute to inimitability see J.W. Rivkin, 'Imitation of complex strategies', *Management Science*, vol. 46, no. 6 (2000), pp. 824–44.

8. The distinction between and importance of characteristic and linkage ambiguity is explained by A.W. King and C.P. Zeithaml, 'Competencies and firm performance: examining the causal ambiguity paradox', *Strategic Management Journal*, vol. 22, no. 1 (2001), pp. 75–99.

9. For a fuller discussion of path dependency in the context of resources and capabilities, see D. Holbrook, W. Cohen, D. Hounshell and S. Klepper, 'The nature, sources and consequences of firm differences in the early history of the semiconductor industry', *Strategic Management Journal*, vol. 21(10–11), 2000, pp. 1017–42.

10. For an extensive discussion about complementary assets and capabilities see D. Teece, 'Profiting from technological innovation', *Research Policy*, vol. 15, no. 6 (1986), pp. 285–305.

11. An extensive discussion of the value chain concept and its application can be found in M.E. Porter, *Competitive Advantage*, Free Press, 1985.

12. The idea of SWOT as a common-sense checklist has been used for many years. For a critical discussion of the (mis)use of SWOT, see T. Hill and R. Westbrook, 'SWOT analysis: it's time for a product recall', *Long Range Planning*, vol. 30, no. 1 (1997), pp. 46–52.

13. For background reading on the pharmaceutical industry see, for example, 'From vision to decision Pharma 2020', PWC, www.pwc.com/pharma, 2012; 'The pharmaceutical industry', Scherer, F.M., *Handbook of health economics*, vol. 1 (2000), part B, pp. 1297–336; 'A wake-up call for Big Pharma', *McKinsey Quarterly*, December 2011.

14. See H. Weihrich, 'The TOWS matrix – a tool for situational analysis', *Long Range Planning* (April 1982), pp. 54–66.

15. David Teece first wrote about dynamic capabilities in D.J. Teece, G. Pisano and A. Shuen: 'Dynamic capabilities and strategic management', *Strategic Management Journal*, vol. 18, no. 7 (1997), pp. 509–34.

16. For a discussion of reorganization as dynamic capability see G. Stephane and R. Whittington, 'Reconfiguration, Restructuring and Firm Performance: Dynamic Capabilities and Environmental Dynamism', *Strategic Management Journal*, 38.5, 2017, pp. 1121–1133.

Case example

Rocket Internet – will the copycat be imitated?

Patrick Regnér

Introduction

Rocket Internet is a Berlin-based start-up incubator and venture capital firm. It starts, develops, funds and operates e-commerce and other online consumer businesses. The company was founded in 2007 and stock listed in 2014 valued at $8.2bn (€6.5bn). It has over 700 employees and over 30,000 across its network of portfolio companies. It has helped create and launch over 150 start-ups and is currently active in more than 100 companies across more than 100 countries on six continents.

The company was founded by the Samwer brothers, Alexander, Oliver and Marc. After going to Silicon Valley in the late 1990s they became inspired by the Californian entrepreneurial culture and especially eBay. The brothers offered to eBay to create a German version of the online auction house, but they received no reply from eBay. Instead they launched their own eBay clone, Alando. A month later they were acquired by eBay for $50m. This was to be their first great online success, but far from the last.

The Samwer brothers
Source: Dieter Mayr Photography

Next the brothers created Jamba, a mobile phone content platform. It was sold to VeriSign, a network infrastructure company, for $273m in 2004. Since then they have become experts in spotting promising business models, especially in the USA, and imitating and scaling them internationally quicker than the originals. Several of their ventures have been acquired by the company with the original idea, like two of their most high-profile ventures: CityDeal, which was sold off to American Groupon, and eDarling sold to American eHarmony.

The company has frequently been criticised for simply being a copycat machine without any original ideas and some have even claimed it is a scam that rips off the originals. The brothers, through Oliver Samwer, defended their model ahead of their IPO in *Financial Times* (Sally Davies, 15 July 2014): 'There is a romantic concept of what tech innovation is... There's always an Einstein, a pioneer who defines the first category. But take the first car – it looked horrible, you would never want to use it, and you would never make a market for it. It took someone like Toyota to work harder, make it cheaper and bring it faster around the world.'

Finance and expert teams

To structure the financial solutions, Rocket Internet has a large team of finance experts at the Berlin headquarters and extensive cooperation externally with high profile investors globally like J.P. Morgan. Besides financial skills Rocket Internet also develops the concepts of new ventures, provides the technology platforms and combines various skills necessary for setting up new ventures. It has about 250 specialists working at the Berlin head office. These specialists are part of diverse expert teams. Engineering including IT software, programming and web design skills are essential for product development and there are around 200 engineers with access to state-of-the art technologies.

The expert team in marketing includes experts in customer management, customer relationship marketing and online marketing. Other teams include Operations, Business Intelligence and HR. Apart from this there is a Global Venture Development programme including a global mobile task force of entrepreneurial talents that can bring further know-how to all international markets. This task force includes venture developers with functional skills in product development, supply management, operations and online marketing. They rotate every 4–6 months to a new venture in another part of the world.

Human resource management and culture

The HR team recruit regular staff support for Rocket Internet and specialists for the expert teams and Global Venture Development programme and, not least, the founders of the ventures. Based on their entrepreneurial spirit they emphasise personal drive rather than good school grades. Head of HR, Vera Termuhlen, explains:

> 'All in all, it doesn't matter if an applicant is from an elite university. For the area of global venture development, we look for applicants that are hands-on, first-class, have analytical skills, describe themselves as entrepreneurs, have a passion for the online start-up scene along and a willingness to work internationally, often in exotic locations like the Philippines or Nigeria.'

The co-founders and managing directors of the individual ventures establish all operations, build the team around a venture, and develop the business; acting as entrepreneurs and holding personal stakes in the venture's equity. Recruiting them is central and Rocket Internet normally recruits extraordinary, ambitious MBA-level graduates with high analytic skills from within the local regions where the venture is set up. As Alexander Kudlich, Managing Director of Rocket Internet, says:

> 'We are looking for those who from an analytical point of view understand the beauty of the business model, understand the rationale and understand what a huge opportunity is. Sometimes we say we are looking for analytical entrepreneurs rather than accidental billionaires.'

The company emphasises not only strong expertise, but 'a close cultural connection to Rocket Internet'. Rocket Internet has an intense entrepreneurial working culture that is highly performance driven including high pressure, long working hours, often from 09.00 to 23.00, and little job security. While this is attractive to some, the culture has also been criticised for being too tough and aggressive. Rocket Internet's Managing Director Alexander Kudlich comments on the culture:

> 'I would describe our culture as very focused, we have young teams – the average age is below 30. There is no place where you get more freedom and where you can take as much responsibility as you want. The only thing we want back is accountability.'

Identification of business models and execution

Rocket Internet is more of an international venture builder and operator compared to many others. Expertise is shared throughout the portfolio of ventures globally and its best practice can be applied across diverse business models (ranging from online fashion to payments to deals to social networking). Compared to many other incubators, the function of the headquarters is central. While entrepreneurs are hired to oversee individual ventures, overall strategy for Rocket Internet is largely shaped at the head office. The managing directors at head office lead the scanning for and identification of novel and proven online and mobile transaction-based business models that are internationally scalable. They have a team of about 25 staff looking for new opportunities, scanning a couple of hundreds companies a month. Former Managing Director Florian Heinemann explains in *Wired*: 'We take a pretty systematic look at business models that are already out there and we basically try to define whether a model suits our competence and is large enough that it's worth it for us to go in there.'

Another significant aspect of Rocket Internet's centralised model is the speed at which it can launch novel business models internationally. This is different compared to many US and European counterparts. Rocket Internet has an international infrastructure and distribution network with the capacity to build ventures on an international scale in just a few months. As Managing Director Kudlich explains in *Wall Street Journal*:

> 'When we identify a business model we can, within a few weeks, build a platform out of our central teams. In the meantime the local Rocket offices will have hired or allocated the people who will execute on the ground . . . That gives us the speed. The combination of access to the best talent in each country combined with highly standardised or modular approach in terms of platform and systems which are rolled out by our headquarters.'

In brief, Rocket Internet specialises in execution rather than innovation. This is also how the management defend their model when they are blamed for simply being a clone machine. Oliver Samwer says that they are 'execution entrepreneurs' rather than 'pioneering entrepreneurs'. Managing Director Kudlich explains to *Inc. Magazine*: 'Which is harder: to have the idea of selling shoes online or to build a supply chain and warehouse in Indonesia? Ideas are important. But other things are more important.'

Paradoxically, even though Rocket Internet often builds on others' ideas it prefers to keep its own ideas for itself as explained by Marc Samwer in the *New York Times*: 'We really don't like to speak about our investments since our track record encourages people to set up competing sites . . . Ideas travel much faster these days.'

The future

Rocket Internet has continued to produce successful start-ups. Zalando, which initially mimicked the online shoe retailing business in the USA by Zappos, now part of Amazon, has expanded into clothing and jewellery. They are now the biggest online fashion retailer in Europe with rapidly growing sales (€4.5bn for 2017) and the company was stock listed in Germany in 2014 at €5.3bn. Other fashion brands have also been launched in the umbrella Global Fashion Group: Dafiti (Latin America), Jabong (India), Lamoda (Russia), Namshi (Middle East) and Zalora (South East Asia and Australia). Two high-profile IPOs in 2017 from Rocket Internet were Delivery Hero, an online takeaway food delivery company and HelloFresh, a meal-kit delivery company. In 2018 the online retailer Daraz was sold to Alibaba.

However, Rocket Internet's stock price has fallen close to 50 per cent since its listing and some investors have complained that the company is too complex to analyse and understand and questions its ability to become profitable and find enough successful exits for its many start-ups.

Rocket Internet has also started to attract imitators of its own. Wimdu, is a copy of Airbnb, which allows individual home and apartment owners to list their properties as holiday accommodation, but they quickly formed a partnership with another Berlin incubator for expansion into Europe. Similarly, the original company responded swiftly when Rocket Internet imitated Fab.com, a designer deal site, with its Bamarang. Fab acquired Casacanda, a parallel European site, and quickly re-launched it as a Fab internationally and Bamarang was closed down.

Rocket Internet is even facing imitators from within. Four of the original managing directors who contributed to the initial success have left the company. They have all become active as venture capitalists and support companies in direct competition with Rocket Internet. Two, together with other former employees, left to set up the Berlin incubator 'Project A Ventures'. Multiple venture capitalist firms and incubators from other parts of Europe have also emerged, like The Hut Group in the UK. There are thus signs that Rocket Internet may eventually be imitated itself. In addition, many of these new competitors are pioneering entirely new online ventures and business models rather than imitating existing ones. 'The day an age of copying seems over' according to Ciaran O'Leary, general partner at BlueYard Capital, a Berlin-based venture capital firm. However, these developments did not worry Rocket Internet CEO Oliver Samwer in an interview with *Reuters*[12]: 'We are planting new seedlings so we can harvest them in 2020 and beyond. . . Small seedlings can suddenly grow big.'

Questions

1 Based on the data from the case (and any other sources available) use the frameworks from the chapter and analyse the resources and capabilities of Rocket Internet:

   a What are its resources and capabilities?

   b What are its threshold, distinctive and dynamic resources and capabilities?

2 Based on your initial analysis and answers to question 1, carry out a VRIO analysis for Rocket Internet. What do you conclude? To what extent does Rocket Internet have resources and capabilities with sustained competitive advantage?

3 What is the importance of the Samwers brothers? What would happen if they left or sold the company?

Sources: J. Kaczmarek, 'An inside look at Rocket Internet', *VentureVillage.com*, 18 November 2012; M. Chafkin, 'Lessons from the world's most ruthless competitor', *Inc. Magazine*, 29 May 2012; B. Rooney, 'Rocket Internet leads the clone war', *The Wall Street Journal*, 14 May 2012; G. Wiesmann, 'Zalando to set foot in seven new countries', *Financial Times*, 26 March 2012; T. Bradshaw, 'Facebook backers to take stake in Zalando', *Financial Times*, 2 February 2012; M. Cowan, 'Inside the clone factory', *Wired UK*, 2 March 2012; R. Levine, 'The copy cat kids', *Cnnmoney.com*, 2 October 2007; *New York Times*, 3 December 2006; *The Economist*, 'Attack of the clones', 6 August 2011 and 'Launching into the unknown', 4 October 2014; S. Gordon and D. McCrum, 'Rocket Internet: Waiting for the lift-off', *Financial Times*, 10 October 2015; J. Kahn., S. Nicola. A. Ricadela and A. Satariano, 'Inside Rocket Internet's ailing startup factory', *Bloomberg Business Week*, 7 October 2016; E. Thomasson and N. Schimroszik, *Reuters*, Business News, 11 January 2018.

Suggested video clip

http://www.youtube.com/watch?v=Tq7WnzY89KE

Chapter 5
Stakeholders and culture

Key terms

Learning outcomes

After reading this chapter you should be able to:

- Undertake *stakeholder analysis* in order to identify the power and attention of different stakeholder groups.

- Analyse the strategic significance of different *ownership models* for an organisation's strategy.

- Relate *corporate social responsibility* and *personal ethics* to strategy.

- Analyse the relationship of *organisational culture* to strategy

5.1 Introduction

Facebook's scandals during 2018 raised major questions regarding the company's social responsibilities, its corporate governance, its culture, and even its basic strategy. Facebook's strategy relies heavily on harvesting private data from its users for selling on to diverse advertisers. But these data are liable to leakage or abuse. In 2018 it was revealed that Cambridge Analytica, a political consulting company, had used Facebook data from 87 million users to secretly influence both the 2016 American Presidential election and the 2016 Brexit referendum in the United Kingdom. Later in 2018, Facebook admitted to a data breach involving 50 million users. Over the year, Facebook's stock price trailed the financial markets by about a fifth. Politicians and regulators increasingly challenged Facebook's data policies. Many doubted whether the 34-year-old company founder and chief executive, Mark Zuckerberg, was fit to govern a company with two billion users, 30,000 employees and a market value of around $600bn. Zuckerberg's shares have enhanced voting rights, so he controls nearly 70 per cent of shareholder votes even while holding only 18 per cent of the shares.

Facebook's troubles highlight four crucial issues in this chapter. First, there is the problem of balancing the interests of diverse *stakeholders* – in Facebook's case, advertisers interested in sales, shareholders concerned for profits, users needing privacy and society anxious about the abuse of power. They also underline the importance of *corporate governance*, with Facebook led by a dominant young founder with just a minority ownership stake. In question too are the *ethics* of a strategy that relies on selling the data of poorly informed users. The company's mistakes may also be attributed to its 'go-along' *culture*, in which ethically doubtful conduct is rarely challenged internally because of the personal authority of its leadership. These four issues are all strategic: strategies to maximise advertisers' interests might be at the cost of users' privacy; a domineering founder may choose bolder strategies than would professional managers; a strategic commitment to high ethical standards might constrain both advertisers and users; a culture of deference may allow mistakes to go unchallenged.

The chapter continues therefore as follows:

- Section 5.2 introduces the various types of *stakeholder* who may be involved in strategy and shows how to map their *power* and *attention* using stakeholder analysis. The section then focuses on one crucial set of stakeholders, that is owners (shareholders), and their roles under different *ownership models.*

- Section 5.3 addresses the formal *corporate governance mechanisms* within which organisations operate. Governance is concerned with the way in which boards of directors influence strategy through formalised processes for supervising executive decisions and actions.

- Section 5.4 is concerned with issues of *corporate social responsibility.* How should managers respond strategically to the expectations society has of their organisations, particularly with regard to environmental, social and governance issues?

- Section 5.5 considers how *organisational culture* can influence the purpose and strategy of an organisation. It also provides a framework – the *cultural web* – by which organisational cultures can be analysed.

5.2 Stakeholders[1]

Strategic decisions are influenced by the expectations of stakeholders. Stakeholders are those who have some kind of *stake* in the future of the business. More formally, **stakeholders are those individuals or groups that depend on an organisation to fulfil their own goals**

and on whom, in turn, the organisation depends. These stakeholders can be very diverse, including owners, customers, suppliers, employees and local communities. Facebook's stakeholders include the shareholders who have invested their wealth in its future, the advertisers who depend on it to access their markets, the employees who are building careers in the company and the users who rely on it for their social lives. To the extent their organisations depend on them, managers must take all stakeholders into account. However, stakeholder demands can diverge widely, especially in the short term: for instance, in many companies profit maximisation on the part of shareholders may come at the expense of customers who want quality products, employees who want good jobs and groups in the wider society who want a clean environment. It is important therefore that managers understand who their stakeholders are, what they want and which have most influence upon their strategies.

5.2.1 Stakeholder groups

External stakeholders can be usefully divided into five (potentially overlapping) types, categorised according to the nature of their relationship with the organisation and how they might affect strategic direction (see Figure 5.1):

- *Economic stakeholders*, including suppliers, customers, distributors, banks and owners (shareholders).
- *Social/political stakeholders*, such as policy makers, local councils, regulators and government agencies that may influence the strategy directly or via the context in which strategy is developed.

Figure 5.1 Stakeholders of a large organisation

Source: Adapted from R.E. Freeman, *Strategic Management: A Stakeholder Approach*, Pitman, 1984. Copyright 1984 by R. Edward Freeman.

- *Technological stakeholders*, such as key adopters, standards agencies and ecosystem members supplying complementary products or services (e.g. applications for particular mobile phones).
- *Community and society stakeholders*, who are affected by what an organisation does: for example, those who live close to a factory or, indeed, groups in the wider society. These stakeholders typically lack the formal powers of social/political stakeholders such as local councils, but may form activist groups to influence the organisation.
- *Internal stakeholders*, who may be specialised departments, local offices and factories or employees at different levels in the hierarchy.

Individuals may belong to more than one stakeholder group and such groups may 'line up' differently depending on the issue or strategy in hand. The influence of different types of stakeholders is likely to vary in different situations. For example, social/political stakeholders are usually particularly influential in the public-sector context or for multinational companies operating in countries with demanding political and legal systems.

Since the expectations of stakeholder groups will differ, it is normal for conflict to exist regarding the importance or desirability of aspects of strategy. For example, in the private sector the pursuit of short-term profit may favour top management bonuses and shareholder dividends, while at the same time endangering the long-term future of the company and its employees. In universities, the prioritisation of research may suit academics concerned to advance their fields and reputations, but be at the expense of the immediate learning of students. In most situations, a compromise will need to be reached.

The stakeholder concept, and its sensitivity to different wants, helps to understand the organisational politics of strategic decision-making. Taking stakeholder expectations and influence into account is also an important aspect of strategic choice.

5.2.2 Stakeholder mapping[2]

Given that there are often so many stakeholders, it is useful to categorise them according to their likely influence on strategic decisions. **Stakeholder mapping identifies stakeholder power and attention in order to understand strategic priorities.** The underlying view is that organisations involve *political coalitions* of stakeholders, each of which has different kinds of power and each of which pays different amounts of attention to strategic issues. Building coalitions of supportive stakeholders is therefore crucial to strategy.

It is therefore important to understand the *power* different stakeholders have and their likely *attention* to issues. These two dimensions form the basis of the power/attention matrix shown as Figure 5.2. The matrix classifies stakeholders according to the power they hold and the extent to which they are likely to attend actively to a particular strategic issue. The matrix allows different stakeholders to be plotted either according to the simple dichotomy of low or high. The positions of different stakeholders on the matrix are likely to vary according to each issue: stakeholders may have more power in some domains than others, and will care more about some issues than others.

The power/attention matrix indicates the type of relationship that managers might typically establish with stakeholders in the different quadrants. Generally, relationships are more intense as they progress from quadrant D up to quadrant A. Thus cultivating the support of key players (quadrant A) is of greatest importance: these might be major investors, for example. However, it is also important to satisfy the sleeping giants in quadrant B: these might be government regulators. Although sleeping giants might generally be relatively passive, difficulties can arise when dissatisfaction awakens their attention and they reposition to segment A: here they may challenge the strategy. The gadflies in quadrant C, for example community campaign groups, can usually be managed largely by information provision.

Illustration 5.1 Oxfam's infamy

Oxfam reveals governance problems as it disappoints stakeholders over Haiti.

Oxfam International is a confederation of 19 national charities – stretching from Australia to the USA – dedicated to fighting poverty and injustice around the world. It started in 1942 as a group of British volunteers called the Oxford Committee for Famine Relief. Ironically, it would be staff at Oxfam GB (Great Britain) that nearly brought down the whole organisation in 2018. That year, *The Times* newspaper revealed that seven senior staff working in Haiti after the 2011 earthquake had been using local prostitutes, some allegedly under-age, and using Oxfam GB accommodation to do so.

Within two weeks of the revelations in 2018, Oxfam GB had seen the cancellation of over 7,000 regular donations. After criticisms from senior politicians, Oxfam GB announced it would suspend its bids for government contracts, the source of about 40 per cent of its funding. The Haitian government banned Oxfam GB from its territory. Two celebrity ambassadors for the charity, Bishop Desmond Tutu and actress Minnie Driver, resigned from their roles in protest. Soon after, Oxfam GB's chief executive, Mark Goldring, announced his early retirement.

Oxfam International is based in the Netherlands. It is a strong believer that good governance is essential to poverty relief, publishing 577 reports on the subject by early 2018. Its own governance has two tiers: a board of supervisors made up of its own chair, its executive director and the chair of each of the 19 affiliates; and an executive board made up of the executive directors of all the affiliates. There are about 80 Oxfam International staff, with an operating budget of around €10m (recent figures are unavailable). Affiliates typically have their own boards of trustees overseeing local executives: for example, Oxfam GB has 11 trustees, with a Chair who had previously been chief operating officer at the British Broadcasting Corporation (BBC). Many affiliates are large: Oxfam GB has over 5,000 employees and an annual income above €500m.

Oxfam GB investigated the Haitian operation back in 2011, and dismissed four members of staff, allowing three more to resign early. However, while the charity had reported problems to its regulator, the UK's Charity Commission, it had concealed their exact nature. One of the departed staff members had since been temporarily hired by Oxfam America. When the scandal broke in 2018, chief executive Mark Goldring explained to *The Guardian* newspaper why the charity had not fully disclosed the Haitian problems: 'It was done in good faith to try to balance being transparent and protecting Oxfam's work. I don't think [Oxfam] wanted to promote a sensation and damage the delivery of [the Haiti] programme.' Goldring suggested some of the attacks on Oxfam GB were political, aimed at undermining the aid sector in general and Oxfam's anti-poverty campaigns in particular: 'The intensity and ferocity of the attack makes you wonder, what did we do? We murdered babies in their cots?'

The increased scrutiny following the revelations brought out new issues. For example, Oxfam GB had suffered 123 cases of alleged sexual harassment and carried out no criminal record checks for its 23,000 volunteers. The BBC also reported widespread allegations about the use of prostitutes in Africa by staff at another prominent international charity, Medecins sans Frontières. During 2018, Oxfam GB introduced stringent new safeguarding policies and declared: 'However difficult it is to meet the demands of transparency, and however hard it is to confront mistakes of the past, we believe that ultimately, this will help us take meaningful action and become more effective in our mission to tackle poverty and help people hit by disaster'.

Sources: www.oxfam.org; *The Times*, 9 February 2018; *The Guardian*, 16 February 2018; *The Lancet*, 23 February 2018.

Questions

1 Identify Oxfam GB's various stakeholders along the lines of Figure 5.1 and assess their engagement in terms of the power/attention matrix in Figure 5.2.

2 Adapt the corporate governance chain described in Figure 5.4 to Oxfam GB. What were the weaknesses in this chain?

Figure 5.2 Stakeholder mapping: the power/attention matrix

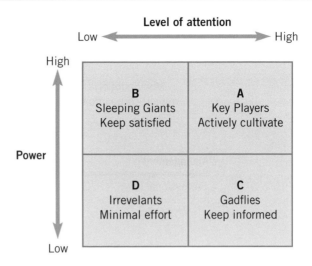

Source: Newcombe, R. (2003) From client to project stakeholders: a stakeholder mapping approach, *Construction Management and Economics*, 21.8, pp. 841–848.

Although not powerful themselves, it is important not to alienate such stakeholders because they can influence more powerful stakeholders: for example, community campaigners might awaken the giants in quadrant B.

The power/attention matrix is a useful tool for analysing potential coalitions of stakeholders for or against particular decisions. Aligning potential supporters for strategic initiatives, and appeasing opponents, are often crucial moves in the process of strategy development. Building stakeholder coalitions is at the core of strategy, therefore. Stakeholder mapping can help in three aspects of the coalition-building process:

- Analysing who the key *blockers* and *facilitators* of a strategy are likely to be.

- *Repositioning* certain stakeholders, for instance diverting the attention of powerful potential blockers so that they transition to quadrant B, while mobilising the attention of powerful potential facilitators so that they move to quadrant A. For example, a regulator might be made alert to the dangers of an aggressive competitor seeking to abuse its market power.

- *Maintaining* the appropriate level of attention or power of some stakeholders: this is what is meant by *keep satisfied* in relation to stakeholders in quadrant B, and to a lesser extent *keep informed* for those in quadrant C.

5.2.3 Owners

Owners are typically key stakeholders in strategic decisions. However, their power and attention can vary according to different *ownership models.*

There are many different ways firms are owned, and the boundaries between them often blur.[3] However, it is useful to distinguish four main ownership models, each with different implications for strategy. Figure 5.3 ranges these four models along two axes. The horizontal axis describes the dominant modes of management, ranging from wholly *professional* (with managers employed for their professional expertise) to wholly *personal* (with managers employed because of their personal relationships with owners). The vertical axis describes the extent to which organisational purpose (Chapter 1) is focused on *profit* as an exclusive goal or on profit as just one of a *mix of motives*. In each case, there is a range along the axes:

Figure 5.3 Ownership, management and purpose

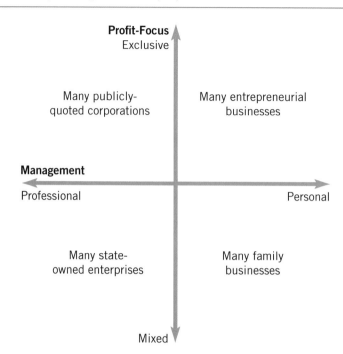

organisations vary in their relative positioning. Also some organisations do not conform to the typical behaviour of their ownership model: these are organisational *hybrids*, for instance pursuing profit and social goals simultaneously.[4] Nonetheless organisations with particular ownership models do tend to behave in distinctive ways.

The four main ownership models are as follows:

- *Publicly-quoted companies* (often called public limited companies) are the most important ownership model in economies such as the USA, Europe, Japan and many others. These companies' shares are 'quoted' on public stock exchanges. In other words, their shares can be bought and sold by the public.[5] Usually owners do not manage publicly-quoted companies themselves, but delegate that function to professional managers. In principle, company managers work to make a financial return for their owners – that is why the public usually buy the shares in the first place. In terms of Figure 5.3 therefore, most publicly-quoted companies focus strongly on profit. However, in practice many managers may not profit-maximise because they respect other stakeholders, for example employees. In relation to the vertical axis in Figure 5.3, publicly-quoted companies may therefore vary in how much they focus on profit objectives.

- *State-owned enterprises* are wholly or majority owned by governments. They are very important in many economies: about 80 per cent of stock market value is accounted for by state-owned companies in China, 60 per cent in Russia and 40 per cent in Brazil.[6] Governments may take over ownership during crises: for example, the Spanish government nationalized private-sector hospitals during the covid-19 crisis. In state-owned enterprises, politicians typically delegate day-to-day control to professional managers, though they may attend more closely to major strategic issues. State-owned enterprises usually have to earn some kind of profit or surplus in order to fund investment and build financial reserves, but they are also likely to pursue a range of other objectives that are in keeping with government policy. For Chinese state-owned enterprises, for example, securing access to overseas resources such as minerals and energy is an important objective, worthwhile sacrificing some profits for.

- *Entrepreneurial businesses* are businesses that are substantially owned and controlled by their founders. Founders head some major companies. For example, Lakshmi Mittal remains chairman and chief executive of his creation, ArcelorMittal, the largest steel company in the world. Nonetheless, as they grow, entrepreneurial businesses are likely both to rely more on professional managers and to draw in external investors in order to fund new opportunities. Typically entrepreneurial companies need to attend closely to profit in order to survive and grow. However, entrepreneurs may attend to some issues more than others.[7] For example, Jeff Bezos as founder of Amazon for a long time has favoured growth strategies over short-term profitability.

- *Family businesses* are typically businesses where ownership by the founding entrepreneur has passed on to his or her family, on account of the founder's death or retirement for instance. Most family businesses are small- to medium-sized enterprises, but they can be very big: Ford, Fiat, Samsung and Walmart, the largest retailer in the world, all have substantial family ownership stakes and retain significant family involvement in top management roles. However, family members may lack the skill and inclination to attend closely to strategy. Family businesses therefore often bring in professional managers, even while retaining ultimate family control: thus the Chief Executive of Ford is a non-family member, but the Executive Chairman is still William Ford Jr. For family businesses, retaining control over the company, passing on management to the next generation and ensuring the company's long-term survival are often very important objectives, and these might rule out profit-maximising strategies that involve high risk or require external finance.[8]

As well as these four main types of ownership model, there are several other variants that play smaller but still significant roles in the economy.[9] *Not-for-profit* organisations, such as Oxfam (Illustration 5.1), are typically owned by a charitable foundation: they may need to make some kind of surplus to fund investment and protect against hard times, but they fundamentally exist to pursue social missions. The *partnership* model, in which the organisation is owned and controlled by senior employees (its partners), is important in many professional services such as law and accounting. There are also *employee-owned* firms, which spread ownership among employees as a whole. Prominent examples of employee-owned firms include W. L. Gore & Associates, famous for Gore-Tex, the Spanish Mondragon Cooperative, with 75,000 employees, and John Lewis, one of the UK's leading retailers. Typically these not-for-profits, partnerships and employee-owned firms are restricted in their ability to raise external finance, making them more conservative in their strategies.

Clearly everybody should know how the ownership of their own organisation relates to its strategy: as above, strategy for a state-owned business is likely to be very different to that of a publicly-quoted company. However, it is also important for managers to understand the ownership of other organisations with which they engage, for example competitors and partners. Without understanding the relationship between ownership and strategies, it is easy to be surprised by competitors and partners with different priorities to your own. For example, Western public mining companies have often found themselves outbid for overseas mining opportunities by Chinese state-owned companies keen to secure raw material supplies at almost any price.

5.3 Corporate governance

The varying power and attention of owners, and their frequent reliance on professional managers, raise issues of corporate governance.[10] **Corporate governance is concerned with the structures and systems of control by which managers are held accountable to those who**

have a legitimate stake in an organisation.[11] Key stakeholders in corporate governance are typically the owners, but may include other groups such as employee representatives. Connecting stakeholder interests with management action is a vital part of strategy. Failures in corporate governance have contributed to calamitous strategic choices in many leading companies, even resulting in their complete destruction: in 2014, Portugal's second largest bank, Banco Espirito Sanctu, disappeared after the discovery of financial irregularities involving €5bn losses. With the survival of whole organisations at stake, governance is increasingly recognised as a key strategic issue.

Managers and stakeholders are linked together via the governance chain. **The governance chain shows the roles and relationships of different groups involved in the governance of an organisation.** In a small family business, the governance chain is simple: there are family shareholders, a board with some family members and there are managers, some of whom may be family too. Here there are just three layers in the chain. However, large publicly-quoted corporations have more extended governance chains, potentially diluting accountability for strategy. Figure 5.4 shows a governance chain for a typical large, publicly-quoted corporation. Here the size of the organisation means there are extra layers of management internally, while being publicly-quoted introduces more investor layers too. Thus individual investors (the ultimate beneficiaries) often invest in public corporations through investment funds, i.e.

Figure 5.4 The chain of corporate governance: typical reporting structures

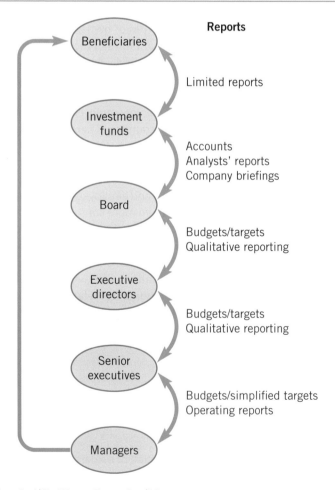

Source: Adapted from David Pitt-Watson, Hermes Fund Management

Illustration 5.2 Too hot in the kitchen? Jamie's family management

British celebrity chef Jamie Oliver's business has run into trouble. Is his brother-in-law the right man to save it?

Cheery chef Jamie Oliver left school at 16 with barely any qualifications at all. A quarter of a century later, after a career as a TV chef and restauranteur, he is believed to be worth £250m (about €300m or $300m). His cookbooks sell so well that he is the biggest non-fiction author in the United Kingdom. But by 2018, Oliver's empire looked as if it might all be falling apart. Could Paul Hunt, Oliver's brother-in-law, save the Jamie Oliver Group of businesses?

The mid-market restaurant segment occupied by many of Oliver's restaurants – most notably, Jamie's Italian – had become very difficult by 2018. The rise of takeaway deliveries via Deliveroo and Uber offered a convenient alternative to going out to eat. The retail shopping areas where many of these restaurants operated were declining in the face of internet competition. Many restaurant chains were closing branches, including the Italian mid-market Carluccio's and premium burger chain Byron.

During 2017–18, Jamie's Italian restaurants cut back heavily, shedding 600 out of their 2,220 employees. The Jamie Oliver Group lost £20m in the financial year. The Group took on a loan of £37m. As Oliver himself put it: 'We had simply run out of cash.'

Although Oliver himself was a notorious workaholic – often getting to work at 5.30 in the morning and returning home at 9.00 in the evening – most of his energy was put into the creative and public side of the business. He was a chef and television star, not a business executive. Oliver owned more than 75 per cent of the business, but he knew he had to delegate its management.

Paul Hunt joined the Jamie Oliver Group as chief executive in 2014. Paul Hunt's own business background was controversial. In the late 1990s, he was fined heavily for misconduct at a City of London financial trading company. Later a finance company he had been chairman of went into administration with £5m debts and nearly 100 job losses just a year after his departure. Two other companies of which he had been director ran into financial and regulatory trouble.

By his account, Hunt found a chaotic group of businesses: 'We had somewhere in the region of . . . 38 different businesses that we were involved in. Everything from talent agencies to graphic design studios, to restaurants. We needed to make the business about Jamie again.' Hunt closed or sold several businesses, with many senior management departures. Notoriously he closed one business on Christmas Eve. But Hunt worked hard, claiming to sleep overnight in the office many times. The end result was a Group reorganised around four main business areas: media and publishing; licensing and endorsements; restaurants; and philanthropy. Hunt brought in a new group of managers to cut costs and bring down restaurant prices.

Hunt made enemies. One former senior employee commented: 'Paul Hunt is an arrogant, incompetent failure. He knows virtually nothing about restaurants and even less about publishing. He's running the business into the ground.' But Jamie Oliver himself is utterly loyal to his brother-in-law. Hunt is married to Oliver's sister, Anna-Marie, who lives just five minutes from his weekend mansion in the country. Oliver explained his support for Hunt to the *Financial Times*: 'Do you know why I chose him?. . . He's honest, and he's fair. I absolutely trust him. His job was to come in and clean up. He has done the hardest and most fabulous job. I'm not saying that because he's my brother-in-law. I'm saying it because it's a fact. . . There are times when you need family and you need the thorough trust that family brings.'

Sources: Financial Times, 1 September 2018; *Daily Mail*, 18 March 2018.

Questions

1 In which respects does the Jamie Oliver Group exemplify issues relevant to entrepreneurial businesses (see Section 5.2.3)?

2 Explain the relevance of the principal–agent model (Section 5.3) to Oliver's trust in CEO Paul Hunt?

---

institutional investors such as unit trusts or pension funds. Investment funds then invest in a range of companies on behalf of beneficiaries, providing them with limited reports on portfolio performance. In turn, the investment funds receive reports from the companies they invest in, in the form of briefings and annual accounts, the responsibility of company boards. Boards are themselves at the top of an internal chain, in which each layer reports on performance against budgets and target, both quantitatively and qualitatively (i.e. verbal reports). In sum, the managers at the bottom are accountable to the ultimate beneficiaries at the top, but only through many layers of reporting. Beneficiaries may not even know in which companies they have a financial stake and have little power to influence companies' strategies directly.

Economists analyse the relationships in such governance chains in terms of the *principal–agent model.*[12] Here 'principals' employ 'agents' to act on their behalf, just as homeowners pay estate agents to sell their homes. Classically, the principal is simply the owner and the agent is the manager. However, the reality for large publicly-quoted corporations is usually more complex, with principals and agents at every level. In Figure 5.4, the beneficiaries are the ultimate principals and fund trustees and investment managers are their immediate agents in terms of achieving good returns on their investments. Further down the chain, company boards can be considered as principals too, with senior executives their agents in managing the company. Thus there are many layers of agents between ultimate principals and the managers at the bottom, with the reporting mechanisms between each layer liable to be imperfect.

The governance issues in principal–agent theory arise from three problems:

- *Knowledge imbalances.* Agents typically know more than principals about what can and should be done. After all, it is they who are actually doing the job and they have presumably been hired for their expertise.

- *Monitoring limits.* It is very difficult for principals to monitor closely the performance of their agents. This limit is made worse because principals usually have many investments, so their attention is likely to be split several ways.

- *Misaligned incentives.* Unless their incentives are closely aligned to principals' interests, agents are liable to pursue other objectives that reward them better. Principals might introduce bonus schemes in order to incentivise desired performance, but then agents may game the system: for example, they might use their superior knowledge to negotiate bonus targets that are in reality easy to meet.

Principal–agent theory therefore stresses the importance of knowledgeable principals, effective monitoring systems and well-designed incentives in order to make sure that large organisations actually pursue the purposes that their owners set for them. Illustration 5.2 asks what implications the principal–agent model has for Jamie Oliver's business.

5.4 Corporate social responsibility[13]

An underlying theme in this chapter is the question of whether organisations are just for the benefit of a primary stakeholder, such as the shareholders of a company, or whether they have a responsibility to a wider group of stakeholders. This section considers the role of *corporate social responsibility* in strategy. Facebook's strategy with which this chapter started arguably showed insufficient regard for corporate social responsibility.

Corporate social responsibility (CSR) **is the commitment by organisations to behave ethically and contribute to economic development while improving the quality of life of the workforce and their families as well as the local community and society at large.**[14]

CSR is therefore concerned with the ways in which an organisation exceeds its minimum legal obligations. Increasingly, a company's CSR stance becomes an integral part of the overall strategy itself: a reputation for social responsibility can be a source of competitive advantage.

Different organisations take different stances on CSR. Table 5.1 outlines four basic types to illustrate these differences. They represent a progressively more inclusive set of stakeholder interests and a greater breadth of criteria against which strategies and performance will be judged. The discussion that follows also explains what such stances typically involve in terms of the ways companies act.[15]

- The *laissez-faire* view (literally 'let do' in French) represents an extreme stance. In this view, organisations should be let alone to get on with things on their own account. Proponents argue that the only responsibility of business is to make a profit and provide for the interests of shareholders.[16] Expecting companies to exercise social duties beyond this only confuses decision making, introduces additional costs and undermines the accountability of managers to their shareholders. In this view, society benefits anyway from the profits: after all, these can either be used for further investment in the business or be paid out to shareholders, who may be pensioners relying on the income or similar.

- *Enlightened self-interest* is guided by recognition of the potential long-term financial benefit to the shareholder of well-managed relationships with other stakeholders. Here the justification for social responsibility is that it makes good business sense. For most organisations a good reputation in the eyes of customers and suppliers is important to long-term financial success. Working constructively with suppliers or local communities can actually increase the 'value' available for all stakeholders to share: for example, supporting education in the local workforce will increase the availability of skilled labour. Indeed, there is mounting evidence that responsible strategies can also reward shareholders.[17]

- A *forum for stakeholder interaction*[18] explicitly incorporates multiple stakeholder interests and expectations rather than just shareholders as influences on organisational purposes and strategies. Here the argument is that the performance of an organisation should be measured in a more pluralistic way than just through the financial bottom line. Such organisations adopt the principle of *sustainability* in strategy, one that ensures a better quality of life by attending to all three dimensions of environmental protection, social responsibility and economic welfare. Performance here is measured and rewarded in terms of *the triple bottom line* – social and environmental benefits as well as profits. Companies

Table 5.1 Corporate social responsibility stances

	Laissez-faire	Enlightened self-interest	Forum for stakeholder interaction	Shaper of society
Rationale	Legal compliance: make a profit, pay taxes and provide jobs	Sound business sense	Sustainability or triple bottom line	Social and market change
Leadership	Peripheral	Supportive	Champion	Visionary
Management	Middle-management responsibility	Systems to ensure good practice	Board-level issue; organisation-wide monitoring	Individual responsibility throughout the organisation
Mode	Defensive to outside pressures	Reactive to outside pressures	Proactive	Defining
Stakeholder relationships	Unilateral	Interactive	Partnership	Multi-organisation alliances

in this category might retain uneconomic units to preserve jobs, avoid manufacturing or selling 'anti-social' products and be prepared to bear reductions in profitability for the social good.

- *Shapers of society* regard financial considerations as of secondary importance or a constraint. These are visionary organisations seeking to change society and social norms. Public-sector organisations and charities are typically committed to this kind of stance. There are also *social entrepreneurs* who found new organisations that earn revenues but pursue a specific social purpose. For example, Traidcraft UK is a public limited company with a chain of retail shops that fights world poverty by promoting 'fair trade'. For shapers of society, the social role is the *raison d'être* of the business, not profits. Financial viability is important only as providing the means for continuing the social mission.

5.5 Culture and strategy

Mark Fields, President of Ford Motor Company in 2006, famously argued that 'culture eats strategy for breakfast', by which he emphasised the importance of culture in defining the strategy of the business. The importance of culture does not mean that strategy is irrelevant of course: culture should be seen as *part* of the strategy, something that can be a source of competitive advantage and, to some degree, something that can be managed too.

5.5.1 Organisational culture

Edgar Schein defines organisational culture as the 'basic assumptions and beliefs that are shared by members of an organisation, that operate unconsciously and define in a basic taken-for-granted fashion an organisation's view of itself and its environment'.[19] Related to this are the taken-for-granted 'ways we do things around here'[20] that accumulate over time. So **organisational culture is the taken-for-granted assumptions and behaviours of an organisation's members.** This culture helps make sense of people's organisational context and therefore contributes to how they respond to issues they face.

An organisation's culture can be conceived as consisting of different layers. The four proposed by Edgar Schein[21] are (see Figure 5.5):

- *Values* may be easy to identify in terms of those formally stated by an organisation since they are often explicit, perhaps written down (see Chapter 1). The values driving a strategy may, however, be different from those in formal statements. For example, in the early 2000s, many banks espoused values of shareholder value creation, careful risk management and, of course, high levels of customer service. But in practice they indulged in highly risky lending, resulting in the need for huge government financial support in the financial crisis of 2008–09. It is therefore important to delve beneath espoused values to uncover underlying, perhaps taken-for-granted, values that can help explain the strategy actually being pursued by an organisation.

- *Beliefs* are more specific. They can typically be discerned in how people talk about issues the organisation faces; for example, a belief that the company should not trade with particular countries or a belief in the rightness of professional systems and standards.

- *Behaviours* are the day-to-day ways in which an organisation operates which can be seen by people both inside and often outside the organisation. This includes the work routines, how the organisation is structured and controlled and 'softer' issues around symbolic behaviours. These behaviours may become the taken-for-granted 'ways we do things around here' that are potentially the bases for inimitable strategic capabilities, but also significant barriers to achieving strategic change if that becomes necessary.

- *Taken-for-granted assumptions* are the core of an organisation's culture which, in this book, we refer to as the organisational *paradigm*. The **paradigm is the set of assumptions held in common and taken for granted in an organisation.** In effect these shared assumptions represent *collective experience* about fundamental aspects of the organisation that, in turn, guide people in that organisation about how to view and respond to different circumstances that they face. The paradigm can underpin successful strategies by providing a basis of common understanding in an organisation but, again, can be a major problem when major strategic change is needed. The importance of the paradigm is discussed further in Section 5.3.2.

The concept of culture implies coherence, hence the common expression of 'corporate culture'. However, most organisations also have *organisational subcultures*, just like national cultures can contain local regional cultures. These subcultures may relate to the structure of the organisation: for example, the differences between geographical divisions in a multinational company, or between functional groups such as finance, marketing and operations. Differences between business functions can also relate to the different nature of work in different functions. For example, in a major oil company differences are likely between those functions engaged in 'upstream' exploration, where time horizons may be in decades, and those concerned with 'downstream' retailing, with much shorter market-driven time horizons. In strategic decision making, therefore, it is important to recognise the different subcultural assumptions managers may be bringing to the processes: finance managers may have different subcultural assumptions to marketing managers, and so on. Illustration 5.3 suggests very different subcultures within the University of Bath.

5.5.2 Analysing culture: the cultural web

In order to understand the existing culture and its effects it is important to be able to analyse an organisation's culture. The cultural web[22] is a means of doing this (see Figure 5.6). The **cultural web shows the behavioural, physical and symbolic manifestations of a culture** that inform and are informed by the taken-for-granted assumptions, or paradigm, of an organisation. It is in effect the inner two ovals in Figure 5.5. The seven elements of the cultural web are as follows:

- The *paradigm* is at the core of Figure 5.5. As previously defined, the paradigm is the set of assumptions held in common and taken for granted in an organisation. The paradigmatic assumptions are, quite likely, very basic. For example, a common problem in technology and engineering firms is the propensity of people to focus on the technical excellence of products rather than customer-perceived needs. Or the paradigm of practitioners in the National Health Service in the UK is about curing illnesses. It is quite likely that, even if the rational view is to build a strategy around the engineering firm' customer needs or the need for prevention (as distinct from curing) of illnesses, people in those organisations may still interpret issues and behave in line with its paradigm. So understanding what the paradigm is and how it informs debate on strategy matters. The problem is that, since it is unlikely to be talked about, or even be something that people are conscious of, trying to identify it can be difficult, especially if you are part of that organisation. Outside observers may find it easier to identify simply by listening to what people say and emphasise. One way of 'insiders' getting to see the assumptions they take for granted is to focus initially on other aspects of the cultural web because these are to do with more visible manifestations of culture. Moreover these other aspects are likely to act to reinforce the assumptions of the paradigm.

Illustration 5.3 Learn the culture proper to each. University pays a price for success

The controversy surrounding the University of Bath's Vice Chancellor raises issues about both corporate culture and organisational field.

In 2018, Glynis Breakwell stepped down after 17 years as Vice Chancellor (chief executive) of the University of Bath. For a new university situated outside any major city, the University of Bath had experienced remarkable success during Breakwell's term of office. She had presided over a doubling in student numbers since her start in post. The University had achieved the highest possible ratings from the government's teaching assessment system, it ranked among the top 12 universities for research in the United Kingdom, and overall it was rated as the country's fifth-best university in the influential *Guardian University 2018* guide. Yet Breakwell retired from her position surrounded in controversy.

The University's motto is taken from the Latin poet Virgil: 'Learn the culture proper to each after its kind.' This is a message of respect. The University's 2016–21 Strategic Plan reinforced this message by describing as one of its five key attributes: 'A supportive culture: creating a welcoming, inclusive community that values the individual and supports the realisation of their potential.' However, by the last year of Breakwell's tenure, one of the University's trade union leaders was accusing her of creating a 'culture of fear'.

Breakwell had been well rewarded for the university's successes. Breakwell's total package increased from £349,000 in 2011 to £451,000 in 2016, a proportional rise far ahead of that of most of her staff. Another pay rise followed in 2015–16, taking Breakwell's pay to the highest among British universities, more than £450,000. The number of other staff paid more than £100,000 in the University rose from just two when Breakwell took over to more than 50 by 2014. The University had also bought a prestigious mansion in the centre of Bath as living accommodation for Breakwell.

At the same time, Breakwell kept a tight grip on other labour costs. Breakwell had always refused to negotiate with local trade unions and non-academic pay lagged other local employers. For academics, the university had become one of the country's leaders in the use of zero-hours contracts, by which staff were hired by the hour, often at short notice. Many postgraduate teachers were stuck on the very lowest pay grade on the national scale and – unlike at other universities – were unable to progress higher.

In 2017, Breakwell was awarded another large pay increase by a committee on which she herself sat and voted. Protests among students and both academic and non-academic staff broke out. A senior member of the University complained: '[Breakwell] represents an idea of the university as "business" that most of us do not share.' Newspapers and politicians denounced Breakwell's pay and four Members of Parliament resigned from the University's advisory board. Among the controversy, student applications for entry to Bath in 2018 fell by nearly 6 per cent, while competitor universities were expanding. Breakwell was obliged to promise her retirement at the end of the academic year.

The university carried out an inquiry, recommending attention to the university's culture 'with a view to improving transparency, rebuilding trust and encouraging two-way communication'. Professor Ian White was appointed as the new Vice Chancellor, at a salary around half of what Breakwell had been paid. The President of the University of Bath Students' Union said: 'The recruitment process for our new Vice-Chancellor was transparent, inclusive and wide-ranging. . . We had the chance to hear about Ian White's values and vision for the University. As a result, I am confident that Ian White is the right choice for Bath. I believe we can all look forward to an exciting and bright future for our University.'

Sources: *Guardian*, 24 November 2017; *Bath Chronicle*, 23 November 2017 and 6 September 2018; University of Bath press release, 3 September 2018, www.bath.ac.uk/announcements/university-of-bath-appoints-new-vice-chancellor/

Questions

1 Identify key elements in the university's traditional organisational culture either in terms of Schein's four layers (Figure 5.5) or the cultural web (Figure 5.6).

2 In what respects did the University of Bath's culture under Breakwell appear to diverge from that outlined in the 2016–21 strategic plan and what could be done to reduce this apparent divergence?

Figure 5.5 Culture in four layers

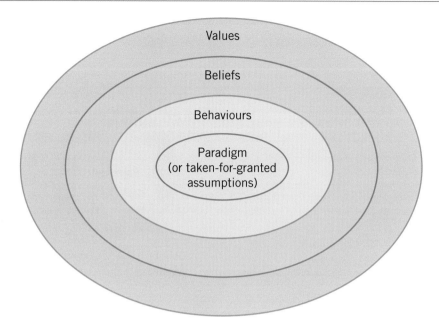

- *Rituals and routines* point to the repetitive nature of organisational cultures. *Routines* refer to 'the way we do things around here' on a day-to-day basis. At their best, routines lubricate the working of the organisation, and may provide a basis for distinctive organisational capabilities. However, they can also represent a taken-for-grantedness about how things should happen which, again, can guide how people deal with situations and be difficult to change. For example, managers trying to achieve greater customer focus in engineering firms often report that customer-facing sales engineers routinely tend to tell customers what they need rather than listening to their needs. The *rituals* of organisational life are particular activities or special events that emphasise, highlight or reinforce what is important in the culture. Examples include training programmes, promotion and assessment procedures, sales conferences and so on. An extreme example, of course, is the ritualistic training of army recruits to prepare them for the discipline required in conflict. However, rituals can also be informal activities such as drinks in the pub after work or gossiping around water coolers.

- The *stories* told by members of an organisation to each other, to outsiders, to new recruits, and so on, may act to embed the present in its organisational history and also flag up important events and personalities. They typically have to do with successes, disasters, heroes, villains and mavericks (who deviate from the norm). They can be a way of letting people know what is conventionally important in an organisation.

- *Symbols* are objects, events, acts or people that convey, maintain or create meaning over and above their functional purpose. For example, office furniture and layouts, cars and job titles have a functional purpose, but are also typically signals about status and hierarchy. Particular people may come to represent especially important aspects of an organisation or historic turning points.

- *Power* was defined earlier as the ability of individuals or groups to persuade, induce or coerce others into following certain courses of action. So *power structures* are distributions of power to groups of people in an organisation. The most powerful individuals or groups are likely to be closely associated with the paradigm and long-established ways of doing things.

Figure 5.6 The cultural web of an organisation

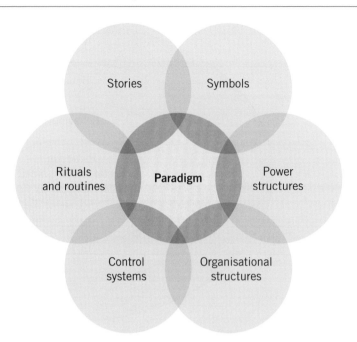

- *Organisational structures* are the roles, responsibilities and reporting relationships in organisations. These are likely to reflect power structures and how they manifest themselves. Formal hierarchical and mechanistic structures may emphasise that strategy is the province of top managers and everyone else is 'working to orders'. Structures with less emphasis on formal reporting relationships might indicate more participative strategy making. Highly decentralised structures may signify that collaboration is less important than competition and so on.

- *Control systems* are the formal and informal ways of monitoring and supporting people within and around an organisation and tend to emphasise what is seen to be important in the organisation. They include measurements and reward systems. For example, public-service organisations have often been accused of being concerned more with stewardship of funds than with quality of service. This is reflected in their control systems, which are more about accounting for spending rather than with quality of service. Remuneration schemes are a significant control mechanism. Individually based bonus schemes related to volume are likely to signal a culture of individuality, internal competition and an emphasis on sales volume rather than teamwork and an emphasis on quality.

Summary

- The purpose of an organisation will be influenced by the expectations of its *stakeholders*. Different stakeholders exercise different influence on organisational strategy, dependent on the extent of their power and attention. Managers can assess the influence of different stakeholder groups through *stakeholder analysis*.

- The influence of some key stakeholders will be represented formally within the *governance structure* of an organisation. This can be represented in terms of a *governance chain*, showing the links between ultimate beneficiaries and the managers of an organisation.

- Organisations adopt different stances on *corporate social responsibility* depending on how they perceive their role in society. Individual managers may also be faced with *ethical* dilemmas relating to the purpose of their organisation or the actions it takes.
- *Organisational culture* is the basic taken-for-granted assumptions, beliefs and behaviours shared by members of an organisation.
- The seven elements of the *cultural web* are useful for analysing organisational cultures and their relationships to strategy.

Recommended key reading

- A good review of important ideas in both corporate governance and corporate social responsibility is A. Rasche and M. Morsing, *Corporate Social Responsibility: Strategy, Communication, Governance*, Cambridge University Press, 2017. Specifically on corporate governance, a leading guide is B. Tricker, *Corporate Governance: Principles, Policies and Practices*, 3rd edn, Oxford University Press, 2015. For a comprehensive and critical explanation of organisational culture see Mats Alvesson, *Understanding Organisational Culture*, 2nd edn, SAGE Publications Ltd, 2012.

References

1. R.E. Freeman, J.S. Harrison and S. Zyglidopoulos, *Stakeholder Theory: Concepts and Strategies,* Cambridge University Press, 2018. Also see L. Bidhan, A. Parmar and R.E. Freeman, 'Stakeholder theory: the state of the art', *Academy of Management Annals*, vol. 4, no. 1 (2010), pp. 403–45.

2. D. Walker, L. Bourne and A. Shelley, 'Influence, stakeholder mapping and visualization', *Construction Management and Economics*, vol. 26, no. 6 (2008), pp. 645–58. In this edition, we have replaced 'interest' by 'attention' in line with recent theoretical literature: for example, D.A. Shepherd, J.S. McMullen and W. Ocasio, 'Is that an opportunity? An attention model of top managers' opportunity beliefs for strategic action', *Strategic Management Journal*, vol. 38, no. 3 (2017), pp. 626–44.

3. See for instance M. Nordqvist and L. Melin, 'Entrepreneurial families and family firms', *Entrepreneurship and Regional Development*, vol. 22, no. 3–4 (2010), pp. 211–39.

4. Haigh, N., Walker, J., Bacq, S. and Kickul, J. 'Hybrid organizations: origins, strategies, impacts, and implications', *California Management Review,* vol. 57, no. 3 (2015), pp. 5–12.

5. In the United Kingdom and associated countries, this kind of corporation is called a public limited company (plc); in Francophone countries, it is the Société Anonyme (SA); in Germany, it is the Aktiengesellschaft (AG).

6. *The Economist,* 'The rise of state capitalism' (21 January 2012).

7. For a discussion, see R. Rumelt, 'Theory, strategy and entrepreneurship', *Handbook of Entrepreneurship Research,* vol. 2 (2005), pp. 11–32.

8. I. Le Bretton-Miller, D. Miller and R.H. Lester, 'Stewardship or agency? A social embeddedness reconciliation of conduct and performance in public family businesses', *Organization Science*, vol. 22, no. 3 (2011), pp. 704–21.

9. The Ownership Commission, *Plurality, Stewardship and Engagement*, London, 2012.

10. Useful general references on corporate governance are: R. Monks and N. Minow (eds), *Corporate Governance*, 4th edn, Blackwell, 2008.

11. This definition is adapted from S. Jacoby, 'Corporate governance and society', *Challenge*, vol. 48, no. 4 (2005), pp. 69–87.

12. For a debate on principal–agent theory, see D. Miller and C. Sardais, 'Angel agents: agency theory reconsidered', *Academy of Management Perspectives*, vol. 25, no. 2 (2011), pp. 6–13.

13. For general coverage of Corporate Social Responsibility, see A. Rasche, M. Morsing and J. Moon (eds), *Corporate Social Responsibility: Strategy, Communication, Governance,* Cambridge University Press, 2017; on ethics, see M.T. Brown, *Corporate Integrity: Rethinking Organisational Ethics and Leadership*, Cambridge University Press, 2005.

14. A good review of current research on corporate social responsibility is the introduction to an *Academy of Management Journal* special issue on the topic: H. Wang, L. Tong, R. Takeuchi and G. George, 'Corporate social responsibility: an overview and new research directions', *Academy of Management Journal*, vol. 59, no. 2 (2016), pp. 534–44.

15. P. Mirvis and B. Googins, 'Stages of corporate citizenship', *California Management Review*, vol. 48, no. 2 (2006), pp. 104–26.

16. See M. Friedman: 'The social responsibility of business is to increase its profits', *New York Times Magazine* (13 September 1970).

17. See M. Porter and M. Kramer, 'Creating shared value', *Harvard Business Review*, vol. 89, no. 1/2 (2011), pp. 62–77; and D. Vogel, 'Is there a market for virtue? The business case for corporate social responsibility', *California Management Review*, vol. 47, no. 4 (2005), pp. 19–45.

18. H. Hummels, 'Organizing ethics: a stakeholder debate', *Journal of Business Ethics*, vol. 17, no. 13 (1998), pp. 1403–19.

19. This definition of culture is taken from E. Schein, *Organisational Culture and Leadership*, 3rd edn, Jossey-Bass, 2004, p. 6.

20. This is how Terrence Deal and Alan Kennedy define organisational culture in *Corporate Cultures: the Rites and Rituals of Corporate Life*, Addison-Wesley, 1982.

21. E. Schein (see reference 19) and A. Brown, *Organisational Culture*, Financial Times Prentice Hall, 1998, are useful in understanding the relationship between organisational culture and strategy.

22. A fuller explanation of the cultural web can be found in G. Johnson, 'Managing strategic change: strategy, culture and action', *Long Range Planning*, vol. 25, no. 1 (1992), pp. 28–36.

Case example
Uber and the ubermensch

The transport network company seeks to change from arrogant start-up to sustainable giant.

Travis Kalanick, Uber's founder.
Source: Justin Lane/EPA/Shutterstock

Uber was only founded in 2010, but already it has a full and controversial history. Its culture has been widely described as 'toxic'. As it aimed for an Initial Public Offering in 2019, with a rumoured target valuation of more than $120bn, it was critical to persuade potential investors that the company had achieved real cultural change.

Uber's foundational years

For Uber, the years to 2017 were heavily marked by its entrepreneurial chief executive and cofounder, Travis Kalanick. A product of the Californian tech culture, Kalanick already had a mixed entrepreneurial record when he started the Uber taxi company. His first business, Scour, was a peer-to-peer sharing business, sued by numerous publishers and bankrupt in 2000. His second business, Red Swoosh, was another peer-to-peer business, which was successfully sold for $19m in 2007, despite Kalanick's committal for tax fraud and perjury. Kalanick's personal style in the early years was unusual: he wore a cowboy hat and referred to himself as the Wolf, after the apparently cool fixer in the violent Tarantino film *Pulp Fiction*. At the same time, Kalanick was a fan of the libertarian philosopher Ayn Rand, adopting as his Twitter avatar the cover of her book *The Fountainhead*, a celebration of heroic individualism.

Given this personal background, Uber's name is probably no accident: it recalls the notion of Übermensch ('superior being') associated with the German philosopher Friedrich Nietzsche (famous for declaring the death of God). Uber's launch was certainly highly aggressive, seeking to be among the first to enter cities internationally and then working quickly to establish local dominance. This search for early-mover advantage frequently involved defying local regulations regarding car-hire businesses. Kalanick's philosophy was one of 'principled confrontation'. The motto was: 'it is easier to ask for forgiveness than for permission.' Uber would typically commence operations in a city, then, if faced by regulatory opposition, mobilise public support and professional lobbyists to campaign for regulatory change. In Portland, Oregon, the transportation commissioner called Uber's management 'a bunch of thugs'. By the end of 2015, however, Uber was already operating in about 400 cities around the world, from Abu Dhabi to Zurich. Revenues were $1.5bn (€1.3bn; £1.1bn).

Many of Uber's practices reflected a strong belief in the free market. For example, Uber uses dynamic (or 'surge') pricing, where prices are adjusted simply according to market demand. This could result in controversial price hikes. In 2014 during a terrorist siege in central Sydney, prices rose by 800 per cent as people rushed to get out of danger. This was widely seen as exploiting people's fear, but for Uber, it was just a matter of supply and demand. Similarly, the contract between drivers and Uber was held to be a simple market transaction, with drivers treated as independent businesses rather than employees. When an Uber driver complained to Kalanick about how difficult it had become to finance his car in the wake of pricing cuts imposed by the company, Kalanick responded that drivers took on car loans at their own risk. Drivers should estimate future prices themselves; Uber would not guarantee their profitability.

Uber could also turn the market against competitors. When Gett and Lyft launched competitive services in New York in 2013–2014, Uber organised its local employees to order cars from the new rivals, only to cancel orders when they were on their way. Uber even provided special phones and credit cards to enable these orders. Lyft was able to identify 177 Uber employees that had ordered and cancelled 5,560 orders over several months.

Uber made use of its software expertise as well. One of its most famous pieces of software was something called Greyball. Greyball was developed to identify individuals who the company suspected of using its services improperly, for instance people suspected of violating terms of service. However, Greyball could also be used to deny service to law enforcement agents and those with credit cards or phones associated with regulatory agencies. This was a tactic used in Portland, Oregon, for instance. Another piece of software was called God View, which allows Uber to track the movements of particular individuals: again, this was used to follow law enforcement agents, but was used widely within the company for personal and entertainment reasons. Finally, Uber developed the Ripley software, a secret 'panic button' that enabled the company to respond to government raids on Uber offices by immediately locking, shutting off and changing passwords on staff computers.

Uber's culture was special too. Kalanick adopted 14 core values for the company, including: Big bold bets, a champion's mindset, principled confrontation, always be hustlin' (sic) and meritocracy and toe-stepping. The result was a culture with few restraints, where the successful seemed to be forgiven for conduct that might otherwise be punished. When Emil Michael, one of Uber's senior vice presidents, was caught up in a scandal about digging into the private lives of journalists perceived as hostile to the company, Kalanick defended him, and indeed pulled him on-stage at a major meeting to praise him as an exemplar of Uber's culture.

This culture created a challenging work environment, particularly for women. Kalanick has referred to his company as 'Boob-er' because of how its high profile boosted his personal dating. In 2017, only 15.1 per cent of Uber's engineers, product managers and scientists were female. During 2017, the female engineer Susan Fowler published an account of her time at Uber that went viral on the internet. She recorded sexual harassment by her manager and very weak responses from the company to her complaints: 'Upper management told me he was a high performer . . . and they wouldn't feel comfortable punishing him for what was probably just an innocent mistake on his part'. Investigation with other female colleagues discovered that this kind of harassment and response was very common within the company. More generally, Fowler described 'a game-of-thrones political war raging within the ranks of upper management'.

Susan Fowler's blog captured widespread attention in part because of its resonance with the MeToo movement, then newly emerging to advance the cause of women in the workplace, particularly with regard to harassment. It also prompted more general criticisms of Uber's practices, and particularly the conduct of Travis Kalanick. Uber's employees stopped wearing proudly their company t-shirts in the streets of San Francisco, their headquarters city. Fearing for the value of its investment in the company, the venture capital firm Benchmark brought together investors holding 40 per cent of Uber's voting shares to demand Kalanick's resignation. In June 2017, Kalanick finally stepped down as Chief Executive of the firm he himself had founded.

New leadership

In August 2017, Dara Khosrowshahi, former Chief Executive of Expedia, took over as CEO. One of his first tasks was to change Uber's culture. He wrote on his LinkedIn page: 'The culture and approach that got Uber where it is today is not what will get us to the next level . . . our culture needs to evolve.' Using 20 working groups of Uber employees, Khosrowshahi developed eight new 'cultural norms'. Some were the same as Kalanick's old core values, for example on the importance of big, bold bets. Others were new, for example with regard to employee diversity: 'We celebrate differences.' One cultural norm in particular seemed to mark a sharp change from the Kalanick era: 'We do the right thing. Period.'

Khosrowshahi moved rapidly to repair relations with local city administrations, with London and New York particularly important. In London, where Uber had 3.6 million users and 45,000 drivers, the local administration had refused to renew its licence to operate, with the company's policy regarding the reporting of crimes a particular complaint. The UK and Ireland General Manager who had ultimate responsibility was replaced by Tom Elvidge, who had previously run Uber London locally. Three non-executive directors from outside the company were appointed to the local company's board, and policies were changed in a range of areas, from crime reporting to drivers' hours. In 2018, the company had its licence renewed, but on a probationary basis for just 18 months. Elvidge reflected that the threat to its London licence had been 'a wake-up call for a company that had grown incredibly fast but that needed to grow up'.

In New York, Uber's largest North American market with 75,000 drivers, there was trouble too, with an Uber driver being charged with kidnapping a female passenger and local regulators imposing a cap on new drivers. Again, Uber put in new management, bringing in their Houston manager to run the local operation. The new manager, Sarfaz Maredia, adopted a less combative stance with regulators and introduced more safety measures. Maredia declared: 'We're trying to build a successful, sustainable business, a company we can be proud of, not next year or the year after, but for many years down the road.'

Khosrowshahi also established a central safety team in Phoenix, Arizona, to handle the growing number of complaints regarding both drivers and passengers. The team had been just 23 strong in July 2017, but by the beginning of 2019 it had grown to 125. Eighty per cent of complainants are contacted personally within one hour of first notification. For complaints that are deemed potentially serious, drivers or passengers are immediately suspended. The company promised to report statistics on complaints. A company representative commented: 'The numbers are going to be disturbing because anything over one is disturbing, but then when you think about the fact that we do 100m. rides a week around the world, it's a lot of rides.'

Khosrowshahi's new regime was not untroubled. The company's head of human resources, Liane Hornsey, suddenly resigned a year into her tenure following an investigation into how she had handled employee grievances in the company. At a company 'all-hands' meeting in late 2018, Khosrowshahi faced tough employee questions about the culture of Uber's Advanced Technology Group (ATG) following *Business Insider*'s investigations into the killing of a pedestrian by an Uber test-car in self-driving mode. ATG engineers had turned off the ability to stop the car quickly. One employee asked: '*Business Insider* called ATG's culture "toxic" and referred to "missed warning signs, vast dysfunction and rampant infighting". Any truth to this?'. Khosrowshahi defended ATG's top management, calling *Business Insider* sensationalist. None the less he conceded: 'We have screwed up. . . It [the investigation] does reflect what is true, which is we have gone through a lot. . . Our test now is: Can the team come together and build something better?'

The new Chief Executive was not entirely free of the company's founder either. Travis Kalanick was one of Uber's largest shareholders and continued to sit on the company's board of directors. He also had the expertise of somebody who had been there right from the start. Initially, Khosrowshahi talked privately with Kalanick on at least a monthly basis: 'I would be foolish not to use Travis's incredible genius'. However, during 2018, Khosrowshahi admitted that relations with the company's founder were 'strained'. He commented: 'There was a lot that happened in the past that wasn't right. . . While you don't want to blame individuals, in the end the CEO of the company has to take responsibility.'

Main sources: Business Insider, 24 January and 29 November 2018; *Evening Standard*, 24 May 2018; *Financial Times*, 25 June and 28 December 2018; *New York Times,* 1 December 2018.

Questions

1 If you were a large shareholder in Uber contemplating buying more stock in the Initial Public Offering of 2019, how satisfied would you be with Uber's governance and what changes would you seek, in particular with regard to the company's governance chain (Figure 5.5)?

2 Referring to Section 5.3.1, analyse Uber's culture under Travis Kalanick in terms of values, beliefs, behaviours and taken-for-granted assumptions (the 'paradigm'). How much has this culture changed and how consistent is it across Uber as a whole?

Chapter 6
Business strategy and models

Key terms

Learning outcomes

After reading this chapter, you should be able to:

- Assess business strategy in terms of the generic strategies of *cost leadership, differentiation*, *focus* and *hybrid* strategy.

- Apply principles of *game theory* and the benefits of *competition vs. cooperation* to business strategy.

- Identify and apply *business model* components: *value creation, configuration* and *capture.*

6.1 Introduction

This chapter is about two fundamental strategic choices: what business strategy and what business model should a company, business unit or other organisation adopt in its market? Business strategies are about how to compete in a market place so that a restaurant, for instance, has to decide a range of issues such as food concept, menus, décor and prices in the light of local competition from other restaurants. Business strategy questions are fundamental both to standalone small businesses and to all the many business units that typically make up large diversified organisations. Large diversified corporations thus typically include many decentralised 'strategic business units' in different product or market areas each with its own business strategy depending on the specific needs of their served market. **A strategic business unit (SBU) supplies goods or services for a distinct domain of activity** (sometimes these SBUs are called 'divisions' or 'profit centres'). For example, Nestlé's ice-cream SBU has to decide how to compete against smaller and local artisanal companies with new imaginative flavours and different customer focus, distribution channels and pricing. These kinds of business strategy issues are distinct from the question as to whether Nestlé should own an ice-cream business in the first place: this is a matter of corporate strategy, the subject of Chapter 7.

Another important choice is to identify the relationship between the value created for customers and other participants, the organisational activities that create this value and how the organisation and other participants can capture value from this – a *business model*. For instance, Amazon was a pioneer with its e-commerce business model that contrasted with bricks-and-mortar retailers. Over time, however, this business model was imitated and many other retailers also entered into e-commerce. This shows that organisations need to consider what business model to build on; established or new ones or both.

Three themes that provide the structure for the rest of the chapter:

- *Generic competitive strategies*, including cost leadership, differentiation, focus and hybrid strategies.
- *Game theory*, including choices between competition and cooperation.
- *Business models*, including the three basic components of value creation, value configuration and value capture.

Business strategy and business models are not just relevant to the private business sector. Charities and public-sector organisations also compete and have business models. Hence, charities compete between each other for support from donors. Public-sector organisations also need to be 'competitive' against comparable organisations in order to satisfy their stakeholders, secure their funding and protect themselves from alternative suppliers from the private sector. Schools compete in terms of examination results, while hospitals compete in terms of waiting times, treatment survival rates and so on. Likewise, these sectors need to consider what value is created for whom and how organisational activities contribute to this in a business model. Although some of the detailed implications may vary between sectors, wherever comparison is possible with other similar organisations, basic principles of business strategy and models are likely to be relevant. Very few organisations can afford to be demonstrably inferior to peers. Most have to make choices on key competitive variables such as costs, prices and quality.

6.2 Generic competitive strategies

This section introduces the competitive element of business strategy, with cooperation addressed particularly in Section 6.3. **Competitive strategy is concerned with how a company, business unit or organisation achieves competitive advantage in its domain of activity.** Competitive strategy therefore involves issues such as costs, product and service features and branding. In turn, **competitive advantage is about how a company, business unit or organisation creates value for its users both greater than the costs of supplying them and superior to that of rivals.** Competitive advantages should underpin competitive strategies. There are two important features of competitive advantage. To be *competitive* at all, an organisation must ensure that customers see sufficient value that they are prepared to pay more than the costs of supply. To have an *advantage*, the organisation must be able to create greater value than competitors. In the absence of a competitive advantage, an organisation's competitive strategy is always vulnerable to competitors with better products or offering lower prices.

There are two fundamental means of achieving competitive advantage. An organisation can have structurally lower *costs* than its competitors. Or it can have products or services that are *differentiated* from competitors' products or services in ways that are so valued by customers that it can charge higher prices that covers the additional costs of the differentiation. In defining competitive strategies, Michael Porter adds a further dimension based on the *scope* of customers that the business chooses to serve.[1] Businesses can choose to focus on narrow customer segments, for example a particular demographic group such as the youth market. Alternatively, they can adopt a broad scope, targeting customers across a range of characteristics such as age, wealth or geography. Porter's distinctions between cost, differentiation and scope define a set of 'generic' strategies: in other words, basic types of strategy that hold across many kinds of business situations. These three generic competitive strategies are illustrated in Figure 6.1.

Figure 6.1 Three generic strategies

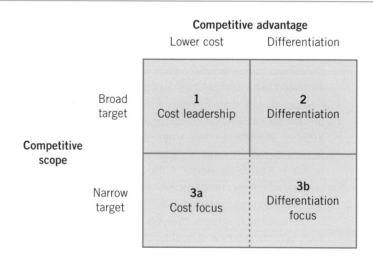

Source: Adapted from *Competitive Advantage: Creating and Sustaining Superior Performance* by Michael E. Porter. The Free Press, a Division of Simon & Schuster, Inc.

6.2.1 Cost-leadership strategy

Cost-leadership strategy involves becoming the systematically lowest-cost organisation in a domain of activity. For example, Ryanair pursues a relentless low-cost strategy in the European airline industry. The airline saves costs in virtually every aspect of its operation from purchasing a single type of aircraft (without reclining seats) to selling tickets primarily online (over 90 per cent of sales) to low employee costs (second lowest in Europe). There are four key *cost drivers* that can help deliver cost leadership, as follows:

- *Input costs* are often very important, for example labour or raw materials. Many companies seek competitive advantage through locating their labour-intensive operations in countries with low labour costs. Examples might be service call centres in India or manufacturing in South East Asia and China. Location close to raw material sources can also be advantageous, as for example the Brazilian steel producer CSN which benefits from its own local iron-ore facilities.

- *Economies of scale* refer to how increasing scale usually reduces the average costs of operation over a particular time period, perhaps a month or a year. Economies of scale are important wherever there are high fixed costs. Fixed costs are those costs necessary for a level of output: for example, a pharmaceutical manufacturer typically needs to do extensive R&D before it produces a single pill. Economies of scale come from spreading these fixed costs over high levels of output: the average cost due to an expensive R&D project halves when output increases from one million to two million units. Economies of scale in purchasing can also reduce input costs. The large airlines, for example, are able to negotiate steep discounts from aircraft manufacturers. For the cost-leader, it is important to reach the output level equivalent to the *minimum efficient scale*. Note, though, that *diseconomies of scale* are possible. Large volumes of output that require special overtime payments to workers or involve the neglect of equipment maintenance can soon become very expensive. As to the left in Figure 6.2, therefore, the economies of scale curve is typically somewhat U-shaped, with the average cost per unit actually increasing beyond a certain point.

- *Experience*[2] can be a key source of cost efficiency. The *experience curve* implies that the cumulative experience gained by an organisation with each unit of output leads to reductions in unit costs (see Figure 6.2 to the right). For example, for many electronic components per unit costs can drop as much as 95 per cent every time the accumulated volume doubles. There is no time limit: simply the more experience an organisation has in an activity,

Figure 6.2 Economies of scale and the experience curve

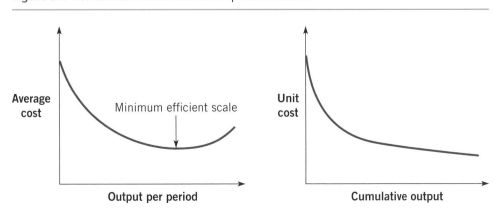

111

the more efficient it gets at doing it. The efficiencies are basically of two sorts. First, there are gains in labour productivity as staff simply learn to do things more cheaply over time (this is the specific *learning curve* effect). Second, costs are saved through more efficient designs or equipment as experience shows what works best. The experience curve has three important implications for business strategy. First, entry timing into a market is important: early entrants into a market will have experience that late entrants do not yet have and so will gain a cost advantage. Second, it is important to gain and hold market share, as companies with higher market share have more 'cumulative experience' simply because of their greater volumes. Finally, although the gains from experience are typically greatest at the start, as indicated by the steep initial curve to the right in Figure 6.2, improvements normally continue over time. Opportunities for cost reduction are theoretically endless. Figure 6.2 compares the experience curve (to the right) and economies of scale (to the left) in order to underline the contrast here. Unlike scale, where diseconomies appear beyond a certain point, the experience curve implies at worst a flattening of the rate of cost reduction. However, completely new production technologies from competitors can potentially introduce even steeper experience effects and further improved cost savings.

- *Product/process design* also influences cost. Efficiency can be 'designed in' at the outset. For example, engineers can choose to build a product from cheap standard components rather than expensive specialised components. Organisations can choose to interact with customers exclusively through cheap web-based methods, rather than via telephone or stores. Organisations can also tailor their offerings in order to meet the most important customer needs, saving money by ignoring others.

There are two tough requirements for cost-based strategies. First of all, the principle of competitive advantage indicates that a business's cost structure needs to be systematically *lowest* cost (i.e. lower than all competitors'). Having the second-lowest cost structure implies a competitive disadvantage against somebody. Competitors with higher costs than the cost-leader are always at risk of being undercut on price, especially in market downturns. For businesses competing on a cost basis, systematic cost leadership is always more secure than being second or third in terms of costs. The US financial investments company Vanguard is a good example of this as discussed in Illustration 6.1.

The second requirement is that low cost should not be pursued in total disregard for quality. To sell its products or services, the cost-leader has to be able to meet market standards. For example, low-cost Chinese car producers exporting to Western markets need to offer not only cars that are cheap, but cars that meet acceptable norms in terms of style, safety, service network, reliability, resale value and other important characteristics. Cost-leaders have two options here:

- *Parity* (in other words, equivalence) with competitors in product or service features valued by customers. Parity allows the cost-leader to charge the same prices as the average competitor in the marketplace, while translating its cost advantage wholly into extra profit (as in the second column of Figure 6.3). The Brazilian steel producer CSN, with its cheap iron-ore sources, is able to charge the average price for its steel and take the cost difference in greater profit.

- *Proximity* (closeness) to competitors in terms of features. Where a competitor is sufficiently close to competitors in terms of product or service features, customers may only require small cuts in prices to compensate for the slightly lower quality. As in the third column in Figure 6.3, the proximate cost-leader still earns better profits than the average competitor because its lower price eats up only a part of its cost advantage. This proximate cost-leadership strategy might be the option chosen initially by Chinese car manufacturers in export markets, for example.

Illustration 6.1 Vanguard's low-cost strategy comes to Europe

The US company Vanguard pioneered a distinct low-cost strategy in the mutual fund industry and is now exporting it world-wide.

Mutual funds are managed by investment companies that raise money from multiple customers and invest the money in a group of assets (stocks, bonds, money market instruments, etc.). Each customer, often as part of a retirement plan, then owns shares that represent a portion of the holdings of the fund. They are charged an annual fee or 'expense ratio' that covers investment advisory fees, administrative costs, distribution fees, and other operating expenses. The traditional way of competing in the industry was by actively managed and differentiated investments that tried to generate as high returns as possible and thus being able to charge higher fees. The emphasis was on the business performance end of the business by offering differentiated funds with higher returns. Vanguard instead focused on the cost end of the business and offered customers considerably lower annual fees and costs. Most comparisons showed that Vanguards fees or expense ratios were 65–80 per cent less than the industry average depending on investment asset. The company also launched the industry's first index mutual fund that passively followed a stock market index without ambitions to generate a better performance than the market, but which outperformed many actively managed funds.

Vanguard has started to export its low-cost focus worldwide and has about $400bn (€300bn, £240) in non-US assets and reach over $45bn (€34bn, £30bn) under management in Europe. 'Lowering the cost of investing is in our DNA' blogged Tom Rampulla, former head of Vanguard Europe. Their low-cost strategy involved several components. First, unlike competitors it did not need to make a profit. Tim Buckley, chief investment officer explained:

'We are not a listed company. We're a mutual company. We're owned by our clients. So when we make a profit, we have two choices. We can roll that profit back into the business or we can pay it out to our owners, our clients, in the form of lower expenses. Over the years we have lowered expenses and that has attracted more clients.'[1]

Second, Vanguard distributed their funds directly to customers and did not need to pay commissions of around 8 per cent to brokers. Third, the company had internalised investment advisory functions of the funds at cost instead of using external investment advisors that would charge a premium. Fourth, Vanguard relied on a no-nonsense thrifty organisational culture where managers were incentivised to control cost and no one, not even senior executives flew first class. Fifth, the company had only a few retail centres and spent less on advertising than anyone else in the industry. Last, but not least, as one of the largest asset managers globally they gained large economies of scale.

The next step for Vanguard is to do to the financial advisory services industry what they had done to the mutual fund industry. Based on webcam chats and other cost reductions the aim was to offer advisory services at a fraction of the cost of competitors. They would charge annually 0.3 per cent on assets compared to the industry average of 1 per cent, according to former Vanguard CEO Bill McNabb:[2]

'Can we provide really super-high quality advice at a very low cost and do that in a very large way, and change the market? I think we can. We continue to think of our primary mission to reduce the complexity and cost of investing across the board.'

Source: (1) D. Oakley, *Financial Times*, 4 March 2015; (2) S. Foley, *Financial Times*, 8 December 2014.

Questions

1 What type of competitive strategy, low-cost, differentiation, focus or hybrid would you suggest as a way of competing with Vanguard?

2 Using webcam chats is one approach to lower costs in financial advisory services as indicated above. What other ways could there be to lower costs to support a low-cost strategy in this area?

Figure 6.3 Costs, prices and profits for generic strategies

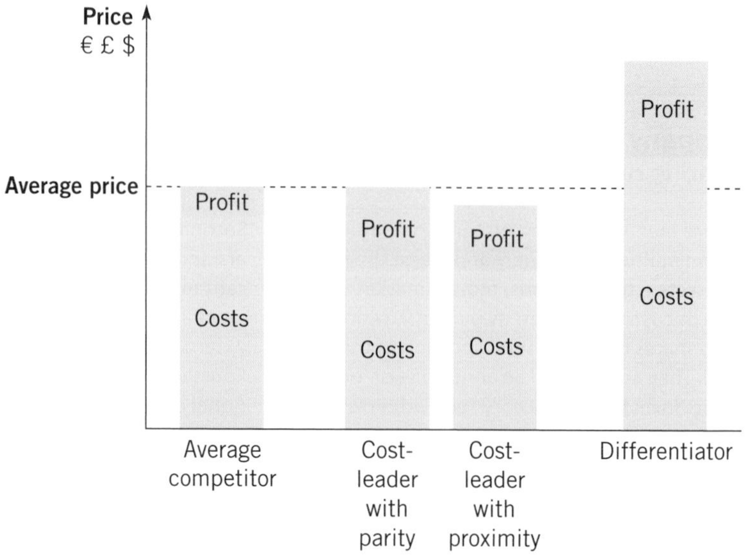

6.2.2 Differentiation strategy

The principal alternative to cost leadership is differentiation.[3] **Differentiation strategy involves uniqueness along some dimension that is sufficiently valued by customers to allow a price premium.** For example, German manufacturer Miele pursues a differentiation strategy in the domestic appliance industry. Their European manufactured, high-quality and durable dishwashers, washing machines and stoves are targeted towards higher income households at a price premium. Relevant points of differentiation vary between markets. Within each market too, businesses may differentiate along different dimensions. In clothing retail, competitors may differentiate by store size, locations or fashion. In cars, competitors may differentiate by safety, style or fuel efficiency. Where there are many alternative dimensions that are valued by customers, it is possible to have many different types of differentiation strategy in a market. Thus, even at the same top end of the car market, BMW and Mercedes differentiate in different ways, the first typically with a sportier image, the second with more conservative values. In brief, there are various aspects to consider in pursuing a differentiation strategy and below are three primary differentiation drivers to consider:

- *Product and service attributes.* Certain product attributes can provide *better or unique features* than comparable products or services for the customer. For example, the Dyson vacuum cleaner with its unique technology provides customers with a better suction performance compared to competitors. The possibilities of product differentiation are, however, virtually endless and only limited by the creativity of an organisation. They may include differences in colour, design, speed, style, taste, etc. For vacuum cleaners other companies may, for example, differentiate themselves on the basis of user convenience or design rather than suction performance. Product innovation and introduction can also be a basis of differentiation. Apple has been able to charge considerable premiums by continuously launching novel products with superior technologies, design and consumer interfaces. Finally, in building a basis for differentiation it is vital to identify clearly the customer on whose needs the differentiation is based. This is not always straightforward; for example, it may be either an intermediate distributor or end customer.

- *Customer relationships.* Besides more tangible differences in product and service characteristics differentiation can rely on the relationship between the organisation providing the product and the customer. This often relates to how the product is perceived by the customer. The perceived value can increase through *customer services and responsiveness*. This can include distribution services, payment services or after sales services among other things. For example, Zalando, Europe's leading online retailer for fashion and shoes, offers not only free shipping to the customer, but free returns and a 'bill-me-later' service. Products can also be differentiated for the individual customer through *customisation*. This is the case for a variety of consumer goods from athletic shoes to cars, but also for business-to-business goods like enterprise software. Finally, *marketing and reputation*, including emotional and psychological aspects, that an organisation projects can be another basis for differentiation. Starbucks, for example, can charge a premium price for its coffee not only because of its product differences, but also because of the ambiance and image that the company displays at its outlets.

- *Complements.* Differentiation can also build on linkages to other products or services. The perceived value of some products can be significantly enhanced when consumed together with other product or service complements compared to consuming the product alone (see Section 3.2.3). Apple has created the complement services iTunes and App Store free of charge for the consumer, which differentiate its products (iPhone, iPad, etc.) with the possibility to charge a premium. Considering how customers benefit from consuming two products or services in tandem and a way of bundling products and services together to increase the value for the customer and thus another way of differentiation.

There is an important condition for a successful differentiation strategy. Differentiation allows higher prices, but usually this comes at a cost. To create valuable differentiation typically involves additional investments, for example in R&D, branding or staff quality. The differentiator can expect that its costs will be higher than those of the average competitor. But, as in the fourth column of Figure 6.3, the differentiator needs to ensure that the additional costs of differentiation do not exceed the gains in price. It is easy to add on additional costs in ways that are not valued sufficiently by customers. Just as cost-leaders should not neglect quality, so should differentiators attend closely to costs, especially in areas irrelevant to their sources of differentiation. Volvo's differentiation strategy in the Indian bus market in Illustration 6.2 also involved keeping an eye on costs besides differentiation.

6.2.3 Focus strategy

Porter distinguishes focus as the third generic strategy, based on competitive scope. A **focus strategy targets a narrow segment or domain of activity and tailors its products or services to the needs of that specific segment to the exclusion of others.** Focus strategies come in two variants, according to the underlying sources of competitive advantage, cost or differentiation. In air travel, Ryanair follows a *cost focus strategy*, targeting price-conscious travellers with little need for connecting flights. In the domestic detergent market, the Belgian company Ecover follows a *differentiation focus* strategy, gaining a price premium over rivals on account of its ecological cleaning products targeted at environmentally conscious customers.

The focuser achieves competitive advantage by dedicating itself to serving its target segments better than others that are trying to cover a wider range of segments. Serving a broad range of segments can bring disadvantages in terms of coordination, compromise

Illustration 6.2 Volvo's different Indian buses

Volvo has a strategy to sell buses at nearly four times the prevailing market price.

The Indian bus market has long been dominated by two subsidiaries of major Indian conglomerates: Tata Motors and Ashok Leyland. They made simple coaches on a design that had hardly changed for decades. On top of a basic truck chassis, the two companies bolted a rudimentary coach body. Engines were a meagre 110–120 horse-power and roared heartily as they hauled their loads up the steep roads. Mounted at the front, the heat from the over-strained engines would pervade the whole bus. Air conditioning was a matter of open windows, through which the dust and noise of the Indian roads would pour. Suspension was old-fashioned, guaranteeing a shaky ride on pot-holed roads. Bags were typically slung on the top of the bus, where they were easily soiled and at high risk of theft. But at least the buses were cheap, selling to local bus companies at around Rs 1.2m (€15,000; $21,000).

In 1996, Swedish bus company Volvo entered, with buses priced at Rs 4m, nearly four times as much as local products. Akash Passey, Volvo's first Indian employee, commissioned a consultancy company to evaluate prospects. The consultancy company recommended that Volvo should not even try. Passey told the *Financial Times*: 'My response was simple – I took the report and went to the nearest dustbin and threw it in.' Passey entered the market in 2001 with the high-priced luxury buses.

Passey used the time to develop a distinctive strategy. His product had superior features. Volvo's standard engines were 240–250 hp and mounted at the back, ensuring a faster and quieter ride. Air conditioning was standard of course. The positioning of the engine and the specific bus design of the chassis meant a roomier interior, plus storage for bags internally. But Passey realised this would not be enough. He commented to the *Financial Times*: 'You had to do a lot of things to break the way business is done normally.'

Volvo offered post-sale maintenance services, increasing life expectancy of buses from three to ten years, and allowing bus operating companies to dispense with their own expensive maintenance workshops. Free training was given to drivers, so they drove more safely and took more care of their buses. The company advertised the benefits of the buses direct to customers in cinemas, rather than simply promoting them to the bus operators. Faster, smoother and more reliable travel allowed the bus operators to increase their ticket prices for the Volvo buses by 35 per cent.

Business people and the middle classes were delighted with the new Volvo services. Speedier, more comfortable journeys allowed them to arrive fresh for meetings and potentially to save the costs of overnight stays. Tata and Ashok Leyland both now produce their own luxury buses, with Mercedes and Isuzu following Volvo into the market. Nonetheless, the phrase 'taking a Volvo' has become synonymous with choosing a luxury bus service in India, rather as 'hoover' came to refer to any kind of vacuum cleaner.

A new state-of-the-art bus factory was opened in Bangalore in 2008 and after further investments in 2012 it doubled the annual capacity to 1,500 buses per year. As Volvo's most efficient bus factory worldwide it has started to export buses to Europe. In 2016 Volvo continued its distinctive strategy and became the first bus company in India to manufacture and sell hybrid buses running on an electric motor and battery as well as diesel. Kamal Bali, President and Managing Director, Volvo Group India says they are very bullish on India: 'We are bringing in hybrid buses now. A lot of automation and connected vehicles are the future plans that we have for India.'

Source: Adapted from J. Leahy, 'Volvo takes a lead in India', *Financial Times*, 31 August 2009; M. Lalatendu, *The Hindu*, 15 February 2016; S. Mathur, Auto.economictimes.indiatimes.com, 19 May 2016.

Questions

1 Rank the elements of Passey's strategy for Volvo in order of importance. Could any have been dispensed with?

2 How sustainable is Volvo's luxury bus strategy?

or inflexibility. Focus strategies are, therefore, able to seek out the weak spots of broad cost-leaders and differentiators:

- *Cost focusers* identify areas where broader cost-based strategies fail because of the added costs of trying to satisfy a wide range of needs. For instance, in the United Kingdom food retail market, Iceland Foods has a cost-focused strategy concentrated on frozen and chilled foods, reducing costs against discount food retailers with a wider product range and more diverse suppliers which have all the complexity of fresh foods and groceries as well as their own frozen and chilled food ranges.

- *Differentiation focusers* look for specific needs that broader differentiators do not serve so well. Focus on one particular need helps to build specialist knowledge and technology, increases commitment to service and can improve brand recognition and customer loyalty. For example, ARM Holdings dominates the world market for smartphone and tablet chips, despite being only a fraction of the size of the leading microprocessor manufacturers, AMD and Intel, which also make chips for a wide range of computers.

Successful focus strategies depend on at least one of three key factors:

- *Distinct segment needs.* Focus strategies depend on the distinctiveness of segment needs. If segment distinctiveness erodes, it becomes harder to defend the segment against broader competitors. For example, Tesla Motors started to target a narrow segment with its expensive premium electric vehicles. However, if the boundaries become blurred between Tesla's focus on electric cars used by affluent environmentally conscious consumers and electric cars used by general consumers it could become easier for competitors to also attack this distinctive niche.

- *Distinct segment value chains.* Focus strategies are strengthened if they have distinctive value chains that will be difficult or costly for rivals to construct. If the production processes and distribution channels are very similar, it is easy for a broad-based differentiator to push a specialised product through its own standardised value chain at a lower cost than a rival focuser. In detergents, Procter & Gamble cannot easily respond to the Belgium ecologically friendly cleaning products company Ecover because achieving the same environmental soundness would involve transforming its purchasing and production processes.

- *Viable segment economics.* Segments can easily become too small to serve economically as demand or supply conditions change.

6.2.4 Hybrid strategy

Michael Porter warned that managers face a crucial choice between the generic strategies of cost leadership, differentiation and focus. As earlier indicated, the lowest-cost competitor can always undercut the second lowest-cost competitor. For a company seeking advantage through low costs, therefore, it makes no sense to add extra costs by half-hearted efforts at differentiation. For a differentiator, it is self-defeating to make economies that jeopardise the basis for differentiation. For a focuser, it is dangerous to move outside the original specialised segment, because products or services tailored to one set of customers are likely to have inappropriate costs or features for the new target customers. Managers are generally best to consider the trade-offs and choose which generic strategy they are pursuing and then sticking to it. Otherwise there would be a danger of being *stuck in the middle*, doing no strategy well.

However, it has been acknowledged that a hybrid type of strategy is possible under certain circumstances. For example, American Southwest Airlines pursues a low-cost strategy with their budget and no-frills offering. However, its brand also signals differentiation based on convenience including frequent departures and friendly service. Some companies start out with one strategy that is later combined with another. McDonald's first followed a product differentiation strategy, but later its fast-food leader position allowed the company to emphasise scale and low costs as well.

As Michael Porter acknowledges there may also be specific circumstances in which the strategies can be combined:[4]

- *Organisational separation.* It is possible for a company to create separate strategic business units (SBUs), each pursuing different generic strategies and with different cost structures. The challenge, however, is to prevent negative spill-overs from one SBU to another. For example, a company mostly pursuing differentiated strategies is liable to have high head office costs that the low-cost SBUs will also have to bear. On the other hand, a cheap cost-leader might damage the brand value of a sister SBU seeking differentiation.

- *Technological or managerial innovation.* Sometimes technological innovations allow radical improvements in both cost and quality. Internet retailing reduces the costs of merchandise, at the same time as increasing differentiation by greater product range and, through online reviews, better advice.

Hybrid strategies are, however, complex and should be pursued with caution. They require careful considerations as the fundamental trade-off between low cost and differentiation has to be resolved.[5] Porter's generic strategies do remind managers that trade-offs and costs are critical. Unless an organisation has some secure cost advantage (such as economies of scale), a hybrid strategy of high-perceived benefits and low prices is unlikely to be sustainable for long unless competition pressures are low. Hence, Porter's warning about the danger of being stuck in the middle provides a useful discipline for managers. It is very easy for them to make incremental decisions that compromise the basic generic strategy. As profits accumulate, the successful cost-leader will be tempted to stop scrimping and saving. In hard times, a differentiator might easily cut back the R&D or advertising investments essential to its long-term differentiation advantage. Consistency with generic strategy provides a valuable check for managerial decision-making.

6.3 Game theory

Generic strategies need to be chosen and adjusted in the light of competitors' strategies. If everybody else is chasing after cost leadership, then a differentiation strategy might be sensible. Thus, business strategy choices *interact* with those of competitors. This suggests that competitors need to consider not only their own competitive moves, but their competitors potential counter-moves and whether to compete or try to cooperate. Game theory can help managers choose between competition and more cooperative strategies.

Competition can sometimes escalate in a way that is dangerous to all competitors. It can thus be in the self-interest of organisations to restrain competition and even to collaborate. Game theory provides important insights into competitor interaction and when to compete and when to cooperate.[6] The 'game' refers to the kinds of interactive moves two players make in a game of chess. **Game theory encourages an organisation to consider competitors' likely moves and the implications of these moves for its own strategy.** Game theorists are alert to two kinds of interaction in particular. First, game theorists consider how a *competitor response* to a strategic move might change the original assumptions behind that move: for example, challenging a competitor in one area might lead to a counter-attack in another. Second, game theorists are sensitive to the *strategic signals*, or messages, their moves might convey to competitors, for example with regard to how fiercely they seem willing to defend their position in a particular market. In the light of possible attacks and counter-attacks, game theorists often advise a more cooperative approach than head-to-head competition.

Game theory is particularly relevant where competitors are *interdependent*. Interdependence exists where the outcome of choices made by one competitor is dependent on the choices made by other competitors. For example, the success of price cuts by a retailer depends on the responses of its rivals: if rivals do not match the price cuts, then the price-cutter gains market share; but if rivals follow the price cuts, nobody gains market share and all players suffer from the lower prices. Anticipating competitor counter-moves is clearly vital to deciding whether to go forward with the price-cutting strategy.

There are two important guiding principles that arise from interdependence:

* *Get in the mind of the competitors.* Strategists need to put themselves in the position of competitors, take a view about what competitors are likely to do and choose their own strategy in this light. They need to understand their competitors' game-plan to plan their own.

* *Think forwards and reason backwards.* Strategists should choose their competitive moves on the basis of understanding the likely responses of competitors. Think forwards to what competitors might do in the future, and then reason backwards to what would be sensible to do in the light of this now.

One of the most famous illustrations of mathematical game theory is the *prisoner's dilemma*. Game theorists identify many situations where organisations' strategic decisions are similar to the dilemma of two prisoners accused of serial crimes together and being interrogated in separate prison cells without the possibility of communicating with each other. The prisoners have to decide on the relative merits of: (i) loyally supporting each other by refusing to divulge any information to their interrogators; and (ii) seeking an advantage by betraying the other. If both stay silent, they might get away with most of their crimes and only suffer some lesser punishment, perhaps for just one or two offences. The interrogators, though, will tempt each of them to divulge full information by offering them their freedom if only they betray their fellow criminal. However, if both betray, then the judge is unlikely to be grateful for the confessions and will punish them for all their crimes. The dilemma for each of the prisoners is how much to trust in their mutual loyalty: if they both refuse to divulge, they can both get away with the lesser punishment; on the other hand, if one is sure that the other will not betray, it makes even more sense to betray the loyal one as that allows the betrayer to go totally free. The two prisoners are clearly interdependent. But because they cannot communicate, they each have to get in the mind of the other, think forwards to what they might do, and then reason backwards in order to decide what their own strategy should be – stay silent or betray.

The prisoner's dilemma has its equivalence in business where there are two major players competing head-to-head against each other in a situation of tight interdependence. This is the position of Airbus and Boeing in the aircraft business. It would be relevant to the strategic decisions of two such interdependent companies in a range of situations: for example, if one company was thinking about making a major investment in an innovative new product that the other company could match. For two such competitors to communicate directly about their strategies in these situations would likely be judged illegal by the competition authorities. They therefore have to get into each other's minds, think forwards and reason backwards.

6.4 Business models

Business models have become increasingly popular as internet-based and platform companies such as Airbnb, Spotify and Uber have conquered the world with their new models. They are particularly useful when explaining more complex business interrelationships. Consequently, the business model concept is commonly discussed in relation to strategy today. Building on David Teece's work, this chapter carefully distinguishes business models from business strategy.[7] **A business model describes a value proposition for customers and other participants, an arrangement of activities that produces this value, and associated revenue and cost structures.**[8] Most fundamentally it concerns the manners and mechanisms of an organisation's value creation, configuration and capture. Competitors often have the same or similar business models, but their business strategy and basis for competitive advantage can still differ.

When entrepreneurs in new start-ups have entered old industries with new business models in recent years, they have frequently changed industry dynamics and competition in radical ways. The new models often involve more complex interrelationships than traditional ones and generate value and profits for more parties than just a buyer and seller. This shows that both entrepreneurs and managers, whose organisations may be threatened by new start-ups, need to understand business models. Illustration 6.3 discusses how Uber's business model has revolutionised the taxi industry globally. The remainder of this section first discusses three fundamental elements of business models, some typical business model patterns and finishes with an examination of a common business model: the multi-sided platform.

6.4.1 Value creation, configuration and capture

Business models describe business transactions and interrelationships between various parties and are best explained in terms of three interrelated components (see Figure 6.4).[9] The first emphasises *value creation*, a proposition that addresses a specific customer segment's needs and problems and those of other participants. The second component is the *value configuration* of the resources and activities that produces this value. The final *value capture* part explains revenue streams and cost structures that allow the organisation and other stakeholders to gain a share of the total value generated.

Figure 6.4 Business model components

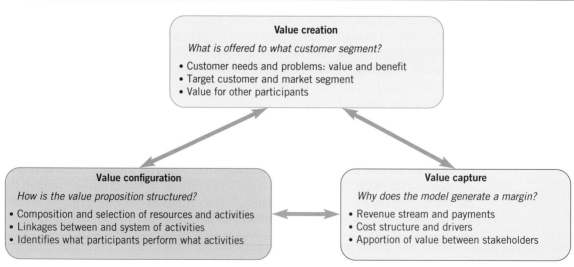

Illustration 6.3 Uber's ubiquitous business model

The on-demand transportation service that has revolutionised the taxi industry.

Source: Narapirom/Shutterstock

With an estimated market value of between $60 and100bn Uber has been predicted to become the world's dominant transportation company without owning a single vehicle. After its start in San Francisco 2009 it has quickly expanded to over 68 countries and 600 cities worldwide. Uber only employs 12,000, but has over 6 million drivers and 50 million users and generates over 4 billion rides a year. The company is growing at exponential rates and has received over $22bn of equity funding so far.

Uber's smartphone app is at the centre of their business model. Customers download the app, create an account and put in their credit card information. By tapping the app they request a car and a notification is sent to the nearest driver who can accept or reject the ride and if rejected it is sent to another driver in the area. Customers can track the estimated time of arrival and the meter via the app. Payment is made to Uber via the app with a later payment to the driver. The customer gets an option to rate the driver and the driver also has the option to rate the customer.

Through the Uber app customers can search, book, pay and rate the taxi service. They are offered a convenient, reliable and fast taxi service either through luxury rides, priced less than conventional limousine services (Uber Black), or through regular rides priced less than normal taxi fares (Uber Pop or UberX). The value for drivers is an extra source of income and flexible working hours. The review and rating system is a key difference compared to regular taxis. Customers can avoid drivers' with low ratings and drivers can avoid passengers with low ratings.

The basic resources of Uber include their technological platform and app, but they do not own any cars or employ any drivers. Drivers own the cars and are self-employed and apply to Uber to become a driver. Uber's activities are configured to match customers with a nearby driver and car. In addition to match making, the platform and app includes pricing and payment, car tracking and review systems. Uber thus structures the value for both customers and drivers through the development of sophisticated software and algorithms that optimise matchmaking, pricing and reviews for different cities and local markets.

Uber captures their profit and value by typically taking a 20–25 per cent cut on all rides except for special promotions to customers and/or drivers and in areas where they face competition from similar services. Besides generating a margin these revenues should cover their expenses to cover R&D, technology development, marketing, local infrastructure and own local employees in each city.

Even though the business model has been a success there are several significant challenges. The UberPOP service has faced regulatory pushbacks in several European countries and even been forced to shut down in some markets. Uber is also facing an increasing number of competitors with similar business models; Lyft is a significant competitor in the US and in China they were defeated by Didi Chuxing that acquired their operations. However, the CEO Dara Khosrowshahi has expanded their food delivery service UberEATS further and entered into new services such as bike- and scooter-sharing with a vision to be present in all the different ways people move within an urban environment: 'We want to be the Amazon of transportation.'

Sources: J. Bhuiyan, 'Uber powered four billion rides in 2016. It wants to do more – and cheaper – in 2018', 5 January 2018; K. Korosec, 'Uber CEO: ride hailing will be eclipsed by scooters, bikes and even flying taxis', *Techcrunch.com*, 2018; M. Ahmed, 'Uber: Backseat driver', *Financial Times*, 16 September 2015; A. Damodaran, 'A disruptive cab ride to riches: The Uber payoff', *Forbes*, 6 October 2014; *Techtrends.tech*, 2018.

Questions

1 In terms of Figure 6.4, what are Uber's value creation, value configuration and value capture components?

2 If you were the head of a traditional taxi company: how could you change your business model to compete with Uber?

The business model of the San Francisco-based accommodation broker Airbnb, for example, *creates value* for both the customers that rent the apartment, house or private room and for the hosts that offer their homes for rent. The Airbnb website conveniently provides a platform for exchange activities between the hosts and guests. These activities are *configured* via the web platform so that hosts list, describe and present pictures of their homes and customers are thus offered a wide selection of accommodations to choose from and rent. A review system of both accommodations and guests is available to build references and prevent deception. Finally, both hosts and Airbnb *capture value* from this business model. Hosts receive guest payments and Airbnb gets a 6–12 per cent commission fee on guest reservations, a 3 per cent to process the payment to the host and guest credit card processing fees. This points managers and entrepreneurs to three basic and interdependent attributes of business models:

- *Value creation.* A key part of a business model describes what is offered and how value is thus created for the various parties involved: customers, partners and other participants. The main concern here is thus the targeted customer segment and how their needs are fulfilled and their problems solved, but also how to create value for any other parties involved.

- *Value configuration.* A second component explains how various interdependent resources and activities in the value chain underlie the value proposition, for example technology, equipment, facilities, brands, managerial processes, etc. (for a discussion of the value chain see Section 4.4.2). These factors are part of an activity system that not only explains what activities create value, but how they are linked and what participants perform them. While this system is centred on the organisation it can also involve activities conducted by customers, partners and other participants.

- *Value capture.* A business model also describes the cost structure of resources and activities and the revenue stream from customers and any other parties. In addition, this component shows how the value created will be apportioned between the organisation and any other stakeholders involved. For a company, then, this last component also describes how profit is made while for non-for-profits and the public sector there are of course no expectations of financial gain.[10]

Two points need to be emphasised here:

- First, once established in an industry, business models are often taken for granted. All businesses rely on business models, but as they mature and become standardised they are rarely questioned. Until Airbnb and others started their services few thought about or challenged the 'hotel business model' and how value creation, configuration and capture were interrelated in this model. There may have been efforts to change individual business model components, but few changed or differentiated the whole model and the relationships between the components as Airbnb did.

- Second, while competitors may share business models their business strategy can still differ. Walmart, for example, shares the same discount retailer model with several competitors, but has a distinct lowest-cost strategy, cutting costs systematically throughout its value chain. Likewise, Airbnb in the example above have the same business model as Wimdu and many other competitors. However, Airbnb's extensive selection of accommodations from close to one million listings in 34,000 cities in 200 countries surpasses any competitor and thus differentiates them. Because of this size both customers and hosts are likely to prefer Airbnb over competitors as guests are offered more accommodations and hosts more guests. The more customers that use their service the better it is for every customer in their network of guests and hosts and Airbnb thus have an advantage based on network effects (see Section 3.2.3 for network effects).

6.4.2 Business model patterns

Even though business model patterns often become established within industries over time companies use them competitively. New entrants often use new business models to be able to compete successfully with established players. Dell, for example, entered the PC and laptop industry many years ago based on a different business model compared to the established one. Instead of going via middlemen of retailers and wholesalers as HP, IBM and others did, they sold directly to customers. It is thus important for managers to understand what type of business model pattern their business build on and how it may differ from other competitors. It should be noted, however, that business model patterns are described at various levels of detail and sometimes only emphasise one or two business model components. There are multiple business models around, but four typical patterns include the following:

- *Razor and blade.* This is perhaps the most well-known business model pattern, but its primary focus is on the value capture component, which makes it more of a revenue model. It builds on Gillette's classic model of selling razors at a very low price and the compatible replacement blades at a quite high price. This model of selling two technically interlinked products separately is quite common. For example, mobile operators offering consumers a cheap or even a free mobile phone and then catching them through a two-year fee-based subscription plan.

- *Freemium.* This business model pattern name comes from combining 'free' and 'premium' and it primarily relates to online businesses. It refers to how a basic version of a service or product is offered for free so as to build a high volume of customers and eventually convince a portion of the customers to buy a variety of premium services. Revenue is generated by the premium buying customers. They are often only a small portion of the total user volume, but their revenues can be enough. The photo-sharing service Flickr uses this business model pattern. Flickr offers the basic service of uploading and sharing photos for free while generating revenues through extra services for a subscription fee including unlimited uploading and storing of photos. Other businesses that use this model are the business-oriented social networking service LinkedIn and the streaming music service Spotify. The aim of freemium, however, is not only to convince premium customers, but to attract a larger volume of customers as the value of the service increases with more users.

- *Peer-to-peer (P2P).* This model brings people and/or businesses together without necessarily having to go through a middle man. It is based on co-operation among individuals aided by an app, website or some other online or communication service and can include all sorts of peer to peer transactions. Transactions include offerings of specific services such as education, lending personal things that may be rarely used but expensive such as hobby building tools, or providing loans peer to peer. An example of the latter is California-based Kiva, an international non-profit micro-finance website that aims to alleviate poverty by allowing everyday people in developed nations to finance low-income entrepreneurs and students in developing nations. Airbnb is a peer-to-peer model and so is Uber, but they build on for-profit platforms. They are often referred to as 'multi-sided platform' business models and are discussed in the next section.

- *Multi-sided platforms.* [11] This business model is behind some of the most valuable firms in the world. The so-called US 'FAANG' (Facebook, Apple, Amazon, Netflix and Google) and Chinese 'BAT' (Baidu, Alibaba and Tencent) companies all build on platforms. A multi-sided platform brings together two or more distinct, but interdependent groups of participants to interact on a platform. They are distinct as they perform separate functions on the platform and they are interdependent as the platform is of value to each group of participants only if the other group is also present. The platform YouTube, for example, includes creators of videos, viewers of videos, and advertisers. A multisided platform comes in many

Table 6.1   Platform providers

Side 1 (Customers/ Users)	Platform provider	Side 2 (Complementors)
Guests	**Accommodation rentals (e.g. Airbnb)**	Hosts
Passengers	**Personal transportation (e.g. Uber)**	Drivers
Searchers	**Search engines (e.g. Google)**	Advertisers
Shoppers	**Shopping malls**	Merchants
Readers	**Newspapers**	Advertisers
Gamers	**Game consoles (e.g. Nintendo)**	Game developers
Buyers	**On-line marketplaces (e.g. Amazon)**	Merchants
Users	**Smartphone operating systems (e.g. Apple)**	App developers

different shapes and can be a technology (e.g. Microsoft's PC operating system), a product (e.g. Nintendo's video game console), or a service (Uber's transportation service; see Illustration 6.3). Multi-sided platforms often overlap with other business model patterns, as at Airbnb for instance with a peer-to-peer model or at Netflix, which primarily is a subscription model. Also, platforms are not an entirely new phenomena; malls, for example, are platforms that allow consumers and merchants to interact directly with each other and newspapers link subscribers with advertisers. As indicated by the name there are several platform sides, most commonly two, that perform different functions. Uber's platform for example has car drivers on one side and passengers on the other (see Illustration 6.3) and Nintendo has game developers one side and gamers on the other: see Table 6.1 for further examples. In contrast, on a single-sided platform, like a telecommunication operator, all participants perform similar functions; making or receiving calls.

Summary

- Michael Porter's generic strategy framework defines various competitive business strategies, including *cost-leadership*, *differentiation*, *focus* and *hybrid* strategies.
- *Game theory* encourages managers to get in the mind of competitors and think forwards and reason backwards about competitive as well as cooperative strategies.
- A *business model* describes the business logic of an enterprise including the domains of *value creation*, *value configuration* and *value capture*.

Recommended key readings

- The foundations of the discussions of generic competitive strategies are to be found in the writings of Michael Porter, which include *Competitive Strategy* (1980) and *Competitive Advantage* (1985), both published by Free Press.

- An introduction to business models including a long list of various model types is included in O. Gassman, K. Frankenberger and M. Csik, *The Business Model Navigator*, Pearson, 2014.

References

1. This section draws on M. Porter, *Competitive Advantage*, Free Press, 1985.
2. P. Conley, *Experience Curves as a Planning Tool*, available as a pamphlet from the Boston Consulting Group.
3. B. Sharp and J. Dawes, 'What is differentiation and how does it work?', *Journal of Marketing Management*, vol. 17, nos 7/8 (2001), pp. 739–59, reviews the relationship between differentiation and profitability.
4. C. Markides and C. Charitou, 'Competing with dual business models: a contingency approach', *Academy of Management Executive*, vol. 18, no. 3 (2004), pp. 22–36.
5. The *Strategy Clock* is a tool that allows for a dynamic approach for examining alternative generic strategies and gives more scope for hybrid strategies. See D. Faulkner and C. Bowman, *The Essence of Competitive Strategy*, Prentice Hall, 1995.
6. For readings on game theory, see B. Nalebuff and A. Brandenburger, *Co-opetition*, Profile Books, 1997; R. McCain, *Game Theory: A Non-technical Introduction to the Analysis of Strategy*, South Western, 2003.
7. For discussion about business models and how they differ from business strategy see: D. J. Teece, 'Business models, business strategy and innovation', *Long Range Planning*, vol. 43, no. 2 (2010), pp. 172–94 and pp. 86–92; C. Zott and A. Raphael, 'The fit between product market strategy and business model: implications for firm performance', *Strategic Management Journal*, vol. 29, no. 1 (2008), pp. 1–26.
8. For a review of the business model literature see C. Zott, A Raphael and L. Massa, 'The business model: recent developments and future research', *Journal of Management*, vol 36, no. 4 (2011), pp. 1019–1042.
9. For a recent evaluation of business model research and a special issue on business models see, Foss, N. J. and Saebi, T., 'Business models and business model innovation: Between wicked and paradigmatic problems', *Long Range Planning*, vol. 51, no. 1 (2018), pp. 9–21.
10. For a discussion of business models for sustainability that also includes not-for profits see B. Cohen and J. Kietzmann, 'Ride on! Mobility business models for the sharing economy', *Organization & Environment*, vol. 26, no. 3, (2014), 269–96.
11. For a discussion of platforms see M.W. Van Alstyne, G. G. Parker and S. P. Choudary, 'Pipelines, platforms, and the new rules of strategy', *Harvard Business Review*, vol. 94, no. 4 (2016), pp. 54–62.

Case example

The IKEA approach

Kevan Scholes[*]

On 28 January 2018 *The Guardian*[1] newspaper reported the death of Ingvar Kamprad, the founder of IKEA, at the age of 91. In the article Neil Saunders, managing director of retail at the analysis firm GlobalData, said:

> *'Few people can claim to have genuinely revolution-ised retail. Ingvar Kamprad did . . . Much of this dif-ference was down to Ingvar's Swedish heritage and instincts. It is no exaggeration to say that his innovative approach changed not just the furniture sector, but the way people decorated and led their lives at home.'*

By the time of his death IKEA was the world's largest home furnishings company with some 10,000 products in 422 stores in 50 markets. For the year ending 31 August 2018[2] revenue had grown to €38.8bn (an increase of 4.5 per cent on 2016) and net profits were €1.4bn. The com-pany had 208,000 co-workers (of which 40,000 were in production and distribution).[3] There were almost 1 billion store visits each year.

IKEA and the home furnishings market

By the late 2010s home furnishings was a huge market worldwide with retail sales almost $US600bn in items such as furniture, household textiles and floor coverings. IKEA sales by region reflected their European heritage with 60 per cent of sales in Europe (including Russia); 19 per cent in North America and 11 per cent in Asia.[4]

IKEA's competitors

The home furnishings market was highly fragmented with competition occurring locally rather than globally and included competitors of several types:

- Multi-national furniture retailers (like IKEA) all of whom were considerably smaller than IKEA. These included, for example, the Danish company Jysk (turn-over – €3.4bn).

- Companies specialising in just part of the furniture product range and operating in several countries – such as Poggenpohl from Germany in kitchens.

- Multi-branch retail furniture outlets whose sales were mainly in one country such as DFS in the UK. The USA market was dominated by such players (e.g. Bed, Bath & Beyond Inc. with revenues of some $US12bn).

- Non-specialist companies that carried furniture as part of a wider product range. In the UK Argos (a subsidiary of Sainsbury's) offered some 60,000 general merchan-dise products through its network of 800+ stores and online sales. Together with Habitat (also Sainsbury's) it was number one in UK furniture retailing. General do it yourself/DIY companies such as Kingfisher (through B&Q in the UK and Castorama in France) were attempting to capture more of the bottom end of the furniture market.

- Small and/or specialised retailers and/or manufactur-ers. These accounted for the biggest share of the mar-ket in Europe.

In 2016 it was estimated that the UK market was about £16.6bn,[5] of which IKEA had £1.62bn share.

IKEA's approach

IKEA had been founded by Ingvar Kamprad in 1943 in the small Swedish town of Älmhult and opened its first furni-ture store 1958. The company's success had been achieved through the now legendary IKEA business approach – revolutionary in the furnishing industry of its early years (see Table 1). The guiding business philosophy of Kamprad was that of improving the everyday life of people by making products more affordable. This was achieved by massive (20 per cent+) reductions in sales prices vs. competitors which, in turn, required aggressive reductions in IKEA's costs.

Reasons for success

In his book *The IKEA Edge*[6] published in 2011 Anders Dahlvig reflected on the reasons for IKEA's success before, during and after his period as CEO (1999–2009). He felt IKEA had five success criteria:

> '1. Design, function, and quality at low prices; 2. Unique (Scandinavian) design; 3. Inspiration, ideas, and complete solutions; 4. Everything in one place; 5. "A day out," the shopping experience. . .

---

[*]This case was prepared by Kevan Scholes, Emeritus Professor of Strategic Management at Sheffield Business School. It is intended as a basis for class discussion and not as an illustration of good or bad management practice. Copyright Kevan Scholes 2019. Not to be reproduced or quoted without permission.

Table 1 IKEA's 'upside-down' approach

Element of the approach	Traditional furniture retailer	IKEA
Design	Traditional	Modern (Swedish)
Target households	Older, established	Families with children
Style of shop	Small specialist shops	All furnishing items in big stores
Location	City centre	Out-of-town
Product focus	Individual items	'Room sets'
Marketing	Advertising	Free catalogue [203 million in 32 languages in 2016]
Price	High	Low
Product Assembly	Ready assembled	Flat pack – self-assembly
Sourcing	Local	Global
Brand	Manufacturers	IKEA
Financial focus	Gross margin	Sales revenue
Overheads	Often high	Frugal – no perks

You may well say that they are similar to those of most companies. The difference, in my opinion, is that IKEA is much better at delivering on these customer needs than are other retailers. . . . Most competitors focus on one or at most two of these customer needs. High-street shops focus on design and inspiration. Out-of-town low-cost retailers focus on price. Department stores focus on choice. The real strength of IKEA lies in the combination of all five.'

IKEA's competitive strategy

Dahlvig explained IKEA's approach to competition:

'You can choose to adapt your company's product range to the markets you are operating in, or you can choose to shift the market's preference toward your own range and style. IKEA has chosen the latter. By doing this, the company can maintain a unique and distinct profile. This is, however, a more difficult path to follow. . . . A significant under-standing of the customer's situation at home is the basis for IKEA's product development.[7] . . . For most competitors, having the lowest price seems to mean being 5 to 10 percent cheaper than the competition on comparable products. At IKEA, this means being a minimum 20 percent cheaper

and often up to 50 percent cheaper than the competition.'[8]

Managing the value chain

Dahlvig explained that IKEA's strategy crucially requires the 'design' and control of their wider value chain in detail:

'The secret is the control and coordination of the whole value chain from raw material, production, and range development, to distribution into stores. Most other companies working in the retail sector have control either of the retail end (stores and distribution) or the product design and production end. IKEA's vertical integration makes it a complex company compared to most, since it owns both production, range development, distribution, and stores.[9] . . . This included backward integration by extending the activities of Swedwood (IKEA's man-ufacturing arm) beyond furniture factories, into control over the raw materials, saw mills, board suppliers, and component factories.'[10]

The Franchise system[11]

By 2018 all but one of the 422 stores were run by 11 fran-chisees (partners).The role of IKEA Group was to provide the best possible support for franchisees to implement the

IKEA concept worldwide. For this the Group received 3 per cent of the franchisees' sales. This was provided through the following activities:

- Maintaining the IKEA concept and marketing communications.
- Developing the product range.
- Managing suppliers relationships, procuring product and distributing/selling to franchisees.
- In addition IKEA themselves manufactured about 10 per cent of products and materials (mainly wood-based) through 40 production units.

So, of the €38.8bn IKEA sales in 2018 the revenue of the Group was €24.9bn (the remainder being the franchisees' 'mark-up').

Global expansion

Despite IKEA's strong global position when Dahlvig took over as CEO in 1999 he felt there was need for improvement. Earlier growth had come from going 'wide but thin' with limited market shares, but now they would go 'deep' and concentrate on their existing markets.[12]

He explained his reasoning:

'Why make the change? . . . the competition had been very fragmented and local in nature. However, many of the very big retail companies were shifting strategy. From being local, they were looking to a global expansion, not least in the emerging markets like China, Russia, and Eastern Europe. . . [and] broadening their product range. . . with much more muscle than IKEA's traditional competitors. . . One way to dissuade them from entering into the home furnishing arena was to aggressively reduce prices and increase the company's presence with more stores in all local markets in the countries where IKEA was operating.'[13]

China

By 2015 around 60 per cent of IKEA stores were still in Europe and expansion into Asia was crucial, but the company had come to realise that emerging markets could be particularly challenging as head of research Mikael Ydholm remarked: 'The more far away we go from our culture, the more we need to understand, learn, and adapt.'[14]

IKEA first opened in China in 1998 and today it is the company's fastest growing market. By 2009 they had eight of its ten biggest stores there. The Chinese market was extremely challenging for a company that had built global success through standardisation.[15] The main problems were that in emerging markets IKEA products were expensive relative to local competitors and the consumer shopping expectations were centred on small, local shops and personal service. IKEA thus had to be flexible and presented an image as exclusive Western European interior

Source: Kevin Foy/Alamy Stock Photo

design specialists – popular with younger, affluent, city dwellers. Their shops were smaller than usual for IKEA and typically nearer city centres. Because DIY was not well developed in China they offered home delivery and assembly services. Catalogues were only available *in store*. Crucially stores were allowed to source almost 50 per cent locally (against company average of about 25 per cent) in order to keep prices competitive.

India

India has been an important country in the IKEA supply chain for more than 30 years. By 2018 the company sourced €315m of product there through 48 suppliers employing 45,000 co-workers directly. However, in 2012 it was announced that IKEA was to enter the Indian market by investing €1.5bn in 25 stores over 15 to 20 years[16] with the first store opening in Hyderabad in 2018.

The Chinese experience was useful when IKEA entered India. However, India also proved challenging as a third of a retailer chains' merchandise had to be produced locally. IKEA had significant problems in finding enough producers that could live up to their strict corporate social responsibility requirements.

Growing IKEA and reaching more customers

Although the IKEA approach remained central to the company's strategy the yearly report for financial year 2015[17] explained how new challenges were being addressed:

'We want to be even more accessible to the many people. This means working hard to ensure we make it easier for customers to shop with us, wherever and whenever they want to visit our stores and shopping centres, or our website and apps.' This included the following:

- **Shopping centres.** By 2016[18] IKEA operated 43 shopping centres and 25 retail parks (in 15 countries) and had 20 projects in the pipeline across several markets. These family-friendly shopping centres had an IKEA store as one of the main attractions. There were 460 million shopping centre visits.

- **Online.** By 2018 online sales were about 5 per cent of revenue. There were 2.5bn visits to IKEA.com and 2.5bn hits on the IKEA catalogue and store apps.[19] The company was continually exploring how they could improve the ways that customers could find out about IKEA products and be inspired by the product range through digital channels, such as website, apps and catalogue.

- **Pick up (order and collection) points.** Much smaller than the usual stores. Order and Collection points were designed to offer the same range and, with most products available to order and collect, with a small range of products available to take home on the day. They also offer home deliveries.

- **Pop up stores.** Pop up stores are temporary spaces (max. six months) that concentrate on specific themes, events or messages.

- **New leadership.** Anders Dahlvig finished as CEO in 2009 (but joined the Supervisory Board and was Chairman from 2016). He was succeeded as CEO by Michael Ohlsson – who had already worked for IKEA for 30 years. In turn he was succeeded in 2013 by another internal appointee – Peter Agnefjäll (18 years at IKEA) and then in 2016 by Jesper Brodin (20 years at IKEA). It appeared that the key credential for IKEA leaders was the time they had been emerged in the company culture.

The future

In a rapidly changing retail environment CEO Jasper Brodin was eager to restate the IKEA vision that continued to guide everything that the company did:

'Our business idea is to offer a wide range of well-designed, functional, home furnishings at prices so low that as many people as possible will be able to afford them.'[20]

Questions

1 Identify where (in their value system) and how IKEA have achieved cost leadership.

2 Identify how IKEA have achieved differentiation from their competitors.

3 Explain how IKEA tries to ensure that their 'hybrid' strategy remains sustainable and does not become 'stuck-in-the-middle'.

4 How would you explain IKEA's business model in terms of value creation, configuration and capture?

Notes and references:

1. J. Kollewe and R. Orange, www.theguardian.com, 28 January 2018.
2. IKEA financial summary FY18.
3. IKEA yearly summary FY16.
4. IKEA yearly summary FY16.
5. British Furniture Confederation (www.britishfurnitureconfederation.org.uk)
6. Anders Dahlvig, *The Ikea Edge*, McGraw Hill, 2011.
7. Ibid., p. 63.
8. Ibid., p. 64.
9. Ibid., p. 65.
10. Ibid., p. 83.
11. IKEA annual report FY18.
12. Anders Dahlvig, *The Ikea Edge*, McGraw Hill, 2011, p. 120.
13. Ibid., p. 123.
14. B. Kowitt, 'How Ikea took over the world', *Fortune*, 15 March 2015.
15. U. Johansson and A. Thelander, 'A standardised approach to the world? IKEA in China', *International Journal of Quality and Service Sciences*, vol 1, no. 2, (2009), pp. 199–219.
16. Reuters, 23 June 2012.
17. IKEA yearly report FY15.
18. IKEA yearly summary FY16.
19. IKEA financial summary FY18.
20. IKEA yearly summary FY18.

Video:

https://fortune.com/2015/03/10/ikea/

Chapter 7
Corporate strategy

Key terms

Learning outcomes

After reading this chapter, you should be able to:

- Identify alternative strategy options, including *market penetration, product development, market development* and *diversification*.

- Distinguish between different diversification strategies (*related, unrelated* and *conglomerate* diversification) and evaluate *diversification drivers*.

- Assess the relative benefits of *vertical integration* and *outsourcing*.

- Evaluate the ways in which a *corporate parent* can add or destroy value for its portfolio of business units.

- Analyse *portfolios* of business units and judge which to invest in and which to divest.

- Identify an appropriate *international strategy*.

- Understand how to choose between *organic development, mergers and acquisitions* and *strategic alliances* for growth.

7.1 Introduction

Chapter 6 was concerned with business strategy and models – the ways in which a single business unit or organisational unit can compete in a given market space, for instance through cost leadership or differentiation. However, organisations may choose to enter many new product and market areas. For example, Tata Group, one of India's largest companies, began as a trading organisation and soon moved into hotels and textiles. Since that time Tata has diversified further into steel, motors, consultancy, technologies, tea, chemicals, power, communications. As organisations add new units and capabilities, their strategies may no longer be solely concerned with *competitive strategy* in one market space at the business level, but with choices concerning different businesses or markets. **Corporate strategy is about the overall scope of the organisation and how value is added to the constituent businesses of the organisation as a whole.** Choices about business areas, industries and geographies to be active in will determine the direction(s) an organisation might pursue for growth, which business unit(s) to buy and dispose of, and how resources may be allocated efficiently across multiple business activities. For Tata, the corporate strategy questions are whether it should enter any more industries, whether it should exit some, and how far it should integrate the businesses it retains. For large public-sector organisations and charities these choices also have to be made. These choices, indicated in Figure 7.1, inform decisions about how broad an organisation should be. Thus 'scope' of an organisation is central to *corporate strategy* and the focus of this chapter.

Scope is concerned with how far an organisation should be diversified in terms of two different dimensions: products and markets. As the Tata example shows, an organisation may increase its scope by engaging in industries different to its current ones. Section 7.2 introduces a classic product market framework that uses these categories for identifying different growth directions for an organisation. This indicates different *diversification* strategies open to an organisation, according to the novelty of products or markets. Underpinning diversification choices are a range of drivers, which are discussed in Section 7.3, including increasing market power, reducing risk and exploiting superior internal processes. The performance implications of diversification are, then, reviewed in Section 7.4.

Another way of increasing the scope of an organisation is *vertical integration*, discussed in Section 7.5. It allows an organisation to act as an internal supplier or a customer to itself (as for example an oil company supplies its petrol to its own petrol stations). Alternatively the organisation may decide to *outsource* certain activities – to 'dis-integrate' by subcontracting an internal activity to an external supplier – or *divest* as both may improve organisational focus and efficiency. The scope of the organisation may therefore be adjusted through growth or contraction.

Diversified corporations, such as Tata, that operate in different areas of activity will have multiple SBUs (strategic business units) with their own strategies for their specific markets. They can be held accountable for their success or failure. Nevertheless, corporate head office, the 'corporate level', needs to select an appropriate portfolio of individual SBUs and manage them by establishing their boundaries, perhaps by market, geography or capability, so they add value to the group.[1] The value-adding effect of head office to individual SBUs that make up the organisation's portfolio is termed **parenting advantage** (see Section 7.5). Their ability to do this effectively may give them a competitive advantage over other corporate parents in acquiring and managing different businesses. The importance of parenting is underlined by a recent study that found a SBU's corporate parent accounts for more financial performance than the industry in which the SBU competes.[2] But just how do corporate-level activities, decisions and resources add value to businesses?

Figure 7.1 Strategic directions and corporate-level strategy

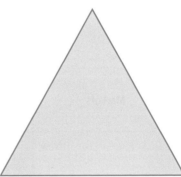

Scope
How broad to make the portfolio?

Corporate parenting
How should the 'parent' add value?

Portfolio matrices
Which SBUs to invest in?

In order to decide which industries and businesses organisations should invest in or dispose of, the corporate centre needs to assess whether the *portfolio* of businesses is worth more under its management than the individual businesses would be worth standing alone. Section 7.6 reviews portfolio matrices, which are useful techniques to help structure corporate-level choices about businesses in which to invest and those to divest.

7.2 Strategy directions

A central corporate strategy choice is the direction in which a company should grow. Ansoff's classic corporate strategy matrix[3] (Figure 7.2) suggests four basic directions for organisational growth. Typically an organisation starts in zone A and may choose between *penetrating* still further within zone A or increasing its diversity along the two axes of increasing novelty of markets or products. Increasing the diversity of products and/or markets is known as 'diversification'. **Diversification involves increasing the range of products or markets served by an organisation. Related diversification involves expanding into products or services with relationships to the existing business.** Thus in Ansoff's matrix the organisation has two related diversification strategies available: moving to zone B, *product/service development* for its existing markets or moving to zone C by taking its existing products into *new markets*. In each case, the further along the two axes, the more diversified the strategy. Alternatively, the organisation can move in both directions at once, following an *unrelated diversification* strategy with altogether new markets and new products/services (zone D). Thus **unrelated diversification involves moving into products or services with no relationships to existing businesses.**

Ansoff's axes can be used for brainstorming strategic options, checking that all four zones have been properly considered. Illustration 7.1 traces the evolution of giant supermarket Tesco, raising questions about how businesses might choose their next strategic direction. The next section will consider each of Ansoff's four main directions in detail.

Figure 7.2 Corporate strategy directions

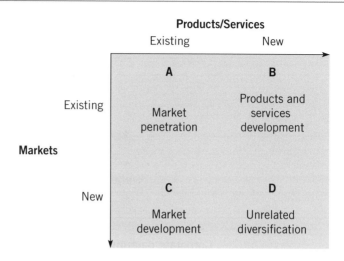

Source: Adapted from H.I. Ansoff, *Corporate Strategy*, Penguin, 1988, Chapter 6. Ansoff originally had a matrix with four separate boxes, but in practice strategic directions involve more continuous axes. The Ansoff matrix itself was later developed – see reference 1.

7.2.1 Market penetration

For a simple, undiversified business, the most obvious strategic option is often increased penetration of its existing market, with its existing products. **Market penetration implies increasing share of current markets with the current product or service range.** This strategy builds on established capabilities and does not require the organisation to venture into uncharted territory. The organisation's scope is exactly the same. Moreover, greater market share implies increased power vis-à-vis buyers and suppliers (in terms of Porter's five forces), greater economies of scale and experience curve benefits.

However, organisations seeking greater market penetration may face three constraints:

- *Retaliation from competitors* as they seek to defend their market shares. This might take the form of price wars or expensive marketing battles.

- *Legal constraints*, as official competition regulators become concerned about excessive market power. Most countries have regulators with the powers to restrain powerful companies or prevent mergers and acquisitions that would create such excessive power.

- *Economic constraints*, where market downturn or public sector funding crisis might negate market penetration as an option. Here organisations might consider withdrawing from the market or follow other directions suggested by the Ansoff matrix, as follows.

7.2.2 Product and service development

Product and service development is where organisations deliver modified or new products (or services) to existing markets. This can involve varying degrees of diversification along the horizontal axis of Figure 7.2. For Apple, developing its products from iPhone to iPad to Apple Watch involved little diversification: although the technologies differed, Apple was targeting the same customers and using very similar production processes and distribution

Illustration 7.1 Choosing new directions at Tesco?

Why has Tesco's successful growth strategy changed?

Source: Daniel Leal-Olivas/AFP/Getty Images and Bloomberg/Getty Images.

Starting in 1919 when Jack Cohen sold surplus groceries on an East London stall, Tesco has grown to become the UK's largest grocer with 440,000 employees, 6,800 stores in 10 countries, revenues of £64.5bn and profits of £1.6bn. However, Tesco posted a record-breaking loss of £6.4bn in 2015 and experienced several poor years due to much tougher competition in the supermarket sector. This has caused investors to speculate whether Tesco's dominance is coming to an end. Is it time for a new strategic direction?

From its humble beginnings, Tesco showed expansionary zeal in the 1950s and 1960s, buying up hundreds of shops from competitors. In 1961 Tesco entered the *Guinness Book of Records* with the largest store in Europe and soon opened its first superstore in 1968. Shortly afterwards in 1974 Tesco opened its first petrol stations and soon became the UK's largest independent petrol retailer. Tesco continued to open more stores and in addition took over supermarket rival Hillards for £220m in 1987. By 1995 Tesco overtook Sainsbury's to become the largest food retailer in the UK, helped by the launch of the Tesco Clubcard. There then followed a great deal of overseas expansion with shops opened in Hungary (1995), Poland, the Czech Republic and Slovakia (1996), Thailand (1998) and South Korea (1999).

By 2000 Tesco was offering more than just food and petrol, with a wider range of products including clothes, electricals and personal financial products. Further international expansion followed, with stores being opened in Malaysia (2001), Japan and Turkey (2003), China (2004) and in the US (2006) using the name 'Fresh and Easy'. However, many of these overseas initiatives did not work out, with closures and sales in Japan, South Korea, Turkey and the USA, and in China the operation became a joint venture with a local partner. Nevertheless in 2008 Tesco managed to complete opening stores in every UK postcode by taking over rivals Somerfield on remote Scottish islands. Tesco then decided to create Tesco's Bank in a joint venture with the Royal Bank of Scotland in 2009.

In 2013 Tesco saw its profits fall for the first time in 20 years, with a record-breaking loss of $6.4bn in 2015. This underperformance persisted as competitive pressures intensified, with discounters Lidl and Aldi making deep inroads, and premium stores such as Waitrose and Marks & Spencer continuing to be very profitable. In addition Sainsbury was bidding for Asda (numbers two and three in the industry) in 2018, in order to increase their buying power, and Amazon's purchase of Whole Foods and launching 'Fresh', an online delivery service in the UK, would further intensify competition.

In response, Tesco acquired the UK's largest food wholesaler Bookers, which supplies food to caterers, retailers and businesses, for £3.7bn. The competition authorities said they were in sufficiently different businesses to not harm competitors. Tesco also entered into a strategic alliance with French giant Carrefour, giving them annually £80bn purchasing power over suppliers and helping them achieve £400m savings. In October 2018 Tesco's shares fell as the retailer missed first-half profits forecasts. Weak trading in Thailand and Poland was blamed for eclipsing accelerating sales growth in the UK. In 2019 Tesco announced a major overhaul of its larger stores, which could result in thousands of job losses, as it tries to achieve cost savings of £1.5bn.

Sources: T. Clark and S.P. Chan, 'A history of Tesco: the rise of Britain's biggest supermarket', *Telegraph*, 4 October 2014; J. Kollewe, 'Tesco and Carrefour plan "strategic alliance" to buy products', *Guardian*, 2 July 2018; J. Davey, 'Tesco shares suffer as pressures abroad overshadow UK growth', *Business News*, Thomson Reuters, 3 October 2018; 'Thousands of jobs affected in Tesco', *Belfast Telegraph*, 27 January 2019.

Questions

1 Using the Ansoff matrix, plot Tesco's growth over time. What do you notice about the pattern of expansion?

2 How has Tesco's corporate strategy changed over time?

channels. Despite the potential for benefits from relatedness, product development can be an expensive and high-risk activity for at least two reasons:

- *New resources and capabilities.* Product development strategies typically involve mastering new processes or technologies that are unfamiliar to the organisation. For example, the digital revolution, accelerated by the recent covid-19 pandemic, is forcing universities to reconsider the way learning materials are acquired and provided to students and the nature of the student/academic interface. High-quality content available free online and virtual engagement with students now raise the question of how universities should add new digital products and how they should consider redeploying their resources in the future. Success is likely to depend on a willingness to acquire new technological capabilities, to engage in organisational restructuring and new marketing capabilities to manage customer perceptions. Thus product development typically involves heavy investments and can have high risk of project failures.

- *Project management risk.* Even within fairly familiar domains, product development projects are typically subject to the risk of delays and increased costs as extension of current strategy focus often leads to growing project complexity and changing project specifications over time. For example, the UK's high-speed rail project, HS2, was originally projected to cost £32.7bn in 2010, estimated to cost £56bn in 2018 and now it is estimated to be £106bn, making it the world's most expensive railway.

7.2.3 Market development

Market development can be more attractive than product/service development by being potentially cheaper and quicker to execute. **Market development involves offering existing products/services to new markets.** Again, the degree of diversification varies along Figure 7.2's downward axis. Typically, of course, market development entails some product development as well, if only in terms of packaging or service. Nonetheless, market development remains a form of related diversification given its origins in similar products. Market development takes two basic forms:

- *New users.* Here an example would be aluminium, whose original users, packaging and cutlery manufacturers are now supplemented by users in aerospace and automobiles.

- *New geographies.* The prime example of this is internationalisation but it would also include the spread of a small retailer into new towns.

In all cases, it is essential that market development strategies be based on products or services that meet the *critical success factors* of the new market. Strategies based on simply offloading traditional products or services in new markets are likely to fail. Moreover, market development faces similar problems to product development. In terms of capabilities, market developers often lack the right marketing skills and brands to make progress in a market with unfamiliar customers. On the management side, the challenge is coordinating between different users and geographies, which might all have different needs.

7.2.4 Unrelated diversification

Whereas related diversification takes the organisation beyond existing markets and its existing products, where operational links remain with the core business, **unrelated diversification is when an organisation expands into markets, products and services completely different from its own** (i.e. zone D in Figure 7.2). Here value can be created at the strategic level as businesses may benefit from being part of a larger group: consumers may have greater confidence in the business unit's products and services than before, and a larger organisation can reduce the costs of finance.

Illustration 7.2 From Sat nav to driverless cars

Sat Nav manufacturer TomTom diversifies to survive.

Dutch manufacturer TomTom's fortunes dived in 2008 with sales down 36 per cent to €959m (2014) and profits down 71 per cent to €25.4m (2014). From its peak of $15bn, multinational TomTom's market value was just €2.3bn by 2015. How did this decline come about and what could management do about it?

Originally a software developer for business-to-business mobile applications and personal digital assistants (PDAs), TomTom became market leader in PDA software in just two years with satellite navigation (Sat-Nav) applications RoutePlanner and Citymaps. In 2002 the TomTom Navigator was launched, providing European customers with an easy-to-use, affordable, portable navigation device (PND) for the first time. Demand was strong for the PND, which was not just a new product but an entirely new consumer electronics category. TomTom GO, launched in 2004, revolutionised the way millions of drivers got from A to B. Affordable and accessible to everyone, it became the fastest selling consumer technology device ever. Since then, over 75m devices have been sold in 35 countries, guiding drivers over 280bn kilometres.

During 2008 TomTom's sales fell dramatically due to an increasingly saturated sat nav market, plus smartphone alternatives from Google and Nokia. TomTom was forced to reconsider its business and diversified into fleet management and vehicle telematics, where it is now a recognised leader. TomTom evolved from just a hardware business, selling sat navs to stick on windscreens, to a software and services provider that offered free mapping on smartphones and integrated traffic management systems used by governments to quell traffic and manage roads.

After partnering with Nike on the Nike+ SportWatch, TomTom launched its own TomTom Runner and TomTom Multi-Sport watches in 2013, to help runners, cyclists and swimmers keep moving towards their fitness goals, by providing essential performance information at a glance. Both have GPS sensors, allowing them to tap into TomTom's navigation platform. TomTom is now straying further from its roots by launching Bandit, an action camera, to challenge American market leader GoPro. It will contain GPS sensors allowing users to find and tag exciting moments in their video footage, based on speed, altitude, G-force and acceleration. Bandit's real selling point is its video editing and sharing capabilities.

Although SatNav devices, sports watches and action cameras may seem unlikely bedfellows, co-founder Vigreux, explains that TomTom is a collection of start-ups under one umbrella. Employees are actively encouraged to be entrepreneurial in product development. 'We're a tech brand at the end of the day – the only consumer electronic brand to come out of Europe in the last 15 years with a global footprint,' she said. If there is one thing that unites TomTom products it is that 'we make things easy for consumers'.

The decline in TomTom's valuation challenges their existing strategy. Nonetheless TomTom still feels there is a market for standalone Sat Nav for people to avoid roaming charges on mobile phones and the need to buy a new car if they want an in-built system. They are also working with car manufacturers to build embedded navigation systems into their vehicles as the era of the 'connected car' – where manufacturers do everything from updating car entertainment to suspension adjustment – has forced automakers into partnerships with technology companies. Competitive concerns mean manufacturers are unwilling to share data with rivals so rely on third parties for services such as traffic management as it is not always cost-effective for them to make the investment themselves. In 2019 TomTom announced the sale of its telematics business for £800m to enable it to reduce costs and fund further investments into real-time map updates for driverless cars in the face of tough competition from Google and Apple.

Sources: 'About TomTom', www.corporate.tomtom.com, July 2014; Curtis, S., 'TomTom: from satnavs to driverless cars', *The Telegraph*, 20 August 2015; Robinson, D., 'TomTom signs deal to supply satnavs in Volkswagen cars', *Financial Times*, 12 February 2015; Bernal, N., 'TomTom sells telematics unit to Bridgestone for £800m', *The Telegraph*, 22 January 2019.

Questions

1 Explain the ways in which relatedness informed TomTom's post-2008 strategy.

2 Were there alternative strategies open to TomTom post 2008?

It is important to note that the distinction between related and unrelated diversification is often a matter of degree as relationships that might have seemed valuable in related diversification may not turn out to be as valuable as expected. Thus the large accounting firms have often struggled in translating their skills and client contacts developed in auditing into effective consulting practices. Similarly, relationships may change in importance over time, as the nature of technologies or markets changes: see, for example, the decision by TomTom to move into different product offerings (Illustration 7.2).

An extreme form of unrelated diversification is conglomerate diversification, where there are no operational or strategic linkages between multiple business, as each remains on its own. The logic of conglomerate diversification is a financial one of balancing a portfolio of investments. Such conglomerate strategies are often not trusted by many observers because there are no obvious ways in which the businesses can work together to generate additional value, over and above the businesses remaining on their own. In addition, there is often an additional bureaucratic cost of the managers at headquarters who control them.

7.3 Diversification drivers

Diversification might be chosen for a variety of reasons, including response to macro-competitive changes and managerial ambitions,[4] with some more value-creating than others.[5] Growth in organisational size is rarely a good enough reason for diversification on its own: growth must be profitable. Indeed, growth can often be merely a form of 'empire building', especially in the public sector. Diversification decisions need to be approached sceptically.

Four potentially value-creating drivers for diversification are as follows.

- *Exploiting economies of scope.* **Economies of scope** refer to efficiency gains through applying the organisation's existing resources or capabilities to new markets or services.[6] If an organisation has under-utilised resources or capabilities that it cannot effectively close or sell to other potential users, it is efficient to use these resources or capabilities by diversification into a new activity. In other words, there are economies to be gained by extending the scope of the organisation's activities. For example, many universities have large resources in terms of halls of residence, which they must have for their students but which are under-utilised out of term-time. These halls of residence are more efficiently used if the universities expand the scope of their activities into conferencing and tourism during holiday periods. Economies of scope may apply to both *tangible* resources, such as halls of residence, and *intangible* resources and competences, such as brands or staff skills.

- *Stretching corporate management capabilities ('dominant logics').* This is a special case of economies of scope, and refers to the potential for applying the skills of talented corporate-level managers (referred to as 'corporate parenting skills' in Section 7.6) to new businesses. The **dominant logic is the set of corporate-level managerial capabilities applied across the portfolio of businesses.**[7] Corporate-level managers may have capabilities that can be applied even to businesses not sharing resources at the operating-unit level. Thus the French luxury-goods conglomerate LVMH includes a wide range of businesses – from champagne, through fashion, jewellery and perfumes, to financial media – that share very few operational resources or business-level capabilities. However, LVMH creates value for these specialised companies by applying corporate-level competences in developing classic brands and nurturing highly creative people that are relevant to all its individual businesses.

- *Exploiting superior internal processes.* Internal processes within a diversified corporation can be more efficient than external processes in the open market. In emerging markets, where markets for capital and labour do not work so well and where there is a lack of market and competitive pressures, conglomerates may work when regional growth rates are between 5 and 15 per cent. For example, China has many conglomerates because they are able to mobilise internal investment, develop managers and exploit networks in a way that standalone Chinese companies, relying on imperfect markets, cannot.

- *Increasing market power.* Being diversified in many businesses can increase power vis-à-vis competitors in at least two ways. First, having the same wide portfolio of products as a competitor increases the potential for *mutual forbearance*. The ability to retaliate across the whole range of the portfolio acts to discourage the competitor from making any aggressive moves at all. Two similarly diversified competitors are thus likely to forbear from competing aggressively with each other. Second, having a diversified range of businesses increases the power to *cross-subsidise* one business from the profits of the others. The ability to cross-subsidise can support aggressive bids to drive competitors out of a particular market and, being aware of this, competitors without equivalent power will be reluctant to attack that business.

Where diversification creates value, it is described as 'synergistic'.[8] **Synergies** **are benefits gained where activities or assets complement each other so that their combined effect is greater than the sum of the parts** (the famous 2 + 2 = 5 equation). Thus a film company and a music publisher would be synergistic if they were worth more together than separately – if the music publisher had the sole rights to music used in the film company productions for instance. However, synergies are often harder to identify and more costly to extract in practice than managers like to admit.[9]

Some drivers for diversification involve negative synergies, in other words value destruction. Three potentially value-destroying diversification drivers are: *responding to market decline* by investing in a new business when conventional finance theory suggests it is usually best to let shareholders find new growth investment opportunities for themselves; *spreading risk* across a range of markets when shareholders can easily spread their risk by taking small stakes in dozens of very different companies themselves; *managerial ambition* to satisfy personal lifestyle and image agendas.

7.4 Vertical integration

Another form of diversification, and another direction for corporate strategy is vertical integration. **Vertical integration** **describes entering activities where the organisation is its own supplier or customer.** Thus it involves operating at another stage of the value system (see Section 4.4.2). This section considers both vertical integration and vertical disintegration, particularly in the form of outsourcing.

7.4.1 Forward and backward integration

Vertical integration can go in either of two directions:

- **Backward integration** is movement into input activities concerned with the company's current business (i.e. further back in the value system). For example, acquiring a component supplier would be backward integration for a car manufacturer.

- **Forward integration** is movement into output activities concerned with the company's current business (i.e. further forward in the value network). For a car manufacturer, forward integration would be into car retail, repairs and servicing.

Thus vertical integration, like other forms of diversification, increases corporate scope. The difference is that it brings together activities up and down the same value network, while diversification typically involves more or less different value networks. However, because realising synergies involves bringing together different value networks, diversification (especially related diversification) is sometimes also described as *horizontal integration*. For example, a company diversified in cars, trucks and buses could find benefits in integrating aspects of the various design or component-sourcing processes. The relationship between horizontal integration and vertical integration is depicted in Figure 7.3.

Vertical integration often appears attractive as it seems to 'capture' some of the profits gained by retailers or suppliers in a value network – the retailers' or suppliers' profits. However there are two dangers. First, vertical integration involves investment. Expensive investments in activities that are less profitable than the original core business will be unattractive to shareholders because they are reducing their *average* or overall rate of return on investment. Second, even if there is a degree of relatedness through the value network, vertical integration is likely to involve quite different resources and capabilities. Thus car manufacturers forwardly integrating into car servicing found managing networks of small service outlets very different to managing large manufacturing plants. Growing appreciation of both the risks of diluting overall returns on investment and the distinct capabilities involved at different stages of the value network has led many companies in recent years to vertically *dis*-integrate.

7.4.2 To integrate or to outsource?

Where a part of vertically integrated operations is not adding value to the overall business, or a partner organisation can manage it better, it may be replaced through outsourcing or subcontracting. **Outsourcing is the process by which value chain activities previously carried out internally are subcontracted to external suppliers.** In other words, the organisation

Figure 7.3 Diversification and integration options: car manufacturer example

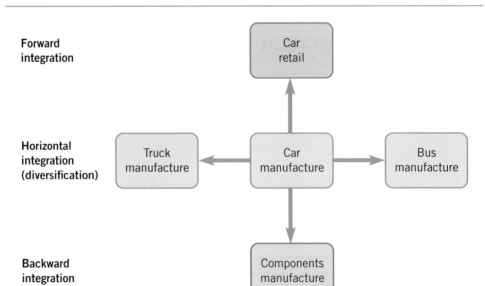

continues to offer its products and services based on external inputs instead of providing those in-house. The argument for outsourcing to suppliers is often based on their unique capabilities that allow lower costs to the sourcing organisation. Suppliers may have lower wages, scale economies, expertise, more professional employees and better incentives. Suppliers may have access to better technology and may be more effective than the sourcing organisation. Outsourcing may also allow the organisation to be more flexible in reducing the size of its balance sheet and allowing it to adjust to market demand. Specialists in a particular activity are therefore likely to have superior capabilities than an organisation for a particular activity not central to its business. A specialist IT contractor is usually better at IT than the IT department of a healthcare company.

However, Nobel prize-winning economist Oliver Williamson has argued that the decision to integrate or outsource involves more than just relative capabilities. His *transaction cost framework* helps analyse the relative costs and benefits of managing ('transacting') activities internally or externally.[10] Assessing whether to integrate or outsource an activity, Williamson warns against underestimating the long-term costs of *opportunism* by external subcontractors. Subcontractors are liable over time to take advantage of their position, either to reduce their standards or to extract higher prices. Market relationships tend to fail in controlling subcontractor opportunism where:

- there are *few alternatives* to the subcontractor and it is hard to shop around;
- the product or service is *complex and changing*, and therefore impossible to specify fully in a legally binding contract;
- investments have been made in *specific assets*, which the subcontractors know will have little value if they withhold their product or service.

Under these conditions it is likely to be better to vertically integrate rather than outsource. In sum, the decision to integrate or subcontract rests on the balance between:

- *Relative resources and capabilities.* Does the subcontractor have the potential to do the work significantly better?
- *Risk of opportunism.* Is the subcontractor likely to take advantage of the relationship over time?

7.5 Value creation and the corporate parent

Sometimes corporate parents do not add value to their constituent businesses. Where there is no added value, or where there may be a better parent, it is usually best to divest the relevant businesses from the corporate portfolio. The following section examines how corporate parents can both add and destroy value, and considers three different parenting approaches that can be effective.[11]

Corporate parents need to demonstrate that they create more value than they cost. This applies to both commercial and public-sector organisations. For public-sector organisations, privatisation or outsourcing is likely to be the consequence of failure to demonstrate value. Companies whose shares are traded freely on the stock markets face a further challenge. They must demonstrate they create more value than any other rival corporate parents could create. Failure to do so is likely to lead to a hostile takeover or break-up. Rival companies that think they can create more value out of the business units can bid for the company's shares, on the expectation of either running the businesses better or selling them off to other potential parents. If the rival's bid is more attractive and credible than what the current parent can promise, shareholders will back it at the expense of incumbent management.

In this sense, competition takes place between different corporate parents for the right to own and control businesses. In this 'market for corporate control', corporate parents must show that they have *parenting advantage*, on the same principle that business units must demonstrate competitive advantage. They must demonstrate that they are the best possible parents for the businesses they control. Parents therefore must be clear on how they create value. In practice, however, parenting activities can be value-destroying as well as value-creating.

7.5.1 Value-adding activities[12]

There are five main types of activity by which a corporate parent can potentially add value:

- *Envisioning.* The corporate parent can provide a clear overall vision or *strategic intent* for its business units.[13] This should guide and motivate business unit managers to maximise corporation-wide performance through commitment to a common purpose. Envisioning should also provide stakeholders with a *clear external image* about what the organisation as a whole is about: to reassure shareholders about the rationale for having a diversified strategy in the first place.[14] Finally, a clear vision provides a *discipline* on the corporate parent to stop its wandering into inappropriate activities or taking on unnecessary costs.

- *Facilitating synergies.* The corporate parent can facilitate cooperation and sharing across business units, so improving *synergies* from being within the same corporate organisation. This can be achieved through incentives, rewards and remuneration schemes.

- *Coaching.* The corporate parent can help business unit managers develop capabilities, by coaching them to improve their skills and confidence. Corporate-wide management courses are one effective means of achieving these objectives, as bringing managers across the business to learn strategy skills also allows them to build relationships between each other and perceive opportunities for cooperation.

- *Providing central services and resources.* The centre can provide capital for *investment* as well as central services such as treasury, tax and human resource advice. If these are centralised they may have *sufficient scale* to be efficient and can build up *relevant expertise*. Centralised services often have greater *leverage*: for example, combining many business unit purchases increases bargaining power for shared inputs such as energy. This leverage can be helpful in *brokering* with external bodies, such as government regulators, or other companies in negotiating alliances. Finally, the centre can have an important role in managing expertise within the corporate whole, for instance by *transferring managers* across the business units or by creating shared *knowledge management* systems via corporate intranets.

- *Intervening.* Finally, the corporate parent can also intervene within its business units to ensure appropriate performance. The corporate parent should be able to closely *monitor* business unit performance and *improve performance* either by replacing weak managers or by assisting them in turning around their businesses. The parent can also *challenge and develop* the strategic ambitions of business units, so good businesses are encouraged to perform even better.

Value-destroying activities

However, there are three ways in which the corporate parent can inadvertently destroy value:

- *Adding management costs.* Most simply, corporate staff and facilities are expensive. If corporate centre costs are greater than the value they create, then corporate staff are value-destroying.

Illustration 7.3 Chipotle: Doing things differently

Struggling to find parenting advantage.

Chipotle Mexican Grill had always done things rather differently to the rest of the restaurant industry. Its outlets were not in the busiest locations, it spent lots on food, rarely added to the menu, didn't serve breakfast, do drive-throughs, franchises, or much advertising. And yet by 2015 it was a $22bn burrito empire. Despite its success, why did owner McDonald's sell it, especially when McDonald's own sales and stock price had dropped, as it became associated with America's obesity epidemic?

Founded in 1993 in Denver, USA by Steve Ells, and relying initially on parents and wealthy friends for initial funding, Chipotle's fast casual dining business soon needed significant capital to expand beyond its 13 stores. In 1998 McDonald's made a $50m investment in Chipotle as part of the group's expansion that included Boston Market, Donatos Pizza, Pret a Manger, Aroma Cafe. It also investigated other businesses such as dry cleaning, a maid service and mowing the lawn.

McDonald's brought distribution systems, real estate expertise, construction knowledge and organisational structure along with its capital investment. To McDonald's, Chipotle brought new products – fresh cilantro, red onions and avocados. 'Our Portland distribution centre smelled like a produce house – our product is fresh but sealed in bags for shelf-life purposes' (McDonald's executive). Only one product was common to both companies – a five-gallon bag of Coca-Cola syrup.

Coming from a standardised, rules-based, efficiency-oriented culture, McDonald's executives were startled when they first visited Chipotle's headquarters. People brought their dogs into the office and Steve Ells walked around in blue jeans. Chipotle employees showed McDonald's executives how they scrubbed the grill by hand – 'there's got to be a better system – maybe a power-tool' (McDonald's executive)? They showed food could be customised as customers walked down the line. 'If you want a bit more or less, nobody ever says no. They might charge you but it doesn't slow the process.'

By 2005, McDonald's owned 90 per cent of Chipotle. They pressed Chipotle to do drive-throughs, breakfasts and advertising, and suggested the name Chipotle Fresh Mexican Grill. Steve Ells hated the idea and was beginning to be resented at McDonald's for rejecting everything.

Chipotle did franchise eight restaurants for McDonald's but they didn't succeed, costing a lot to be bought back. 'We just do it differently – the way we approach our food and our culture' (Steve Ells). McDonald's invited Steve to visit their chicken farm in Arkansas but he was repelled and soon realised sourcing from small farms dramatically improved the taste of his food. Chipotle food costs ran at 30–32 per cent of total costs, similar to up-market restaurants and McDonald's executives found this difficult to accept: 'that's ridiculous: that's like a steakhouse.' But Steve Ells was now focusing on ingredients and food integrity.

After seven years Chipotle's contribution to McDonald's bottom line was small, despite 500 restaurants which investors wanted co-branded. Franchisees were getting distracted and Chipotle was increasingly unhappy about McDonald's supply chain. Jim Cantalupo, McDonald's CEO, had already begun to sell off partner brands and the stock price had begun to rise. It was time for a McSplit.

Since leaving McDonald's, Chipotle worth had risen to $15bn (2015), with 1,800 locations and business was booming. McDonald's pocketed $1.5bn (after $360m investment).

Sources: Chipotle: the definitive oral history, https://www.bloomberg.com/graphics/2015-chipotle-oral-history/

Questions

1 What parenting advantages did McDonald's perceive it might bring to Chipotle?

2 Despite its success, why was Chipotle spun-off?

- *Adding bureaucratic complexity.* As well as these direct financial costs, there is the 'bureaucratic fog' created by an additional layer of management and the need to coordinate with sister businesses. These typically slow down managers' responses to issues and lead to compromises between the interests of individual businesses.

- *Obscuring financial performance.* One danger in a large diversified company is that the under-performance of weak businesses can be obscured. Weak businesses might be cross-subsidised by stronger ones and this diminishes the incentives for business unit managers to strive as hard as they can for their businesses. Externally, shareholders and financial analysts cannot easily judge the performance of individual units within the corporate whole and so diversified companies' share prices are often marked down.[15]

To avoid value destruction corporate parents should keep a close eye on centre costs, both financial and bureaucratic, ensuring that they are no more than required by their corporate strategy. They should also do all they can to promote financial transparency, so that business units remain under pressure to perform and shareholders are confident that there are no hidden disasters.

There are three ways in which corporate parents can add value:[16]

- The *portfolio manager*, who operates as an active investor identifying and acquiring under-valued assets or businesses. They improve their performance over short periods of time by financial target setting, evaluating portfolios of businesses and by intervention through providing or withdrawing investment.

- The *synergy manager*, who seeks to enhance value for business units by managing synergies across business units. Synergies are likely to be particularly rich when new activities are closely related to the core business. Value can be created by envisioning building a common purpose; facilitating cooperation across businesses; and providing central services and resource. However synergies may prove illusory when managers attempt to put them into practice (see Illustration 7.2).

- *The parental developer*, who seeks to employ central capabilities to add value to its businesses. This is not so much about how the parent can develop benefits *across* business units or transfer capabilities between business units, as in the case of managing synergy. Rather parental developers focus on the resources or capabilities they have as parents which they can transfer *downwards* to enhance the potential of business units, such as exchanges of managers and provision of central services and resources. It would seem that McDonald's believed it had identified a parenting opportunity with its acquisition of Chipotle (Illustration 7.3).

7.6 The BCG (or growth/share) matrix[17]

There are many models that managers can use to determine financial investment and divestment within their portfolios of business. Each model gives more or less attention to at least one of three criteria:

- the *balance* of the portfolio (e.g. in relation to its markets and the needs of the corporation);

- the *attractiveness* of the business units in terms of how strong they are individually and the growth rates of their markets or industries; and

- the '*fit*' that the business units have with each other in terms of potential synergies or the extent to which the corporate parent will be good at looking after them.

One of the most common and longstanding portfolio methods is the Boston Consulting Group (BCG) matrix (see Figure 7.4). The **BCG matrix uses market share and market growth criteria for determining the attractiveness and balance of a business portfolio.** High market share and high growth are, of course, attractive. However, the BCG matrix also warns that high growth demands heavy investment, for instance to expand capacity or develop brands. There needs to be a balance within the portfolio, so that there are some low-growth businesses that are making sufficient surplus to fund the investment needs of higher-growth businesses.

The growth/share axes of the BCG matrix define four sorts of business:

- A *star* is a business unit within a portfolio that has a high market share in a growing market. The business unit may be spending heavily to keep up with growth, but high market share should yield sufficient profits to make it more or less self-sufficient in terms of investment needs.

- A *question mark* (or problem child) is a business unit within a portfolio that is in a growing market, but does not yet have high market share. Developing question marks into stars, with high market share, takes heavy investment. Many question marks fail to develop, so the BCG advises corporate parents to nurture several at a time. It is important to make sure that some question marks develop into stars, as existing stars eventually become cash cows and cash cows may decline into dogs.

- A *cash cow* is a business unit within a portfolio that has a high market share in a mature market. However, because growth is low, investment needs are less, while high market share means that the business unit should be profitable. The cash cow should then be a cash provider, helping to fund investments in question marks.

- *Dogs* are business units within a portfolio that have low share in static or declining markets and are thus the worst of all combinations. They may be a cash drain and use up a disproportionate amount of managerial time and company resources. The BCG usually recommends divestment or closure.

The BCG matrix has several advantages. It is a good way of visualising different needs and potentials of all the diverse businesses within the corporate portfolio. It warns corporate parents of the financial demands of what might otherwise look like a desirable portfolio of high-growth businesses. It also reminds corporate parents that stars are likely eventually to wane.

Figure 7.4 The growth share (or BCG) matrix

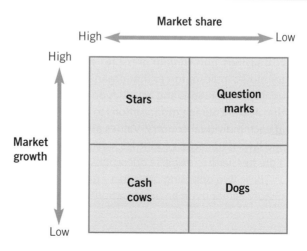

Finally, it provides a useful discipline to business unit managers, underlining the fact that the corporate parent ultimately owns the surplus resources they generate and can allocate them according to what is best for the corporate whole. Cash cows should not hoard their profits.

However, there are at least four potential problems with the BCG matrix: it can be hard to decide what high and low growth or share mean in particular situations; there is an assumption that a balanced portfolio is necessary for financing investment from internal sources (cash cows) when capital can be raised from external markets; cash cows and dogs receive ungenerous treatment, the first being simply milked, the second terminated or cast out of the corporate home and these actions can cause *motivation problems* as managers in these units see little point in working hard for the sake of other businesses; *commercial linkages* between business units are ignored when there may be important dependencies.

7.7 International diversification strategy

The Ansoff matrix (Figure 7.2) identifies various directions in which an organisation might grow. Many organisations expand through market development into different geographic markets where they face new customer needs and may be challenged by local economic, regulative, political and cultural institutions that often differ substantially from home. Coming from abroad the foreign organisation typically is at a considerable disadvantage to local competitors who will have superior knowledge of local market, institutions, supply chain and the like. The foreign entrant must thus have significant firm specific competitive advantages to compete. There are two principle opportunities available to a foreign entrant, namely the exploitation of particular *locational advantages*, often in the entrant's home country, and sourcing advantages abroad via an *international value system*. For instance, Volvo Trucks, the Swedish truck and construction equipment manufacturer, achieved global success by building on a local network of sophisticated engineering partners and suppliers and a local demand oriented towards reliability and safety which gave it an advantage when it internationalised. An example of the value of an international value system is the National Health Service in the UK, which sources medical personnel from overseas to offset a skills shortage at home.

Even with organisation-specific advantages and the ability to obtain sources of international competitive advantage through geographic home-based factors or international value systems, organisations still face difficult questions about what kind of international strategy to pursue. The fundamental issue in formulating an international strategy is to balance pressures for *global integration* versus those for *local responsiveness*.[18] Pressures for *global integration encourage organisations to coordinate their activities across diverse countries to gain efficient operations*. Internationalisation drivers such as market demand, the potential for cost savings, government pressures and inducements and the need to respond to competitor moves indicate forces that organisations can build on to achieve lower costs and higher quality in operations and activities on a global scale. However, there are conflicting pressures that also encourage organisations to become locally responsive and meet the specific needs in each individual country. Values and attitudes, economics, political institutions, cultures and laws differ across countries, which means high pressure for *local responsiveness implies a greater need to disperse operations and adapt to local demand*.

These two opposing pressures – global integration vs. local responsiveness – put contradictory demands on an organisation's international strategy. This key problem is sometimes referred to as the **global–local dilemma: the extent to which products and services may be standardised across national boundaries or need to be adapted to meet the requirements of specific national markets.** For some products and services – such as TVs – markets appear similar across the world, offering huge potential scale economies if design, production and delivery can be centralised. For other products and services – such as processed food – tastes still seem highly national-specific, causing companies to decentralise operations and control as near as possible to the local market.

This dilemma between global integration and local responsiveness suggests several possible international strategies[19] (see Figure 7.5).

- *Export strategy.* This strategy leverages home country capabilities, innovations and products in different foreign countries because the company has a strong reputation such as Google.

- *Multi-domestic strategy.* This is a strategy that maximises local responsiveness and is loosely coordinated internationally. It is particularly appropriate when there are strong benefits to adapting to local needs and when there are limited efficiency gains from integration.

- *Global strategy.* This strategy maximises global integration and focuses on capturing scale economies through standardisation and exploiting location economies worldwide with geographically dispersed value chain activities being coordinated and controlled centrally from headquarters.

- *Transnational strategy.* This strategy tries to maximise responsiveness and integration and maximise learning and knowledge exchange between dispersed units. Therefore strategy products and services and operational activities are adapted to local conditions in each country but learning and innovation are leveraged across units in different countries. The value chain configuration includes an intricate combination of centralised manufacturing to increase efficiency combined with distributed assembly and local adaptations. Although attractive, the complexity of transnational strategy makes it difficult to implement.[20]

Figure 7.5 International strategies: global integration vs. local responsiveness

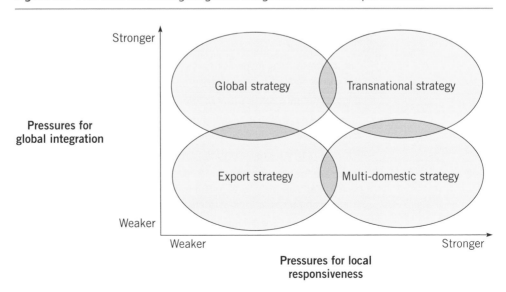

7.8 Growth methods: organic, acquisition and alliances

Key methods for expansion are *organic growth*, *acquisitions*[1] and *alliances*.

- **Organic growth is achieved by building on and developing an organisation's own capabilities**. This can enhance knowledge and learning, enable the spread of investment over time, it is not dependent on the availability of targets for acquisition and the risks of culture clash are avoided.

- **Acquisition is when an acquirer *takes control* by purchasing a majority of shares in a target company**. It can enable the acquirer to reach new geographies, products or markets, allow increases in market power and supplier power through consolidation, increase internal efficiencies through combining operations and increase the acquirer's stock of capabilities, such as acquiring technology and know-how.[21]

- **Strategic alliance is where two or more organisations share resources and activities to pursue a common strategy**. This combination can achieve economies of scale in the production of outputs (products or services) and might also provide economies of scale in terms of inputs, for example by reducing purchasing costs of raw materials or services. Alliances may allow an organisation to gain access to the capabilities, products and distribution systems of another organisation as well as intangible resources such as knowledge and social/political connections. Where the organisations are complementary in nature, this access can help each partner overcome particular weaknesses. Occasionally organisations secretly collude together in order to increase their market power, by combining together into cartels. These are generally illegal, and regulators will act to discourage them although they may be justified politically in sensitive industries such as defence or aerospace due to national interests. They do take place in not-for-profit sectors.

Each of the main growth methods of organic, acquisition and strategic alliance have strengths and weaknesses and the choice of which one is most appropriate is determined by three key factors, urgency, uncertainty and type of capabilities being combined.

Summary

- Corporate strategy involves the decisions and activities above the level of business units. It is concerned with choices concerning the scope of the organisation.

- Organisational *scope* is often considered in terms of *related* and *unrelated* diversification.

- Corporate parents may seek to add value by adopting different parenting roles: the *portfolio manager*, the *synergy manager* or the *parental developer*.

- The *BCG matrix* helps corporate parents manage their portfolios of businesses.

- There are four main types of international strategy, varying according to extent of coordination and geographical configuration: export strategy, multi-domestic strategy, global strategy and transnational strategy.

- There are three broad methods for pursuing a growth strategy: *acquisitions*, *alliances* and *organic development*.

[1]Often known as Mergers and Acquisitions (M&A), real mergers between equal companies, where no company is dominant, are rare and so not commented on here. For fuller treatment see *Exploring Strategy*, 12th edition.

Recommended key readings

- An accessible discussion of corporate strategy is provided by P. Puranam and B. Vanneste, Corporate Strategy. *Tools for analysis and strategic decision making*, Cambridge University Press, 2016.

- An invigorating perspective on international strategy is provided by G.S. Yip and G.T. Hult, *Total Global Strategy*, Pearson, 2012.

- A comprehensive book on M&A is: D. DePamphilis, *Mergers, Acquisitions and other Restructuring Activities*, 10th edn, Academic Press, Elsevier, 2019. For some alternative perspectives, see the collection by D. N. Angwin (ed.), *Mergers and Acquisitions*, Blackwell, 2007.

References

1. For a detailed discussion as to how organisational structures might 'address' an organisation's mix of SBUs, see M. Goold and A. Campbell, *Designing Effective Organizations: How to Create Structured Networks*, Jossey-Bass, 2002. Also K. Eisenhardt and S. Brown, 'Patching', *Harvard Business Review*, vol. 77, no. 3 (1999), p. 72.

2. B.S. Vanneste, 'How much do industry, corporation and business really matter? A meta-analysis', *Strategy Science*, vol. 2, no. 2 (2017) pp. 121–39.

3. This figure is an extension of the product/market matrix: see I. Ansoff, *Corporate Strategy*, 1988, Chapter 6. The Ansoff matrix was later developed into the one shown above.

4. J. Hautz, M. Mayer and C. Stadler, 'Macro-competitive context and diversification. The impact of macroeconomic growth and foreign competition', *Long Range Planning*, vol. 47 (2013) pp. 337–52.

5. For discussions of the challenge of sustained growth and diversification, see D. Laurie, Y. Doz and C. Sheer, 'Creating new growth platforms', *Harvard Business Review*, vol. 84, no. 5 (2006), pp. 80–90.

6. On economies of scope, see D.J. Teece, 'Towards an economic theory of the multi-product firm', *Journal of Economic Behavior and Organization*, vol. 3 (1982), pp. 39–63.

7. See R. Bettis and C.K. Prahalad, 'The dominant logic: retrospective and extension', *Strategic Management Journal*, vol. 16, no. 1 (1995), pp. 5–15.

8. M. Goold and A. Campbell, 'Desperately seeking synergy', *Harvard Business Review*, vol. 76, no. 2 (1998), pp. 131–45.

9. A. Pehrson, 'Business relatedness and performance: a study of managerial perceptions', *Strategic Management Journal*, vol. 27, no. 3 (2006), pp. 265–82.

10. For a discussion and cases on the relative guidance of transaction cost and capabilities thinking, see R. McIvor, 'How the transaction cost and resource-based theories of the firm inform outsourcing evaluation', *Journal of Operations Management*, vol. 27, no. 1 (2009), pp. 45–63.

11. A recent empirical study of corporate headquarters is D. Collis, D. Young and M. Goold, 'The size, structure and performance of corporate headquarters', *Strategic Management Journal*, vol. 28, no. 4 (2007), pp. 383–406.

12. M. Goold, A. Campbell and M. Alexander, *Corporate Level Strategy*, Wiley, 1994, is concerned with both the value-adding and value-destroying capacity of corporate parents.

13. For a discussion of the role of clarity of mission, see A. Campbell, M. Devine and D. Young, *A Sense of Mission*, Hutchinson Business, 1990.

14. T. Zenger, 'Strategy: the uniqueness challenge', *Harvard Business Review* (2013) November pp. 52–58.

15. E. Zuckerman, 'Focusing the corporate product: securities analysts and de-diversification', *Administrative Science Quarterly*, vol. 45, no. 3 (2000), pp. 591–619.

16. The first two rationales discussed here are based on M. Porter, 'From competitive advantage to corporate strategy', *Harvard Business Review*, vol. 65, no. 3 (1987), pp. 43–59.

17. For a more extensive discussion of the use of the growth share matrix see A.C. Hax and N.S. Majluf in R.G. Dyson (ed.), *Strategic Planning: Models and Analytical Techniques*, Wiley, 1990. For the BCG matrix see B.D. Henderson, *Henderson on Corporate Strategy*, Abe Books, 1979.

18. The integration–responsiveness framework builds on the original works by C.A. Bartlett, 'Building and managing the transnational: the new organizational challenge', in M.E. Porter (ed.), *Competition in Global Industries*, Harvard Business School Press, 1986, pp. 367–401.

19. The typology builds on the basic framework of C.A. Bartlett and S. Ghoshal, *Managing across Borders: the Transnational Solution*, The Harvard Business School Press, 1989 (2nd updated edn, 1998); and S. Ghoshal and N. Nohria, 'Horses for courses: organizational forms for multinational corporations', *Sloan Management Review*, vol. 34 (1993), pp. 23–35.

20. For an analysis of the transnational strategy and ABB as an example, see C.A. Bartlett and S. Ghoshal, *Managing Across Borders: The Transnational Solution*, 2nd edn, Harvard Business School Press, 1998, pp. 259–72.

21. D.N. Angwin, 'Motive archetypes in mergers and acquisitions (M&A): the implications of a configurational approach to performance', *Advances in Mergers and Acquisitions*, vol. 6 (2007), pp. 77–105.

Case example

Grand strategies in vision

by Peter Barton

Seeing opportunities

Most wearers of prescription eyewear and sunglasses are aware of the large retail brands on their high street and, increasingly online, as well as many of the brand names that they sell. What many are less aware of is the giant companies that operate the manufacturing of the vast majority of the products behind this industry, which was worth $109bn (£82bn/€93bn) in 2018 and is set to grow 7.4 per cent each year until 2023 to around $167bn (£125bn/€142bn) (ResearchAndMarkets.com, 2018).

While the continued growth in prescriptive eyewear came about in part due to a rapid worldwide population increase, the number of those requiring corrective prescriptions has also risen dramatically. This may be partially down to wider awareness and eye testing but it is also due to a lack of time spent outdoors, increased use of screens and LED lighting, and, the impact of most populations living longer. Notably, there is a global epidemic of myopia (short-sightedness), which has increased roughly two-fold in just a couple of decades. Reportedly, in the 1950s in China, around 10 to 20 per cent of the population were short-sighted but this has risen to around 90 per cent.[1]

Vision as fashion

Up until the 1980s, glasses were largely seen as medical devices with functional designs despite labels such as Christian Dior and Pierre Cardin attempts to bring fashion to the market. It wasn't until the early 1990s that the global manufacturing giant Luxottica played a large part in bringing fashion to the industry through the licensing of the fashion brand Giorgio Armani, and then Prada, Ralph Lauren, Gucci and Chanel. Other major brand manufacturers have since emerged, including Safilo, the world's second largest manufacturer of eyewear, which manages rival fashion brands such as Carrera, Dior, Fendi, BOSS, Tommy Hilfiger and Jimmy Choo.

Luxottica (formerly)

Luxottica was founded by Italy's current highest individual taxpayer Leonardo Del Vecchio who originally started with a workshop in Agordo, in Italy, in 1961. He grew his company into the world's largest maker of frames with two notable objectives: to do everything itself, and to focus on fashion. Progressively, he set about controlling

List of Luxottica brands: http://www.luxottica.com/en/eyewear-brands.

every element in the supply chain, sourcing raw materials, making all parts of the frames which involves around 200 manufacturing stages to produce and, later, the stores where they were sold. Del Vecchio, the current Chairman, was recently quoted as saying: 'Although today we are strong, life has taught me that you should never think of having arrived; I believe that you should always have the courage to reinvent yourself and innovate' (Luxottica Report, 2016). This attitude to ownership, control and innovation has enabled Luxottica to control standards, bringing higher quality products to market faster and in higher quantities.

The most valuable optical brand in the world is Ray-Ban, which now generates more than $2bn (£1.5bn) in sales for Luxottica each year, making it an impressive brand turnaround. Luxottica bought Ray-Ban from Bausch & Lomb in 1999 at a time when the brand was at a notable low with Ray-Bans reportedly being sold at petrol stations for just $19 (£14/€16). Having promised to protect thousands of jobs at four factories in the USA and Ireland, Del Vecchio quickly closed the plants and shifted production to Italy and China. His next move was perhaps less expected as he withdrew Ray-Ban from 13,000 retail outlets, increasing their prices and significantly improving quality: the number of layers of lacquer on a pair of Wayfarers increased from just two to over 30. Once the brand had regained its prestige across its core styles, including Aviators, Wayfarers and Clubmasters, he then introduced a highly successful prescription glasses range.

The other important frame brand to Luxottica is Oakley but this was a brand acquired through much hostility. In 2000, Luxottica asked all its suppliers to reduce its prices to them, but despite its stores making up over 25 per cent of Oakley's business, Oakley refused to comply. Del Vecchio's response was to produce Ray-Bans reportedly more similar to Oakley's designs leading to Oakley suing them in 2001, which ultimately ended in an out-of-court settlement. Perhaps as a show of strength from Del Vecchio, in 2007, Luxottica purchased Oakley for $2.1bn (£1.5bn).

As a result of many acquisitions and significant brand growth, Luxottica now supplies over 25 per cent of the world's frames, catering for multiple market segments. As quoted in the *Guardian* (2018), Luxottica's Chief Operating Officer Striano says: 'Luxottica has around 27,000 models in production at any one time and turns out 400,000 frames a day catering for global fashion demands as well as widely different face shapes that vary from country to country.'

While establishing its business in frame manufacturing, in the 1990s Luxottica sought to diversify its portfolio of optical businesses across the optical supply chain. Del Vecchio listed Luxottica on the New York stock exchange and, in 1995, acquired a conglomerate five times larger than itself called US Shoe through a hostile takeover for $1.4bn (£1.05bn/€1.2bn). US Shoe was founded in 1879 and included LensCrafters, the US's largest optical store. Del Vecchio promptly sold all non-optical elements of the business and filled all the stores with Luxottica's own glasses putting it in competition with thousands of competing opticians that it already supplied. Jeff Cole, the former chief executive of Cole National Corporation, an even larger optical retailer that sold out to Luxottica in 2004, said: 'When they buy a company, they spend a little time figuring it out and kick out all the other suppliers.'[2]

This is a growth formula that they have continued to adopt around the world including through Sunglass Hut, John Lewis Opticians and David Clulow in the UK, Óticas Carol in Brazil, Xueliang Glasses in Shanghai or Ming Long Store in Hong Kong. Luxottica now has almost 9,000 stores and supplies over 100,000 opticians around the world.

HAL Holdings

Two other giants in the global optical market include designer frame manufacturer Safilo, and retail focused Grand Vision, both of which are owned and controlled by HAL Holdings.

Safilo operates an extensive wholly-owned global distribution and wholesale network in over 40 countries servicing almost 100,000 selected stores with its diverse brand portfolio. The direct management of proprietary brands ensures bigger margins, while licensed brands

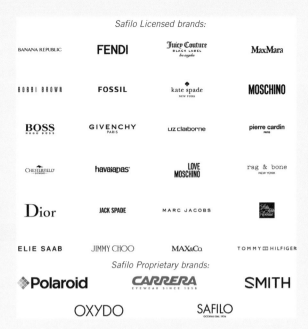

Safilo Licensed brands:

List of Safilo brands: http://www.safilogroup.com/en/2-licensed-brands.

allow for a larger portfolio, through different consumer and distribution segments.

While HAL Holding's other major interest, GrandVision, has some of its own frame brands as well as contact lens brands, its main operation is the overarching control and governance of over 7,000 optical stores serving over 150 million customers across 44 countries and with sales of over €3.6bn (£3.1bn) in 2017. GrandVision sources a large portion of its premium designer frames from Safilo but is also free to source from other suppliers including Luxottica.

Figure 1 GrandVision's historical revenue

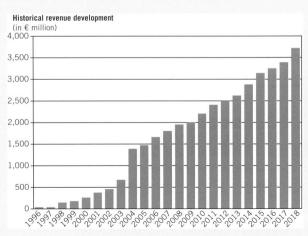

Historical revenue development
(in € million)

Source: Key Figures, https://investors.grandvision.com/key-figures

Figure 2 Recent GrandVision M&A activity

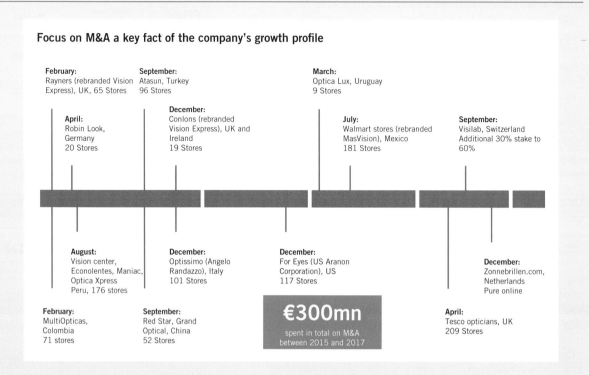

Focus on M&A a key fact of the company's growth profile

February:
Rayners (rebranded Vision Express), UK, 65 Stores

September:
Atasun, Turkey
96 Stores

March:
Optica Lux, Uruguay
9 Stores

April:
Robin Look, Germany
20 Stores

December:
Conlons (rebranded Vision Express), UK and Ireland
19 Stores

July:
Walmart stores (rebranded MasVision), Mexico
181 Stores

September:
Visilab, Switzerland
Additional 30% stake to 60%

August:
Vision center, Econolentes, Maniac, Optica Xpress
Peru, 176 stores

December:
Optissimo (Angelo Randazzo), Italy
101 Stores

December:
For Eyes (US Aranon Corporation), US
117 Stores

December:
Zonnebrillen.com, Netherlands
Pure online

February:
MultiOpticas, Colombia
71 stores

September:
Red Star, Grand Optical, China
52 Stores

€300mn
spent in total on M&A between 2015 and 2017

April:
Tesco opticians, UK
209 Stores

GrandVision can trace its roots back to 1891 when Christian Nissen opened its first store in Helsinki, Finland. However, it wasn't until 1996 that HAL Holdings stepped in by first acquiring the Dutch and Belgian operations of Pearle Vision, which then led to the eventual merger of Pearle to create GrandVision in 2011. Since then, GrandVision has continued to seek growth in new markets as well as acquire and merge into existing retail brands, rolling out its largely standardised formula across each market. For example, in the UK, Vision Express increased its number of stores from around 300 stores to over 600 stores in the space of five years (see Vision Express Industry Case example). This rapid expansion has helped to grow the manufacturing part of the business as well as other products sold through its stores. While its relationship to Safilo remains at arm's length, as GrandVision's principal designer frame supplier, the knock-on effect has seen Safilo's revenues exceed €1bn in 2018 despite still failing to make a profit for the previous three years.

Operating a two-tier governance structure consisting of a Management Board and Supervisory Board, GrandVision is set up and structured to deliberately ensure that the subsidiaries in each country can be close to their own markets. Its strategic priorities are to continue expansion into new markets as well as expand and enhance existing ones.

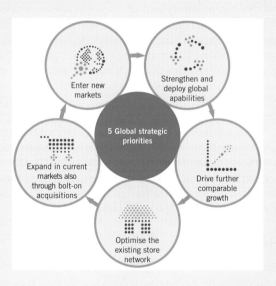

Enter new markets

Strengthen and deploy global capabilities

5 Global strategic priorities

Expand in current markets also through bolt-on acquisitions

Drive further comparable growth

Optimise the existing store network

'For Vision Express in the UK, all our department teams, from marketing to purchasing, make it their job to understand the market and its needs. GrandVision's role is to support us in delivering it to the market. A large part of this comes from the economies of scale and leverage of synergies on a greater scale than if it was just us. So this model enables us to have preferential buying to ensure the delivery of economic value. We are also hungry to learn best practices from others that have had success and relate it back to opportunities within our own market. The longevity of retail brands such as Vision Express in the UK, Apollo-Optik in Germany, Grand Optical in France is clear testament to their commitment and they have no intention to destroy that or create a homogenous brand.'

CEO of Vision Express, Jonathan Lawson

When rival giants collide

On 1 October 2018, GrandVision's and Safilo's biggest competitor, and the world's largest supplier of eyewear, Luxottica merged with global giant Essilor, which itself supplies over 45 per cent of the world's prescription lenses.

The merging of Luxottica with the French multinational Essilor has made the newly named company 'EssilorLuxottica' comfortably the world's largest optical company valued at around $50bn (£37bn) with over 140,000 employees and a customer base of over 1.4 billion, which, to put it perspective, is more than either Microsoft (1.2 billion) or Apple have (1.3 billion). Essilor's chairman and chief executive, Hubert Sagnières, believes that the merger between Luxottica and Essilor will enable them to equip the planet with eyewear over the coming decades. 'The Luxottica frames with our lenses will be a hugely powerful force' (Stothard, 2017, *Financial Times*).

Essilor itself was the merger of two French optical companies, Essel and Silor, which merged in 1972. Specialising in plastic lenses, as opposed to glass, they were renowned for inventing the first progressive/multi-focal lens, allowing people to see both close up and far away, which they branded under the name 'Variux'. Essilor has acquired more than 250 other companies in the past 20 years, including online glasses retailer MyOptique in 2016. It now supplies around 350,000 stores around the world, which is over three times that of Luxottica. It also holds over 8,000 patents and it is focused on new technologies in lenses, such as building upon Google's failed concept of Google Glass with the idea to project information from the internet such as emails, maps, message and social media.

While most people have heard of neither Luxottica or Essilor, the creation of EssilorLuxottica is likely to have a great impact upon the industry as the control of supply within the industry is held by fewer manufacturers operating more brands across diverse retail and legal environments. The Guardian quotes Dr Gorny (Head of R&D Essilor) as saying: 'There is nothing close to that firepower once the combination is done. You have the global footprint. You can play all the courts.'

However, its ability to integrate effectively is yet to be seen and will not be without a potential clash of cultures.

Insiders say that Luxottica is run like a monarchy with little clear management structure, whereas Essilor is clearly defined and organised with 55 per cent of its employees as shareholders. Furthermore, despite inherent optimism, both companies reported an early sales dip in 2018, with Essilor dropping 5.8 per cent and Luxottica 11 per cent, which they put down to fluctuating currencies, bad weather and a dip in wholesale revenue.

Sources: S. Knight, 'The spectacular power of Big Lens', *The Guardian*, 10 May 2018, https://www.theguardian.com/news/2018/may/10/the-invisible-power-of-big-glasses-eyewear-industry-essilor-luxottica; 'AOP Profession Threat and Opportunities': www.aop.org.uk/advice-and-support/threats-and-opportunities-in-the-profession; R. Calver, 'The Health and Social Security Act 1984 and the price of spectacles among corporate practices in the United Kingdom (1980–2007): a review', *Ophthalmic and Physiological Optics*, vol. 30, no. 2 (2010), pp. 113–23; C. Fulop and K. Warren (1993) 'Deregulation and its impact on the opticians' market: a comparison of the forecasts of both proponents and opponents with events in practice', *International Journal of Advertising*, vol. 12, no. 3, pp. 257–78; Essilor Website: https://www.essilor.com/essilor-content/uploads/2016/10/Essilor_Press_Release_Forbes_most_innovating_companies_24_August_2016-.pdf; GrandVision Website: www.grandvision.com/; T. Hockley (2012) 'A giant leap by small steps: The Conservative Party and National Health Service reform' (Doctoral dissertation, The London School of Economics and Political Science (LSE)); Insightnews website: www.insightnews.com.au/Article3/1608/Essilor-Luxottica-sales-dip-ahead-of-merger; Luxottica website: www.luxottica.com/en; Luxottica Group, '2016 Investor and analyst presentation', 2 March 2016, www.luxottica.com/sites/luxottica.com/files/2016_03_02_-_luxottica_2016_investor_and_analyst_presentation_-_transcript_2.pdf; E. McCormick, 'Lens group features on the "100 Most Innovative Companies" list for a sixth year', *Forbes*, 1 September 2016, www.aop.org.uk/ot/industry/eyewear-and-lenses/2016/09/01/essilor-named-on-forbes-list; M. Olczak, 'Chain-store-pricing and the structure of retail markets', *Journal of Industry, Competition and Trade*, vol. 15, no. 2 (2015), pp. 87–104; 'Optical Goods Retailing', February 2018, Mintel; ResearchAndMarkets.com (2018), 'Global $167 Billion Eyewear Market Report 2018 with Forecasts to 2023 by Product, Gender, and Distribution Channel', www.researchandmarkets.com/research/lvw69x/global_167?w=4; Safilo website: www.safilogroup.com/en/; M. Stothard, 'Hubert Sagnières, Essilor CEO, on an eyewear megamerger', *Financial Times*, 11 June 2017, www.ft.com/content/10bde3b0-33ea-11e7-99bd-13beb0903fa3; G.S. Valentina Za, 'Luxottica CEO exits eyewear giant ahead of Essilor merger', 15 December 2017, www.reuters.com/article/us-luxottica-ceo/luxottica-ceo-exits-eyewear-giant-ahead-of-essilor-merger-idUSKBN1E92IB; www.grandvision.com/about-us/exclusive-eyewear-brands/frames-and-sunglasses.

Questions

1 With reference to Ansoff's matrix, show how Luxottica and GrandVision have evolved over time. What can you conclude from each?

2 How does GrandVision compete in its market?

3 How do you think that GrandVision adds or destroys value for its portfolio?

4 With the creation of EssilorLuxottica, what would you recommend for GrandVision's future strategy?

Note: 'Glasses' (or spectacles) are referred to as 'eye-glasses' in the USA.

Chapter 8
Entrepreneurship and innovation

Key terms

Learning outcomes

After reading this chapter, you should be able to:

- Anticipate key issues facing entrepreneurs in *opportunity recognition*, in making choices during the *entrepreneurial process* and in various *stages of growth*, from start-up to exit.

- Identify and respond to key *innovation dilemmas*, such as the relative emphases to place on technologies or markets, product or process innovations and open versus closed innovation.

- Anticipate and to some extent influence the *diffusion* (or spread) of innovations.

- Decide when being a *first-mover* innovator or a fast second-mover imitator is most appropriate in innovation, and how an *incumbent* organisation should respond to innovative challengers.

8.1 Introduction

Apple became the most valuable company in the world through the entrepreneurship of its founder, Steve Jobs (see Illustration 8.1). But Apple's story is one of continuous creativity. Ever since the company's foundation in 1976, and even after Steve Jobs' death in 2011, Apple has continued to innovate with the HomePod, Apple Watch and AirPods. This Apple example illustrates the connections between the two themes of this chapter, entrepreneurship and innovation.

We start with entrepreneurship. **Entrepreneurship is a process by which individuals, start-ups or organisations identify and exploit opportunities for new products or services that satisfy a need in a market.**[1] Entrepreneurship is not confined to new start-up enterprises, but can take the form of corporate entrepreneurship, the pursuit of new products or services by established firms (as Apple has repeatedly done). Entrepreneurship is thus linked to innovation. **Innovation involves the conversion of new knowledge into a new product, process or service *and* the putting of this new product, process or service into actual commercial use.**[2] Strategic entrepreneurship and its outcome, innovation, are thus essential for the long-term survival and success of all organisations and it is the focus of this chapter.[3]

- Section 8.2 addresses *entrepreneurship.* The section starts with a discussion of a central step in strategic entrepreneurship, *opportunity recognition*, which captures conditions under which products and services satisfy market needs or wants in the environment. Other steps in the *entrepreneurial process* then follow. They provide a foundation for further entrepreneurial *growth stages* from start-up to growth, maturity and possibly finally to exit.

- Section 8.3 discusses three fundamental *innovation dilemmas*: technology push as against market pull; product innovation rather than process innovation; and, finally, open versus closed innovation including the importance of ecosystems for the former. None of these are absolute 'either-or' dilemmas, but managers and entrepreneurs must choose where to concentrate their limited resources.

- Once created, innovations will be diffused among users over time and diffusion pace depends on various product and demand features. Section 8.4 considers issues surrounding the *diffusion*, or spread, of innovations in the marketplace.

- Section 8.5 completes the discussion of innovation by considering choices with regard to timing. This includes *first-mover* innovation advantages and disadvantages, the advantages of being '*fast second*' into a market, and the issue of how established *incumbents* can be innovative and respond to innovative challengers.

8.2 Entrepreneurship

Entrepreneurship is for both start-ups and established enterprises. Recognising an opportunity is the very first step in a strategic entrepreneurial process. Opportunity recognition involves more than a simple business idea. It entails a combination of elements that an entrepreneur believes will create value and possibly profit. This section introduces some key issues for entrepreneurial innovators including opportunity recognition and the entrepreneurial process over time.

Illustration 8.1 Entrepreneurs, start-up teams and external relationships

Entrepreneurs are often stereotyped as heroic individuals, but entrepreneurship is rarely done alone – it often builds on a team, pre-existing organisational experience and external relationships.

Hewlett Packard

The entrepreneurial team William Hewlett and David Packard, founders of the famous computing and printer company HP, are oft-quoted examples of the garage stereotype. But digging beneath the stereotype soon reveals a more complex story, in which relationships with large companies can be important right from the start. Often entrepreneurs have worked for large companies beforehand and continue to use relationships afterwards. While Hewlett came fairly directly out of Stanford University's laboratories, Packard worked at General Electric and Litton Industries. They built extensively on their previous social relationships and ties when setting up HP. The company used Litton Industries' foundries early on, and later used relationships at General Electric to recruit experienced managers.

Apple

Steve Jobs has often been celebrated as the heroic innovator and entrepreneur behind Apple, but he too relied heavily on external relationships. From the very beginning Apple computer did not only involve Jobs, but his founding partner Steve Wozniak. They too started in a garage, but similar to HP built heavily on their experiences with more established organisations. Wozniak worked at HP and Jobs at Atari and this helped them gain access to crucial knowledge and contacts for the development of the start-up. When their venture had become more established, they left their employers and incorporated Apple Computer. Apple's much later successes with the iPod and later the iPhone and iPad have also relied on important external relationships. The music player application SoundJam MP was externally acquired early on and an external entrepreneur was vital for developing iTunes. Apple also initially worked with the then leading mobile telephone maker Motorola to develop a smartphone.

Facebook

One of today's most successful and well-known entrepreneurs is Mark Zuckerberg, who started a photo-rating site called Facemash from his dorm room by using Harvard's online student photographs. Zuckerberg did not rely on previous organisational experiences, but built on his programming skills and involved others with complementary skills early on. Based on his previous experience with Facemash he founded the social networking website Facebook together with other fellow Harvard students to develop and grow the site. The team (Dustin Moskovitz, Chris Hughes and Eduardo Saverin) brought various skills including programming, promotion, graphics, financing and other business expertise. To focus entirely on Facebook and attract further talent and financing to their team Zuckerberg and Moskovitz abandoned their education at Harvard and moved to California and Silicon Valley. There Zuckerberg continued to build on external business expertise together with venture capitalist investors to further grow the company.

Sources: P. Audia and C. Rider, 'A garage and an idea: what more does an entrepreneur need?', *California Management Review*, vol. 40, no. 1, 2005, pp. 6–28; D. Kirkpatrick, '*The Inside Story of the Company That Is Connecting the World*', Simon & Schuster, 2010.

Questions

1 Based on the experiences of HP, Apple and Facebook what elements of skills and expertise do you think a new venture requires?

2 How would you form a venture team if you set up your own start-up?

8.2.1 Opportunity recognition

Opportunity recognition means recognising an opportunity, i.e. circumstances under which products and services can satisfy a need in the market or environment.[4] This typically involves an entrepreneur or entrepreneurial team identifying trends in the environment and combining resources and capabilities into the creation of new products or services. Opportunity recognition thus involves three important and interdependent elements: the entrepreneur or entrepreneurial team, the environment and resources and capabilities (see Figure 8.1):

- *Entrepreneur or entrepreneurial team.* The entrepreneur or team drives and integrates the various parts of an entrepreneurial process including scanning and spotting trends in the environment (see Chapter 2), linking these to existing resources and capabilities or acquiring appropriate ones and recombining them. Entrepreneurs come in many different forms. Sometimes they are individuals, but typically they are part of a team which includes the managing of relationships with other partners and sometimes other and bigger companies (see Illustration 8.1).

- *Environment trends and marketplace gaps.* Building on macro trends and possible marketplace gaps is likely to be central in identifying an opportunity. This includes observing economic, technological, social and political trends (as with PESTEL in Chapter 2) and linking them to specific customer needs that are currently not satisfied. For example, the GPS fitness-tracking app Runkeeper, with over 50 million users, built on health awareness and fitness trends, the proliferation of smartphones users and apps, globalisation of markets and the increased possibility to integrate apps across various social media platforms such as Facebook and Twitter.

- *Resources and capabilities.* Having access to resources and capabilities are an important part of opportunity recognition. Various helpful ways of mapping and evaluating them were discussed in Chapter 4 (e.g. VRIO). For small start-ups the necessary resources and capabilities frequently arise from and draw upon the knowledge and experiences and competences of the people involved (see Illustration 8.1).

Figure 8.1 Entrepreneurial opportunity recognition

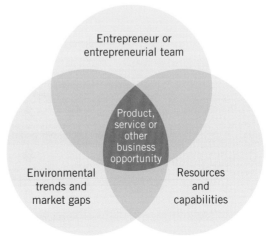

8.2.2 Steps in the entrepreneurial process

The first step of opportunity recognition explained above is likely to be followed by five other steps in the development of an entrepreneurial venture (see Figure 8.2 for an overview of these steps).[5] Before developing a *business plan*, an entrepreneur and start-up can usefully include an initial *feasibility analysis*. This would critically assess an entrepreneurial idea in terms of product or service viability, market opportunity and financing to establish if it can be turned into a business at all. Next, *industry conditions and competitors* are often considered. Competitive positions can be evaluated with the help of five forces and strategic groups analyses (see Chapter 3) and competitors' potential to imitate the venture's resources and capabilities can be examined with the VRIO analysis (see Chapter 4). One of the most important considerations in the entrepreneurial process is to *choose a business model and strategy* (see Chapter 6).[6] A start-up thus needs to consider how to create value for the customers, how to manage revenues and costs, how to generate a margin and whether to build on an established business model or create a new one. In addition to this a distinct competitive strategy position and advantage need to be identified. Thus entrepreneurs will typically have to choose between the generic business strategies of differentiation, cost and focus or any possible hybrid strategy (see Chapter 6). Finally, the new venture's financial strength in terms of *financing and funding* need to be carefully examined.

While these entrepreneurial process steps are important it must be noted that it is an iterative rather than sequential process and thus not necessarily quite as simple as indicated by Figure 8.2. The steps do not necessarily neatly follow on from each other and typically include setbacks along the way. The process thus often involves continuous experimentation and the original business itself may evolve quite radically. This is sometimes referred to as a '*pivoting*', which means making major changes in some dimension of the venture based on market and external feedback.[7] For example, Starbucks started off in 1971 selling espresso makers and coffee beans rather than brewed coffee. It was after a visit to Italy in 1983 that entrepreneur Howard Schultz (former chairman, president and CEO) started to brew and sell Starbucks coffee in the first coffeehouse. At this time, however, it was a European-style coffee house with classical music and waiters, completely different to the Starbucks café it eventually became. The important role of experimentation or pivoting also suggests that many entrepreneurs will fail (see Illustration 8.2).

Figure 8.2 Steps in an entrepreneurial process

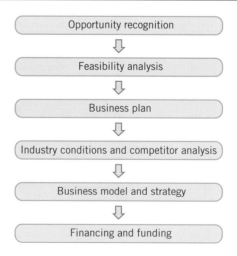

Sources: Adapted from B.R. Barringer and R.D. Ireland, *Entrepreneurship – Successfully launching new ventures*, 4th edn, 2012, Pearson.

Illustration 8.2 Almost Facebook and nearly billionaires

Adam Goldberg and Wayne Ting had the same idea as Facebook's Mark Zuckerberg – and first.

In 2003, Golderg and Ting were engineering students at the prestigious Columbia University, New York. Goldberg was president of his class and hearing lots of complaints about lack of community spirit. Over the summer, he designed a social network for his fellow engineers. Unlike other existing social networks such as MySpace and Friendster, this was the first network which overlaid a virtual community on a real community. Mark Zuckerberg would try the same idea at Harvard the next year.

Three quarters of Columbia's engineering students signed up to the Columbia network over the summer. Goldberg improved the network and relaunched it as CU Community in January 2004, open to all the University's students. Most Columbia students signed up within a month. CU Community was sophisticated for its time. When Facebook launched in February 2004, it only allowed members to 'friend' and 'poke' each other. CU Community also allowed blogging, sharing and cross-profile commenting. Goldberg did not worry about Facebook: 'It was totally different. It had an emphasis on directory functionality, less emphasis on sharing. I didn't think there was much competition. We were the Columbia community, they were Harvard.'

Then in March Facebook launched in other elite American universities such as Yale, Stanford and Columbia. Goldberg, now joined by Wayne Ting, transformed CU Community into Campus Network and launched in elite American universities as well. But Facebook outpaced the new Campus Network. By summer 2004, Facebook had already overtaken Goldberg and Ting's network even at Columbia.

Goldberg and Ting now plunged into the competition full time. They suspended their studies, and moved to Montreal, hiring three other software developers to help them. But resources were tight. Campus Network refused funds from venture capitalists and turned down some large advertisers, including MTV. The two entrepreneurs slept in the office on air mattresses, hiding them away as the three employees turned up for work so they would not know they were homeless.

Nonetheless, Campus Network developed a sophisticated product, with fully-customisable pages, multiple designs and backgrounds. Facebook was simpler. The feel of Campus Network was a bit like Dungeon and Dragons, unlike the clean aesthetics of early Facebook. Ting commented on the logic behind the early development of Campus Network: 'Why would you go to a site that only had poking and a photo [like Facebook then] when you can share photos, share music and share your thoughts on a blog?' Looking back though he observed: 'A good website should have functionalities that 70 or 80% of users want to use. We had functions that only 10% wanted – nobody blogged, nobody even blogs today.'

Campus Network reached 250,000 users by 2005, but at the same point Facebook had reached one million. Goldberg and Ting decided to wind down the network and returned to Columbia as students in the autumn of 2005. The venture had cost them personally something between $100,000 and $200,000, as well as more than a year of their lives. Ting reflected in 2012, when an MBA student at Harvard Business School: 'There are still moments when you feel a deep sense of regret... Could we have succeeded? I think that's a really painful question... There are fleeting moments like that. But I'm much prouder that we took a risk and we learned from it.'

Sources: Slate, 29 September 2010; BBC, 21 December 2010.

Questions

1 What do you learn from the experience of Goldberg and Ting which could be useful to launching a new enterprise?

2 Are there any unmet needs in your community, at college or elsewhere, that could be turned into a business opportunity?

8.2.3 Stages of entrepreneurial growth

Entrepreneurial ventures are often seen as going through four stages of a life cycle (see Figure 8.3). The **entrepreneurial life cycle progresses through start-up, growth, maturity and exit.** Of course, most ventures do not make it through all the stages – the estimated failure rate of new businesses in their first year is more than one-fifth, with two-thirds going out of business within six years.[8] However, each of these four stages raises key questions for entrepreneurs:

- *Start-up.* There are many challenges at this stage, but one key question with implications for both survival and growth is sources of capital. Loans from family and friends are common sources of funds, but these are typically limited. Bank loans and credit cards can provide funding too, and there is often government funding especially for new technologies or economically disadvantaged social groups. *Venture capitalists* are specialised investors in new ventures. Venture capitalist backing has been shown to significantly increase the chances of a venture's success, but they typically accept only about one in 400 propositions put to them.

- *Growth.* A key challenge for growth is management. Entrepreneurs have to be ready to move from 'doing' to 'managing'. Typically this transition occurs as the venture grows beyond about 20 employees. Many entrepreneurs make poor managers: if they had wanted to be managers, they would probably be working in a large corporation in the first place. The choice entrepreneurs have to make is whether to rely on their own managerial skills or to bring in professional managers. In 2019, the founder of the shared-workspace giant WeWork, Adam Neuman, was forced to step aside to allow real-estate veteran Sandeep Mathrani to take charge as CEO.

- *Maturity.* The challenge for entrepreneurs at this stage is retaining their enthusiasm and commitment and generating new growth. This is a period when entrepreneurship can change to *intrapreneurship*, the generation of new ventures from inside the organisation. An important option is usually *diversification* into new business areas, a topic dealt with in Chapter 7. Amazon has moved from book-selling to groceries and clothing and further into a platform for other merchants. It is critical to recall the odds on success at this stage as research suggests that many small high-tech firms fail to manage the transition to a second generation of technology, and that it is often better at this point simply to look for exit.[9]

Figure 8.3 Stages of entrepreneurial growth

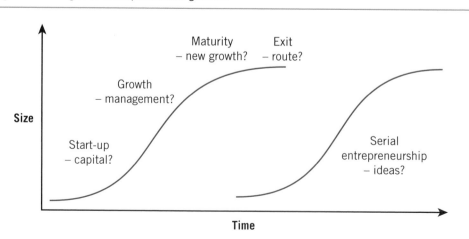

- *Exit.* Exit refers to departure from the venture, either by the founding entrepreneurs, or by the original investors, or both. At the point of exit, entrepreneurs and venture capitalists (early stage investors) will seek to release capital as a reward for their input and risk-taking. In 2014 the founders of the internet-based mobile texting app WhatsApp sold their company to Facebook for $16bn, just four years after starting. It is often said that good entrepreneurs plan for their exit right from start-up, and certainly venture capitalists will insist on this.

8.3 Innovation dilemmas

One important outcome of entrepreneurship is innovation. It is of importance not only for start-ups, but for all firms, including large companies that continuously need to develop new and innovative products and services to compete. Innovation is more complex than just invention. *Invention* involves the conversion of new knowledge into a new product, process or service. Innovation adds an important second stage: putting this new product, process or service into actual commercial use. Strategists involved in innovation have to make choices with regard to three fundamental issues: how far to follow technological opportunity as against market demand; how much to invest in product innovation rather than process innovation and how far to open themselves up to innovative ideas from outside.[10]

8.3.1 Technology push or market pull

People often see innovation as driven by technology. In the pure version of this *technology push* view, it is the new knowledge created by technologists or scientists that pushes the innovation process. Research and development laboratories produce new products, processes or services and then hand them over to the rest of the organisation to manufacture, market and distribute. According to this push perspective, managers should listen primarily to their scientists and technologists, let them follow their hunches and support them with ample resources. Generous R&D budgets are crucial to making innovation happen.

An alternative approach to innovation is *market pull.* Market pull reflects a view of innovation that goes beyond invention and sees the importance of actual use. In many sectors users, not producers, are common sources of important innovations. In designing their innovation strategies, therefore, organisations should listen in the first place to users rather than their own scientists and technologists. Here so-called *lead users* can be important.[11] In medical surgery, top surgeons often adapt existing surgical instruments in order to carry out new types of operation. In extreme sports such as snowboarding or windsurfing, it is leading sportspeople who make the improvements necessary for greater performance. In this view, then, it is the pull of market experts that is responsible for innovation. Managers need to build close relationships with lead users such as the best surgeons or sporting champions.

Technology push and market pull are best seen as extreme views, therefore helping to focus attention on a fundamental choice: how much to rely on science and technology as sources of innovation, rather than what people are actually doing in the marketplace. The key is to manage the balance actively. For a stagnant organisation looking for radical innovation, it might be worth redeploying effort from whichever model currently predominates: the technology push organisation should use more market pull; the market pull organisation should invest more in fundamental research.

8.3.2 Product or process innovation

Just as managers must manage the balance between technology and market pull, so must they determine the relative emphasis to place on product or process innovation. *Product innovation* relates to the final product (or service) to be sold, especially with regard to its features; *process innovation* relates to the way in which this product is produced and distributed, especially with regard to improvements in cost or reliability. Some firms specialise more in product innovation, others more in process innovation. For example, in computers, Apple has generally concentrated its efforts on designing attractive product features (for instance, the iPad tablet), while Dell has innovated in terms of efficient processes, for instance direct sales and build-to-order.

The relative importance of product innovation and process innovation typically changes as industries evolve over time.[12] Usually the first stages of an industry are dominated by product innovation based on new features. Thus the early history of the automobile was dominated by competition as to whether cars should be fuelled by steam, electricity or petrol.[13] Industries eventually coalesce around a *dominant design*, the standard configuration of basic features: after Henry Ford's 1908 Model T, the dominant design for cars was petrol-driven. Once such a dominant design is established, innovation switches to process innovation, as competition shifts to producing the dominant design as efficiently as possible. Henry Ford's great process innovation was the moving assembly line, introduced in 1913. Ford's success was based not only on a great product, the Model T, but the efficiency of his processes, based on the assembly line.

Figure 8.4 provides a general model of the relationship between product and process innovation over time. The model has several strategic implications:

- *New developing industries* typically favour product innovation, as competition is still around defining the basic features of the product or service.

- *Maturing industries* typically favour process innovation, as competition shifts towards efficient production of a dominant design of product or service.

Figure 8.4 Product and process innovation

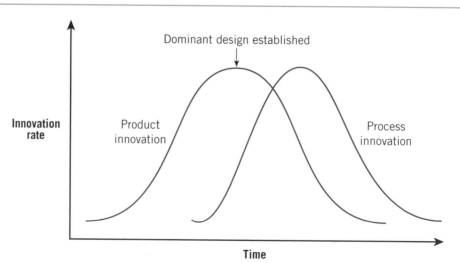

Sources: Adapted from J. Abernathy and W. Utterback, 'A dynamic model of process and product innovation', *Omega*, vol. 3, no. 6 (1975), pp. 639–56.

- *Small new entrants* typically have the greatest opportunity when dominant designs are either not yet established or beginning to collapse. Thus, in the early stages of the automobile industry, before Ford's Model T, there were more than a hundred mostly small competitors, each with its own combination of product features. The recent challenge to the petrol-based dominant design has provided opportunities to entrepreneurial companies such as the Californian start-up Tesla Motors.

- *Large incumbent firms* typically have the advantage during periods of dominant design stability, when scale economies and the ability to roll out process innovations matter most. With the success of the Model T and the assembly line, by the 1930s there were just four large American automobile manufacturers, namely Ford, General Motors, Chrysler and American Motors, all producing very similar kinds of cars.

8.3.3 Open or closed innovation

The traditional approach to innovation has been to rely on the organisation's own internal resources – its laboratories and marketing departments. Innovation in this approach is secretive, anxious to protect intellectual property and avoid competitors free-riding on ideas. This 'closed' model of innovation contrasts with the newer 'open model' of innovation.[14] **Open innovation involves the deliberate import and export of knowledge by an organisation in order to accelerate and enhance its innovation.** The motivating idea of open innovation is that exchanging ideas openly is likely to produce better products more quickly than the internal, closed approach.[15]

Open innovation is widely adopted. For example, technology giant IBM has established a network of 10 'collaboratories' with other companies and universities, in countries ranging from Switzerland to Saudi Arabia. *Crowdsourcing* is an increasingly popular form of open innovation and means that a company or organisation broadcasts a specific problem to a crowd of individuals or teams, often in tournaments with prizes awarded to the best solution.[16] Companies such as Procter & Gamble, Eli Lilly and Dow Chemicals use the network company Inno-Centive to set innovation 'challenges' (or problems) in open competition over the internet.

Open innovation also often involves high-technology firms nurturing innovation by independent companies around their basic technological *platforms*.[17] The communities of companies that form around such platforms are referred to as ecosystems, with the same kind of mutual dependence as in the ecosystems of nature. **An ecosystem consists of a group of mutually dependent and collaborative partners that need to interact to create value for all.** Rather than building on traditional bilateral collaborations, ecosystems build a platform that connects communities of suppliers, software developers, agents, distributors, franchisees, technology entrepreneurs and makers of complementary products.[18] For example, Alibaba, Facebook and Microsoft nurture various ecosystems around their platforms. Most fundamentally the ecosystem partnership includes a platform innovator, a set of complementors, suppliers and customers that create value together rather than doing so independently. However, while they share the interest to grow the whole market around the platform, they compete over how the value is distributed among the various ecosystem participants. Apple has paid out over $100bn to app developers in its ecosystem, but they also charge a 30 per cent fee based on the app sales.[19] See Illustration 8.3 for an overview of ARM's open innovation ecosystem.

The balance between open and closed innovation depends on three key factors:

- *Competitive rivalry.* In highly rivalrous industries, partners are liable to behave opportunistically and steal innovations. Closed innovation is better where such rivalrous behaviours can be anticipated.

Illustration 8.3 ARM's extensive ecosystem

Ecosystems including the alignment of hundreds of partners is central for platform technology companies

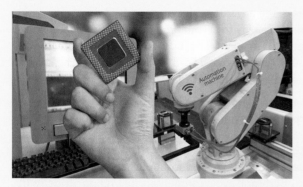

Source: Zapp2Photo/Shutterstock

In the world of connected devices including smartphones, tablets, wearables and storage, British-based and Japanese SoftBank-owned semiconductor company ARM Holdings has an 85–90 per cent market share worldwide. Their success is often explained by their extensive ecosystem. It is central for their business model of only creating and developing its core microprocessor chips and then licensing the technology as intellectual property (IP) for open innovation rather than manufacturing and selling its own set of final products.

ARM designs core processors that read in instructions to perform specific actions that make smartphones, tablets, etc., function. These instructions are linked together in a way that in real time they make up our smartphone or tablet experience; everything we do on these and other devices must be processed by the processor. Whenever we open an app or folder, write a text message or watch a video it requires a core processor.

ARM is a design company that creates the process architecture and an instruction set (a basic set of capabilities and features a processor makes available to software applications). They then license this to partner companies that improve it and pair it with whatever hardware and software seems appropriate (e.g. wireless connectivity, graphics, USB connections and various connected devices or applications).

Although ARM only has 6,000 employees, its partner ecosystem includes over 1,000 partners over the entire semiconductor value chain from device chip design to application software providers (see exhibit below). First, the ARM architecture is only a basic building block including the overall 'intelligence' of a device and thus needs to be designed for any larger system. For example, Apple has a large staff of engineers working on ARM processors and, similarly, Qualcomm and Texas Instruments design larger systems based on ARM. They pair the ARM architecture with a variety of independent 'IP block' suppliers, which make up a central part of the ecosystem. These suppliers develop pre-defined modules supporting specific functions and then re-sell this as a 'system-on-a-chip' for smartphones and tablets. Next there are other partners that conduct the actual manufacturing of the chips, like Samsung. Towards the end of the value chain there are OEM device producers and distributors like Apple and Huawei and, finally, application software companies that develop applications that run on the devices

- *One-shot innovation.* Opportunistic behaviour is more likely where innovation involves a major shift in technology, likely to put winners substantially ahead and losers permanently behind. Open innovation works best where innovation is more continuous, so encouraging more reciprocal behaviour over time.

- *Tight-linked innovation.* Where technologies are complex and tightly interlinked, open innovation risks introducing damagingly inconsistent elements, with knock-on effects throughout the product range. Apple, with its smoothly integrated range of products from computers to phones, has therefore tended to prefer closed innovation in order to protect the quality of the user experience.

8.4 Innovation diffusion

Success relies on the diffusion of innovations after they have been introduced.[20] **Diffusion is the process by which innovations spread among users.** Since innovation is typically expensive, its commercial attractiveness can hinge on the pace – extent and speed – at which the market (e.g. Facebook, Skype). Besides these ecosystem partners there are distributors that provide access to ARM technology for independent software developers, training partners that deliver training information. Some companies, like Samsung and Apple, participate in several parts of ARM's ecosystem.

It's not only the ARM technology itself that attracts ecosystem partners, but their comprehensive web-based developer site including technical support and consultancy, partner forums and blogs, documentations, textbooks, education and research support. ARM not only profits from licensing its chips IP to various ecosystem actors, but also through royalty on every product unit that contains its IP. In brief, both ARM and all the ecosystem participants benefit from a steadily growing ARM ecosystem and its output.

Simplified overview of ARM's ecosystem

ARM	ARM Ecosystem Partners				
Chip Architecture	Chip designers	IP block suppliers	Chip manufacturers	OEM device companies & distributors	Application software companies
ARM processor cores	ARM processor designed into operating systems (e.g. Apple) and larger systems to be used in devices (e.g. Qualcomm, Broadcom, Texas Instruments)	Pre-defined modules supporting specific functions (e.g. camera functions, video processing, blue tooth communication)	Chip manufacturing (e.g. Samsung, Taiwan Semiconductor Manufacturing Company)	Smartphones, tablets, wearables, storage, etc.(e.g. Apple, Huawei, Samsung)	End-user applications: smart phone user interfaces, games, apps, etc. (e.g. Facebook, Skype, Google)

Sources: P.J. Williamson and A. De Meyer, 'Ecosystem advantage: how to successfully harness the power of partners', *California Management Review*, vol. 55, no. 1, Autumn 2012; H. Shaughnessy, 'Intel vs. ARM: battle of the business model', *Forbes*, 24 February 2012; M. Smith, 'What is an ARM processor? Everything you need to know', makeuseof.com, 4 December 2012; ARM.com, 2018; H. Glimstedt, 'Re-thinking Apple's entry and platform leadership in smartphones', mimeo, Stockholm School of Economics, 2019.

Questions

1 How can ARM attract and manage so many ecosystem partners?

2 Can you identify other technology platform companies and their ecosystem partners?

adopts new products and services. This pace of diffusion is something managers can influence from both the supply and demand sides, and which they can also model using the S-curve.

8.4.1 The pace of diffusion

The pace of diffusion can vary widely according to the nature of the products concerned. It took 28 years for the television to reach 50 per cent of ownership and use in the USA; the mobile phone only half that time. The pace of diffusion is influenced by a combination of supply-side and demand-side factors. On the *supply side*, pace is determined by product features such as:

- *Degree of improvement* in performance above current products (from a customer's perspective) that provides incentive to change. For example, 4G mobile phones did not first provide sufficient performance improvement to prompt rapid switch in many markets. Managers need to make sure innovation benefits sufficiently exceed development costs.

- *Compatibility* with other factors: for example HDTV becomes more attractive as the broadcasting networks change their programmes to that format. Managers and entrepreneurs therefore need to ensure appropriate complementary products and services are in place.

- *Complexity*, either in the product itself or in the marketing methods being used to commercialise the product: unduly complex pricing structures, as with many financial service products such as pensions, discourage consumer adoption. Simple pricing structures typically accelerate adoptions.

- *Experimentation* – the ability to test products before commitment to a final decision – either directly or through the availability of information about the experience of other customers. Free initial trial periods are often used to encourage diffusion.

On the *demand side*, simple affordability is of course key. Beyond this, there are three further factors that tend to drive the pace of diffusion:

- *Market awareness*. Many potentially successful products have failed through lack of consumer awareness – particularly when the promotional effort of the innovator has been confined to 'push' promotion to its intermediaries (e.g. distributors).

- *Network effects* refer to the way that demand growth for some products accelerates as more people adopt the product or service. Once a critical mass of users has adopted it, it becomes of much greater benefit, or even necessary, for others to adopt it too. With 1.75 billion users, Facebook became the obligatory social network for many members of society.

- *Customer propensity to adopt*: the distribution of potential customers from early-adopter groups (keen to adopt first) through to laggards (typically indifferent to innovations). Innovations are often targeted initially at early-adopter groups – typically the young and the wealthy – in order to build the critical mass that will encourage more laggardly groups – the poorer and older – to join the bandwagon.

8.4.2 The diffusion S-curve

The pace of diffusion is typically not steady. Successful innovations often diffuse according to a broad *S-curve* pattern.[21] The shape of the S-curve reflects a process of initial slow adoption of innovation, followed by a rapid acceleration in diffusion, leading to a plateau representing the limit to demand (Figure 8.5). The height of the S-curve shows the extent of diffusion; the shape of the S-curve shows the speed.

Figure 8.5 The diffusion S-curve

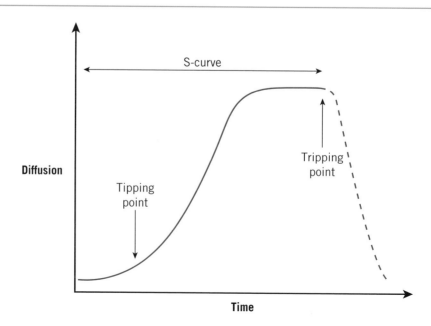

Diffusion rarely follows exactly this pattern, but nonetheless the S-curve can help managers and entrepreneurs anticipate forthcoming issues. In particular, the S-curve points to four likely decision points:

- *Timing of the 'tipping point'.* Demand for a successful new product or service may initially be slow but then reaches a *tipping point* when it explodes onto a rapid upwards path of growth.[22] A tipping point is where demand for a product or service suddenly takes off, with explosive growth. Tipping points are particularly explosive where there are strong *network effects*: in other words, where the value of a product or service is increased the more people in a network use them.

- *Timing of the plateau.* The S-curve also alerts managers to a likely eventual slowdown in demand growth. Again, it is tempting to extrapolate existing growth rates forwards, especially when they are highly satisfactory. But heavy investment immediately before growth turns down is likely to leave firms with over-capacity and carrying extra costs in a period of industry shake-out.

- *Extent of diffusion.* The S-curve does not necessarily lead to one hundred per cent diffusion among potential users. Most innovations fail to displace previous generation products and services altogether. For example, some peoples still prefer traditional LPs for their music. A critical issue for managers then is to estimate the final ceiling on diffusion.

- *Timing of the 'tripping point'.* The tripping point is the opposite of the tipping point, referring to when – sometimes – demand suddenly collapses.[23] This is what happened to social networking site Myspace, as American and European users defected to Facebook. Of course, decline is often more gradual, but the tripping point warns managers that a small dip in sales could presage a more rapid collapse.

To summarise, the S-curve is a useful concept to help managers and entrepreneurs avoid simply extrapolating next year's sales from last year's sales. However, the tripping point also underlines the fact that innovations do not follow an inevitable process, and their diffusion patterns can be interrupted or reversed at any point.[24]

8.5 Innovators and imitators

A key choice for managers is whether to lead or to follow in innovation. First-movers get the easy sales of early fast growth and can establish a dominant position. There are plenty of examples of first-movers who have built enduring positions on the basis of innovation leadership: Coca-Cola in drinks and Hoover in vacuum cleaners are powerful century-old examples. On the other hand, many first-movers fail. Even the powerful Microsoft failed with its first tablet launched in 2001. Nine years later, Apple swept the market with its iPad tablet.

8.5.1 First-mover advantages and disadvantages

A **first-mover advantage** **exists where an organisation is better off than its competitors as a result of being first to market with a new product, process or service.** Fundamentally, the first-mover is a monopolist, theoretically able to charge customers high prices without fear of immediate undercutting by competitors. In practice, however, innovators often prefer to sacrifice profit margins for sales growth and, besides, monopoly is usually temporary. There are six potentially more robust first-mover advantages:[25]

- *Network effects* suggest that a customer of a product or service has a positive effect on the value of that for other customers and if they are present and captured by an individual firm it may be very difficult, if not impossible, for late entrants to catch up and build their own network of customers.
- *Experience curve benefits* accrue to first-movers, as their rapid accumulation of experience with the innovation gives them greater expertise than late entrants still relatively unfamiliar with the new product, process or service.
- *Scale benefits* are typically enjoyed by first-movers, as they establish earlier than competitors the volumes necessary for mass production and bulk purchasing, for example.
- *Pre-emption of scarce resources* is an opportunity for first-movers, as late-movers will not have the same access to key raw materials, skilled labour or components, and will have to pay dearly for them.
- *Reputation* can be enhanced by being first, especially since consumers have little 'mind-space' to recognise new brands once a dominant brand has been established in the market.
- *Buyer switching costs* can be exploited by first-movers, by locking in their customers with privileged or sticky relationships that later challengers can only break with difficulty. Switching costs can be increased by establishing and exploiting a *technological standard.*

But the experience of Microsoft with its tablet computer shows that first-mover advantages are not necessarily overwhelming. Late-movers have two principal potential advantages:[26]

- *Free-riding.* Late-movers can imitate technological and other innovation at less expense than originally incurred by the pioneers. Research suggests that the costs of imitation are only 65 per cent of the cost of innovation.[27]
- *Learning.* Late-movers can observe what worked well and what did not work well for innovators. They may not make so many mistakes and be able to get it right first time.

Given the potential advantages of late-movers, managers and entrepreneurs face a hard choice between striving to be first or coming in later. The most appropriate response to innovation, especially radical innovation, is often not to be a first-mover, but to be a *'fast second'.*[28] A fast second strategy involves being one of the first to imitate the original innovator and thus building an 'early mover advantage'. Thus fast second companies may not literally be the second company into the market, but they dominate the second generation of competitors. For example, the French Bookeen company pioneered the e-book market in the early 2000s, but was soon followed by Amazon's Kindle.[29]

Three factors need to be considered in choosing between innovating and imitating:

- *Capacity for profit capture:* the importance of innovators to capture for themselves the profits of their innovations. This may be challenging if the innovation is *easy to replicate* and if *intellectual property rights* are weak, for example where patents are hard to define or defend.[30]
- *Complementary assets:* the possession of assets or resources necessary to scale up the production and marketing of the innovation.[31] For organisations wishing to remain independent and to exploit their innovations themselves, there is little point in investing heavily to be first-mover in the absence of the necessary complementary assets.
- *Fast-moving arenas:* where markets or technologies are moving very fast and especially where both are highly dynamic, first-movers are unlikely to establish a durable advantage.

8.5.2 The incumbent's response

Definitions of entrepreneurship often emphasise pursuing opportunities and developing innovations without immediately being constrained by the resources under present control. This refers to the fact that incumbent organisations and companies mostly are constrained by their existing resources, capabilities, activities and vested interests. This suggests that for established companies in a market innovation can be challenging and innovations from others can be a threat. Kodak's dominance of the photographic film market was made nearly worthless by the sudden rise of digital photography.

The problem for incumbents can be twofold.[32] First, managers can become too attached to existing assets and skills: understandably, as these are what their careers have been built on. Second, relationships between incumbent organisations and their customers can become too close. Existing customers typically prefer incremental improvements to current technologies, and are unable to imagine completely new technologies. Incumbents are reluctant to 'cannibalise' their existing business by introducing something radically different. After all, as in Figure 8.6, incumbents usually have some scope for improving their existing technology, along the steady upwards trajectory described as Technology 1. Innovations on this trajectory are termed 'sustaining innovations', because they at least allow the existing technology to meet existing customer expectations.

The challenge for incumbents, however, is disruptive innovation. A **disruptive innovation creates substantial growth by offering a new performance trajectory that, even if initially inferior to the performance of existing technologies, has the potential to become markedly superior.** This superior performance can produce spectacular growth, either by creating new sets of customers or by undercutting the cost base of rival existing business models. Such disruptive innovation involves the shift from Technology 1 in Figure 8.6 to Technology 2. Disruptive innovations are hard for incumbents to respond to because poor performance in the early days is likely to upset existing customer relationships and because they typically

Figure 8.6 Disruptive innovation

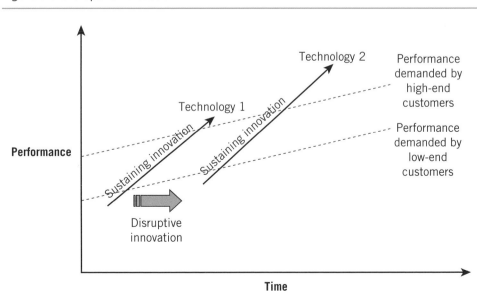

involve changing their whole business model (see Chapter 7). Thus, in the music industry, the major record companies with traditional CDs first responded to online music simply by prosecuting new distribution forms such as Napster, but today streaming services such as Spotify and Apple Music dominate.

Sometimes, however, incumbents do respond. IBM has moved from mechanical tabulators at the beginning of the twentieth century to Artificial Intelligence this century. There are three different approaches to encouraging incumbent innovation and responsiveness:

- *Develop a portfolio of real options.* Real options are limited investments that keep opportunities open for the future. Establishing an R&D team in a speculative new technology or acquiring a small start-up in a nascent market would both be examples of real options, each giving the potential to scale up fast should the opportunity turn out to be substantial.[33]

- *Corporate venturing.* New ventures, especially when undertaken from a real options perspective, may need protection from the usual systems and disciplines of a core business. For this reason, large incumbent organisations often establish relatively autonomous 'new venture units', which can nurture new ideas or invest externally and acquire novel and untried businesses with a longer-term view.[34] BMW, for example, set up a completely separate business unit to develop its first mass-produced electric car, BMW i.

- *Intrapreneurship.* This approach rather emphasises the individuals' ability to perform entrepreneurial activities within a large organisation.[35] Companies can thus encourage employees throughout the organisation to be creative and develop entrepreneurial ideas as part of their regular job. IBM has various initiatives to encourage intrapreneurship and innovation, such as 'Intrapreneurship@IBM'.

Summary

- *Opportunity recognition* involves three important and interdependent elements: the *environment,* the *entrepreneur or entrepreneurial team* and *resources and capabilities.*

- The *entrepreneurship process* typically involves a *business plan*, a *feasibility analysis*, *industry conditions and competitor analysis*, *business model and strategy choice* and *financing and funding.*

- Strategists face three fundamental innovation dilemmas: relative emphasis to put on *technology push* or *market pull*; whether to focus on *product* or *process innovation*; and finally, how much to rely on 'open innovation' and related *ecosystems* or more 'closed innovation'.

- Innovations often diffuse according to *an S-curve model* in which slow start-up is followed by accelerating growth (the 'tipping point') and finally a flattening of demand (and a potential 'tripping point').

- Innovators can capture *first-mover advantages,* but 'fast second' strategies are often more attractive.

- Established incumbents' businesses should beware *disruptive innovations*. Incumbents can stave off inertia by developing *portfolios of real options*, by organising autonomous *new venture units* or by encouraging 'intrapreneurship'.

Recommended key reading

- B.R. Barringer and R.D. Ireland, *Entrepreneurship – Successfully launching new ventures,* 5th edn, Pearson, 2016, provides details of all entrepreneurial process steps. P. Trott, *Innovation Management and New Product Development*, 6th edn, Financial Times Prentice Hall, 2017, provides a comprehensive overview of innovation strategy issues. P.A. Wickham, *Strategic Entrepreneurship,* 5th edn, Prentice Hall, 2013, is a standard European text with regard to entrepreneurial strategy.

References

1. For a good overview of contemporary entrepreneurship theory see S.A. Shane, *A General Theory of Entrepreneurship: The individual-opportunity nexus*, Edward Elgar Publishing, 2000.
2. This definition adapts, in order to include the public sector, the definition in P. Trott, *Innovation Management and New Product Development*, 5th edn, Financial Times Prentice Hall, 2011.
3. On strategic entrepreneurship, see D.F. Kuratko and D.B. Audretsch, 'Strategic entrepreneurship: exploring different perspectives of an emerging concept', *Entrepreneurship Theory and Practice,* vol. 33, no. 1 (2009), pp. 1–17.
4. On opportunity recognition and identification, see A. Ardichvili, R. Cardozo and S. Ray, 'A theory of entrepreneurial opportunity identification and development', *Journal of Business Venturing*, vol. 18, no. 1 (2003), pp. 105–23.
5. For an excellent textbook that provides details of all the steps in the entrepreneurial process see B.R. Barringer and R.D. Ireland, *Entrepreneurship – Successfully launching new ventures*, 4th edn, Pearson, 2012.
6. Please note that business models are discussed in Chapter 6.
7. For a discussion about lean start-ups and pivoting, see S. Blank, 'Why the lean start-up changes everything', *Harvard Business Review*, vol. 91, no. 5 (2013), pp. 63–72.
8. D. Flynn and A. Forman, 'Life cycles of new venture organizations: different factors affecting performance', *Journal of Developmental Entrepreneurship,* vol. 6, no. 1 (2001), pp. 41–58.
9. For a detailed account of Cisco's policy of taking over high-technology firms, see D. Mayer and M. Kenney, 'Economic action does not take place in a vacuum: understanding Cisco's acquisition and development strategy', *Industry and Innovation,* vol. 11, no. 4 (2004), pp. 293–325.
10. A good discussion of the theories underpinning these dilemmas is in R. Rothwell, 'Successful industrial innovation: critical factors for the 1990s', *R&D Management*, vol. 22, no. 3 (1992), pp. 221–39.
11. E. von Hippel, *Democratizing Innovation*, MIT Press, 2005; Y.M. Antorini, A. Muniz and T. Askildsen, 'Collaborating with customer communities: lessons from the Lego Group', *MIT Sloan Management Review*, vol. 53, no. 3 (2012), pp. 73–9.
12. J. Abernathy and W. Utterback, 'A dynamic model of process and product innovation', *Omega,* vol. 3, no. 6 (1975), pp. l42–60.
13. P. Anderson and M.L. Tushman, 'Technological discontinuities and dominant designs: a cyclical model of technological change', *Administrative Science Quarterly*, vol. 35 (1990), pp. 604–33.
14. O. Gasman, E. Enkel and H. Chesbrough, 'The future of open innovation', *R&D Management*, vol. 38, no. 1 (2010), pp. 1–9.
15. For an overview of research on open innovation see E.K.R.E. Huizingh, 'Open innovation: state of the art and future perspectives', *Technovation*, vol. 3, no. 1 (2011), pp. 2–9.
16. L.B. Jeppesen and K. Lakhani, 'Marginality and problem solving: effectiveness in broadcast search', *Organization Science*, vol. 21, no. 5 (2010), pp. 1016–33.
17. For platform strategies see 'Pipelines, platforms, and the new rules of strategy', *Harvard Business Review*, vol. 94, no. 4 (2016), pp. 54–62.
18. For a discussion about innovation strategy and ecosystems, see R. Adner, 'Match your innovation strategy to your innovation ecosystem', *Harvard Business Review*, vol. 84, no. 4 (2006), pp. 98–107.
19. For a discussion of how large corporations can tap into entrepreneurial innovation in start-ups see T. Weiblen and H.W. Chesbrough, 'Engaging with startups to enhance corporate innovation', *California Management Review*, vol. 57, no. 2 (2015), pp. 66–90.
20. Diffusion is discussed in J. Cummings and J. Doh, 'Identifying who matters: mapping key players in multiple environments', *California Management Review,* vol. 42, no. 2 (2000), pp. 83–104.
21. J. Nichols and S. Roslow, 'The S-curve: an aid to strategic marketing', *The Journal of Consumer Marketing*, vol. 3, no. 2 (1986), pp. 53–64.
22. M. Gladwell, *The Tipping Point*, Abacus, 2000.

23. S. Brown, 'The tripping point', *Marketing Research*, vol. 17, no. 1 (2005), pp. 8–13.

24. For a discussion of possibilities to 'jump' the S curve, see P. Nunes and T. Breene, 'Reinvent your business before it's too late', *Harvard Business Review*, vol. 89, no. 1/2 (2011), pp. 80–87.

25. C. Markides and P. Geroski, *Fast Second: How Smart Companies Bypass Radical Innovation to Enter and Dominate New Markets*, Jossey-Bass, 2005.

26. F. Suarez and G. Lanzolla, 'The half-truth of first-mover advantage', *Harvard Business Review*, vol. 83, no. 4 (2005), pp. 121–7.

27. Schnaars S P (1994) *Managing Imitation Strategies – How Later Entrants Seize Markets form Pioneers,* New York: The Free Press.

28. See the discussion of B. Buisson and P. Silberzahn, 'Blue Ocean or fast-second innovation?', *International Journal of Innovation Management*, vol. 14, no. 3 (2010), pp. 359–78.

29. J. Shamsie, C. Phelps and J. Kuperman, 'Better late than never: a study of late entrants in household electrical equipment', *Strategic Management Journal*, vol. 25, no. 1 (2004), pp. 69–84.

30. David Teece refers to the capacity to capture profits as 'the appropriability regime': see D. Teece, *Managing Intellectual Capital*, Oxford University Press, 2000.

31. D. Teece, *Managing Intellectual Capital*, Oxford University Press, 2000.

32. See C.M. Christensen, M.E. Raynor and R. McDonald, 'What is disruptive innovation', *Harvard Business Review*, vol. 93, no. 12 (2015), pp. 44–53.

33. R. Ragozzino, J.J. Reuer and L. Trigeorgis, 'Real options in strategy and finance: current gaps and future linkages', *Academy of Management Perspectives,* vol. 30, no. 4, (2016), pp. 428–40.

34. C. Christensen and M.E. Raynor, *The Innovator's Solution*, Harvard Business School Press, 2003.

35. G. Pinchot, *Intrapreneuring*, London, Macmillan (1985) and P.H. Phan et al., 'Corporate entrepreneurship: current research and future directions', *Journal of Business Venturing*, vol. 24, no. 3 (2009), pp. 197–205.

Case example

Rovio's Angry Birds: The evolution of a global entertainment empire

Daryl Chapman (Metropolia Business School)
Revision by Sandra Lusmägi (Metropolia Business School)

Introduction

Rovio Entertainment Ltd are pioneers in mobile games and are most famous for their Angry Birds characters. In the game, players use a slingshot to catapult colourful birds at their enemies (the egg-stealing pigs), with the goal of destroying them. The game stormed to the top of the charts and became the largest mobile app success the world has ever seen with more than 3 billion downloads globally. Over the years, Rovio has stood firmly behind their intellectual property (IP) and determination to build a lasting brand, despite speculation by critics that Angry Birds were just a one-hit wonder and fears they can lose their fans as quickly as they came due to the short attention span of consumers. The founders, however, have said that the game was always the first step of the vision to build a global entertainment empire that they methodically set out to create.

The early days

The game that took Rovio to the top in the entire mobile gaming industry was neither the company's first game nor was it their first year of operation. The Finnish entrepreneurial venture started in 2003 when the two cousins Mikael Hed and Niklas Hed decided to create their own original intellectual property to take to the global market instead of creating and selling games for other companies. They initially thought they would have to do 10 to 15 titles to get the right one, but the team developed 51 games before Angry Birds. Angry Birds was an overnight success, but it took eight years to build a game for iPhone and abandon other platforms. Conquering the App Store was an integral part of the plan to save the company that was on the brink of bankruptcy in 2009 when the game was released. The App Store enabled worldwide distribution. The cousins' aim was to focus on local markets to begin with rather than the most lucrative English-speaking markets. The game became number one in smaller markets: Finland, Sweden, Denmark, Greece and the Czech Republic before getting any traction in the UK and USA. When it got on the front page of the UK App Store in 2010 it rapidly became the number one app in the US App Store. By 2011, Angry Birds and its various branded spin-offs had earned €50m, on the back of a game which originally cost €100,000 to develop. Forty per cent of that income stemmed from activities not related to the game – from the toys and other licensing deals. As shown in Figure 1, revenues continued to grow considerably, not least thanks to a booming merchandise business.

The evolution of the mobile games industry

The beginning of the mobile games industry can be traced back to 1997, when the iconic Finnish company Nokia introduced the game Snake as a built-in feature to their mobile phones. When Apple introduced the iPhone in 2007, it opened a whole new market for mobile games developers, and the Hed cousins seized that opportunity. Rovio had designed an innovative game based on touch-screen technology and an innovative business model with global distribution through the App Store. In 2011, the American video games company Electronic Arts (EA) boldly estimated that the mobile gaming business would be worth $4.5bn in 2013. Rovio thought that they were in a position to take a slice of that, but it also wanted much more. 'I am convinced that this is not just one game with a slingshot,' said Mikael Hed who was the CEO of the company.[1] In retrospect, the mobile games industry grew to $12.3bn[2] in 2013, surpassing even the most optimistic estimations and easily outpacing all other games segments.

After the massive success with the first Angry Birds game, they launched 14 different Angry Birds themed games, including a racing game Angry Birds Go!, two Star Wars themed Angry Birds puzzle games and then an official sequel, Angry Birds 2. But the newly established mobile gaming industry was changing. By 2013, freemium became the dominant business model. It implies that apps are free to download, and revenues are instead generated by offering additional features in the app that users can buy. Games such as Candy Crush and Clash of Clans exceeded the popularity of Angry Birds and Rovio thus had to tackle the new business model. They had used a pay-to-download game, meaning the game was purchased with a one-time payment and could then be played uninterrupted by ads or waiting times. Rovio then

Figure 1 Rovio Entertainment revenue and operating profit in millions euros

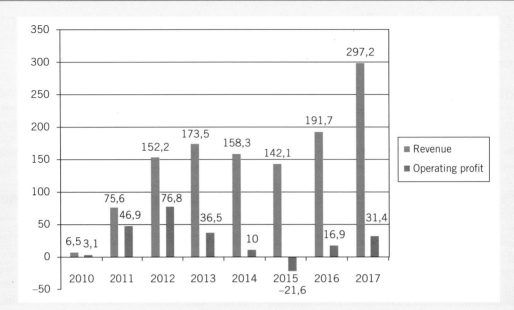

committed to changing their business model to a free-mium model which meant completely redesigning the way they monetised from the games.

However, the massive launch of Angry Birds 2 in 2015 did not meet the company's expectations, but they did not give up and continued to improve the game with new features and it eventually paid off – it is now their most profitable game.

The new Disney?

Like Disney with Mickey Mouse, Rovio saw the potential of transferring its powerful brand to other products. The company has been following in the footsteps of the world's largest entertainment company on the road to building an entertainment empire for the digital age and becoming Disney 2.0. Rovio started building an integrated entertainment franchise where merchandising, activity parks, games, movies, TV, cartoons and comics all came together. Peter Vesterbacka, who has been involved with Rovio since the early days, confidently said in 2015 that Angry Birds will be bigger than Mickey Mouse. Like many other brands, Rovio has set its sights on the vast Chinese market. It opened its first international office in Shanghai in 2011 and introduced localised gaming content and merchandise. 'We want to be more Chinese than the Chinese. We want to be the leading Chinese brand,' Vesterbacka said.[3] Indeed, Angry Birds has become one of the world's strongest brands – 93 per cent of Chinese people know Angry Birds, and the global brand awareness is 97 per cent according to the company's statements.[4]

Rovio has partnered with hundreds of brands globally that license the Angry Birds brand in exchange for royalty fees. The colourful birds were soon on T-shirts, toys, key chains, notebooks, soft drinks and many other consumer products. Rovio's merchandising business is strongly linked to the games; if they become less popular, so will the products that license the brand. At the same time of changing to freemium, Rovio ventured into several new industries – it launched its own video distribution business, started publishing books and opening activity parks.

Rovio also announced its first Hollywood feature movie, having faith in the loyalty of its old fans and in the ability to attract new ones. The movie was self-financed with a budget of €175m, making it the most expensive Finnish movie ever made. Rovio retained creative control of the movie, but hired Sony Pictures Imageworks to produce it, utilising its global marketing and distribution skills. The movie was a significant investment to keep up the momentum of the brand and to boost the licensing and merchandising business through new partnership deals. Indeed, it made deals with big household names, such as the toy makers Lego, Hasbro and the Chinese e-commerce giant Alibaba.

World domination is a tricky business

Despite the seemingly overnight success of the mobile game, creating memorable characters that the world embraced, it was not all smooth sailing for the company. As the company grew in four years from a team of 40 to over 800 employees, the company lost the agility of a start-up company and the organisational culture suffered from the rapid growth. Rovio had to cut 130 jobs in 2014, which was followed by another dramatic downsizing the year after, by eliminating another 260 jobs, more than a third of its workforce. The brain drain continued as many of those who helped build the original success of Rovio left and ventured out to start their own gaming companies. Some of the former managers opened up to the Finnish media to point out the lack of shared strategic vision from the family-owned business, where each member seemed to have a different idea of the kind of company they are building.[5]

Majority owner and chairman of the company Kaj Hed, father to Niklas Hed, explained that after extensive layoffs and financial struggles, Rovio would be restructuring its business operations and going back to its entrepreneurial roots. Part of the restructuring plans was to spin off its books and education businesses and licensing out their activity parks from 2016 onwards. Rovio acknowledged it lost focus and tried to do too many things. After the restructuring, Rovio's operations were divided into two business units: Games and Brand Licensing. Currently the games business is based on two revenue streams: in-game purchases and in-game advertising. A new CEO, Kati Levoranta, was appointed in 2016 and she said it still has the ambition to be a leading entertainment company, with mobile games at its heart.

IPO and future plans

The family-owned business was keeping strong control of its IP and turned down an offer from Zynga, who wanted to buy the company for $2.3bn. Speculations about an initial public offering (IPO) in 2012 had analysts throwing around numbers as high as $9bn.[6] Merchandise sales declined sharply in 2014 and 2015 with great impact on the company's profits (see Figure 1), but the long-awaited Hollywood 3D Angry Birds movie helped Rovio bounce back in 2016. The movie opened at no. 1 in 50 countries around the world, becoming the second highest grossing movie of all time that was based on a video game after earning $352m at the box office. Following the success of the movie, Rovio eventually went public in September 2017, valuing the company at €896m ($1.06bn) with a share price of €11.50. In February 2018, however, Rovio lost half of its market value after warning that revenue and profitability would be significantly below analyst expectations in 2018 (see Figure 2). The CEO Kati Levoranta commented that gaming firms are quite new to the stock market and some volatility is to be expected and instead pointed towards Rovio's new movie and new collaborations.

The Angry Birds 2 movie is released in 2019 and expected to yield further returns from merchandise. Rovio also signed a multi-year shirt sleeve partnership with the English Premier League Club, Everton.[8] The Premier League is the most watched sports league in the world, reaching over 1.5 billion global viewers in more than 200 territories. Together with Rovio's 80 million monthly active users, the Angry Birds' audience can be reached in completely new ways. The partnership allows many new and innovative marketing opportunities in the stadium and in the smartphone space for both companies. Tapping into Everton, Rovio has a multitude of collaboration options for the future, be it Everton-themed plush toys, in-game features or even a standalone Everton game.

Rovio has also spotted the potential to be part of the new booming eSports market with the Everton partnership and made a deal with the National Basketball Association's (NBA) Chicago Bulls: it will install cameras on top of black boards to provide footage from above the basket rim. The new cameras, officially named the 'Angry

Figure 2 Rovio share price development from September 2017 to September 2018[7]

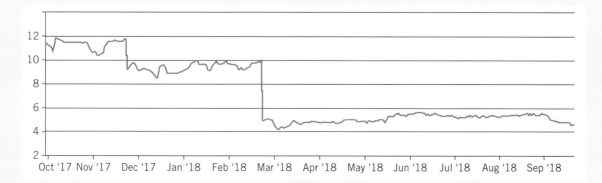

The Angry Birds movie : 'Why are you so mad?'

Source: Collection Christophel/Alamy Stock Photo

Birds Eye View Cam', provide new and exciting ways to experience sports games and are thought to attract the attention of younger audiences. Brand partners hold a key role in the global awareness of the Angry Birds IP. Over the years, Rovio has moved from the quantity of partners to the quality of them. Besides Everton and the Chicago Bulls, Rovio now boasts international partnerships with the likes of Nasa, Chupa Chups, Crocs, Pez, McDonald's and Star Wars.

In 2018 the global mobile games market is worth $70.3bn and growing 25.5 per cent annually.[9] The founders of Rovio could not have foreseen such growth, which might explain scattering their resources across different ventures such as books, cartoons, activity parks, movies, etc. Now, the primary focus is back on games with at least 10 new games under development. In 2018, the first Angry Birds game made its debut on an Augmented Reality (AR) headset Magic Leap[10] and for Rovio it is an opportunity to get in early on yet another burgeoning market. CEO Levoranta saw the Angry Birds coming to life in an entirely new way: 'We are happy to expand the brand and the world of Angry Birds to new platforms like Magic Leap.'

'This will likely be the future of mobile games. We just want to be there, in the first wave,' commented Ville Heijari, Rovio's Chief Marketing Officer. The management thus remains optimistic that the movie sequel, new partnerships and new technologies will help draw new players to their games in the long run and boost the licensing revenues. Rovio has managed to build Angry Birds into a sustainable global brand over the span of a decade. Now it is ready to kick off its next phase of growth by setting its sights on new markets and exploring new technologies.

Questions

1 What contributed to Rovio identifying its business opportunity?

2 Rovio has shifted its products between games, activity parks, movies, licensing etc., how has it handled different steps in the entrepreneurial process?

3 How has Rovio changed its business model over time? What are the advantages and disadvantages of a freemium business model?

4 How has Rovio evolved through the stages of entrepreneurial growth? At what stage of the entrepreneurial life cycle (see Section 8.2) is Rovio currently? Do you agree that the company is ready for its next phase of growth?

References
1. www.wired.co.uk/article/how-rovio-made-angry-birds-a-winner
2. https://newzoo.com/insights/infographics/global-games-market-report-infographics-2013/
3. www.cnbc.com/2016/05/18/creator-talks-about-the-angry-birds-movie-and-the-future-of-the-popular-game.html
4. www.rovio.com/investors/rovio-as-an-investment
5. www.talouselama.fi/uutiset/rovios-ex-managers-reveal-serious-problems-with-strategy-and-management/1d50efce-44f4-36b7-8dc4-59c5c5a353f4
6. www.gamesindustry.biz/articles/2017-09-08-rovio-ipo-a-stark-lesson-in-timing
7. www.nasdaqomxnordic.com/aktier/microsite?Instrument=HEX144044
8. www.rovio.com/node/1874
9. www.gamesindustry.biz/articles/2018-04-30-global-games-market-to-hit-usd137-9-billion-this-year-newzoo
10. www.engadget.com/2018/09/19/angry-birds-magic-leap-hands-on/

Chapter 9
Strategy in action

Learning outcomes

After reading this chapter, you should be able to:

- Analyse main organisational *structural types* in terms of their *fit* with particular strategies.

- Identify key issues in designing organisational *control systems* (such as planning and performance targeting systems)

- Recognise the three main types of leadership style, *transactional, transformational and situational leadership*.

- Identify four *types of strategic change* can be thought of in terms of the *extent* of change required and its *speed*.

- Propose *eight steps for achieving strategic change*, from building a compelling case for change to change institutionalisation.

9.1 Introduction

Strategies only become real when they are put into action. But enacting strategy is no small task. If the American multinational retailer Walmart wants to implement a new strategy, it needs to get 2.2 million employees spread over 12,000 locations worldwide all pointing in the right direction. In just the same way, when a sports team changes its game plan, it has to ensure that all its individual members know not only their own new roles but also those of their team-mates. Thus strategy involves both *organising* and *change*. If the organisation does not change with the strategy, then even the cleverest strategy will fail because of poor implementation.

This chapter examines how organisations put strategies into action – the implementation of strategy (sometimes known as strategy execution). Implementation is important because that is where strategy often goes wrong: strategies may fail not because they are badly chosen but because they are badly executed. **Implementation refers to the translation of a chosen strategy into organisational action in order to achieve strategic goals and objectives.** Implementation involves two key elements: organisation, including establishing the right organisational structures and systems for a particular strategy; and leadership, the human ability to influence employees to enact strategies, particularly strategic change.

The key concepts of this chapter can be defined more formally. **Structures give people formally defined roles, responsibilities and lines of reporting.** These structures can be seen as the skeletons of organisations, providing the basic frameworks on which everything is built. **Systems support and control people as they carry out structurally defined roles and responsibilities.** Systems can be seen as the muscles of organisations, giving them movement and coherence. **Leadership is the process of influencing an organisation (or group within an organisation) in its efforts towards achieving an aim or goal.** Leaders have to put in place the right structures and systems, but they have also to influence constructively the organisational members that work within them. **Strategic change involves either organisational transformation or realignment in the pursuit of a new or adjusted strategy.**

In more detail, the chapter therefore addresses the following topics:

- *Structures*, particularly functional, divisional, matrix, project and transnational structures.
- *Systems*, such as performance targeting and planning.
- *Leadership*, particularly transactional and transformational leadership.
- *Types of strategic change*, both realignment and transformational, and the role of *organisational ambidexterity*.
- *Eight steps* for achieving strategic change, starting with the business case.

9.2 Structural types

Germany's response to the first wave of covid-19 relied on decentralized structures, for instance a network of 150 existing local testing laboratories. The English response on the other hand was centralized, with the London-based Public Health England organization creating three large laboratories from scratch. Germany's decentralized approach contributed to significantly fewer deaths than in England. On the other hand, England gathered far more consistent data, important for the second wave, and had more consistency and lower costs. In other words, different structures lead to different strategic outcomes. It is clearly important that organisations choose the right structures for their strategies. Structural charts define the levels and roles in an organisation. They describe who reports to whom in terms of management and who is responsible for what in terms of activities. They have major implications for how managers interact internally. They also have implications for how organisations face out into the marketplace. Which managers get to interact with customers and suppliers is determined by structural roles. Structure should fit strategy.

There are five basic structural types: functional, divisional, matrix, transnational and project.[1] Broadly, the first two of these tend to emphasise one structural dimension (or 'axis') over another, either functional specialisms or business divisions. The three that follow tend to mix structural dimensions more evenly, for instance trying to give product and geographical units equal weight. The right structure depends on the particular strategy each organisation is following. In the following, we will particularly focus on how the five structural types fit strategies of diversification (Chapter 7) and innovation (Chapter 8).

9.2.1 The functional structure

Even a small entrepreneurial start-up, once it involves more than one person, needs to divide up responsibilities between different people. The functional structure divides responsibilities according to the organisation's primary specialist roles such as production, marketing and finance. It is particularly effective for specialised organisations with undiversified strategies. Figure 9.1 represents a typical organisation chart for such a functional organisation. This kind of structure is particularly relevant to small or start-up organisations, or larger organisations that have retained narrow, rather than diverse, product ranges. Functional structures may also be used within a multidivisional structure (see below), where the divisions themselves may split themselves up according to functional departments (as in Figure 9.1).

There are three key advantages of a functional structure. First, functional structures give top management direct hands-on involvement in key activities, from production to human resources, and centralises operational control at the top. Second, the functional structure provides a clear definition of roles and tasks, increasing accountability: the marketing director is responsible for marketing and should not directly intervene in production, for example. Third, functional departments provide concentrations of expertise, thus fostering knowledge development in functional specialisms. For example, all the marketing executives are together and can learn from each other.

However, there are two potential disadvantages to functional structures. First, centralisation means that functional structures are not good at coping with product or geographical diversity. For example, a central marketing department may try to impose a uniform approach to advertising regardless of the diverse needs of the organisation's various markets around the world. Second, senior managers may focus too much on their functional responsibilities, becoming overburdened with routine operations and too concerned with narrow functional interests: marketing managers focus just on marketing, while production managers focus on production, and both lack an overall strategic view. As a result, functional managers find it hard to respond to long-term strategic issues.

Figure 9.1 A functional structure

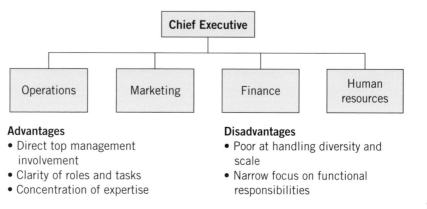

Advantages
- Direct top management involvement
- Clarity of roles and tasks
- Concentration of expertise

Disadvantages
- Poor at handling diversity and scale
- Narrow focus on functional responsibilities

Illustration 9.1 Elon Musk reorganises Tesla: time to shower?

Tesla reorganises as it ramps up production of its new Model 3 electric car.

During 2018, the Silicon Valley electric car company Tesla was struggling to produce enough of its first mass-market electric car, the Model 3. The company had 500,000 customer reservations for the new car, but was not yet reaching its production target of 5,000 cars per week. This target was essential for Tesla to break even financially. Company founder, Chairman and Chief Executive Elon Musk claimed he was working so hard at resolving what he described as 'production hell' that he was sleeping on the factory floor, with no time to go home and have a shower.

Musk was busy not only with the Model 3 Tesla car. He was closely involved in a whole raft of other companies. In 2002, Musk had created SpaceX, a space transport services company, of which he continued to be CEO and lead designer. In 2006, Musk helped found SolarCity, a solar energy services company that is now a subsidiary of Tesla and operates under his chairmanship. In 2015, Musk co-founded OpenAI, a non-profit research company interested in friendly artificial intelligence. The next year he had co-founded Neuralink, a neurotechnology company where he acted as CEO. That same year, after getting stuck in a traffic jam, Musk established The Boring Company, a tunnel-construction company aimed at getting traffic moving faster. The Boring Company's first product in fact turned out to be a flame-thrower.

In resolving the problems at Tesla, Musk naturally had a senior management team to help. The most prominent roles in the company were the Chief Financial Officer, the Chief Technology Officer, the Chief People Officer, the Senior Vice President for Engineering, the Chief Designer, the Vice President for Production and the Vice President for Global Sales. The organisation had grown rapidly in recent years, with total full-time employees reaching 37,000 in 2017, against a couple of thousand in 2012.

However, the financial markets were increasingly sceptical of Tesla's ability to meet its production targets. During the first part of 2018, the stock price fell by nearly a quarter. Musk responded by announcing a new flatter organisation structure in May 2018. In his memo, he wrote:

'To ensure that Tesla is well prepared for the future, we have been undertaking a thorough reorganization of our company. As part of the reorg, we are flattening the management structure to improve communication, combining functions where sensible and trimming activities that are not vital to the success of our mission.'

In the period immediately following the announcement of this new flatter structure, Tesla declared 3,000 employees redundant. During 2018, there were significant senior management departures, including those of the Chief People Officer, the Vice President for Global Sales and the Senior Vice President for Engineering. To fill the gaps, Musk took direct responsibility for both global sales and engineering on a temporary basis.

Musk explained the 2018 reorganisation to financial analysts in a combative conference call. When asked about how much capital Tesla would need to support its growth, he dismissed the question with a curt: 'Boring, bonehead questions are not cool. Next?' A further question about Model 3 reservations met with the response: 'These questions are so dry, they are killing me.' In August 2018, Musk sent out a tweet that he was going to take the company private, meaning that there would be no public shareholders – and no need to talk to financial analysts anymore. The tweet was unfounded and regulators fined both Musk and Tesla separately, $20m each. Musk was obliged to step down from his chairmanship of Tesla, though allowed to continue as CEO.

Sources: Fortune, 14 May 2018; *Wall Street Journal*, 14 May 2018, *Bloomberg*, 7 September 2018.

Questions

1 In the terms of Section 9.2, what kind of structure did Tesla have?

2 Given its strategic challenges, do you agree that for Tesla a flatter organisation was the right way to go?

9.2.2 The divisional structure

A divisional structure is built up of separate divisions organised on the basis of distinct products, services or geographical areas (see Figure 9.2). For example, an organisation might have a chemicals division, a textiles division and a retail division. The key principle is decentralisation. Under divisionalisation, divisional managers typically have sufficient freedom to respond to the specific requirements of their division. Top management typically does not interfere in detailed operations, but monitors the outcomes of divisional managers' choices from corporate headquarters.

There are three potential advantages to divisional structures. First, it is possible for head office to control divisions from a distance simply by monitoring their business performance: top management need only intervene if targets are being missed. Second, there are learning benefits to specialisation within a division, allowing competences to develop with a clearer focus on a particular product group, technology or customer group. Third, having divisions provides flexibility because organisations can add, close or merge divisions as the strategy changes: diversification into a new market can be accommodated simply by adding a new division focused on that market.

However, divisional structures can also have three key disadvantages. First, divisions can become so self-sufficient that they are effectively independent businesses, duplicating the functions and costs of the corporate centre of the company: every division has its own human resources department for instance. Second, divisions may become too autonomous. Here, divisions pursue their own strategies almost regardless of the needs of the corporate parent. Finally, divisionalisation tends to get in the way of cooperation and knowledge-sharing between businesses: divisions can quite literally divide. Expertise is fragmented and division-specific performance targets provide little incentive to collaborate with other divisions.

Figure 9.2 A multidivisional structure

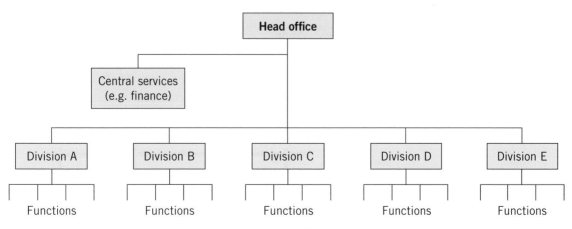

Advantages
- More detached head office control
- Divisions develop specialised expertise
- Strategic flexibility in entering and exiting business areas

Disadvantages
- Functional duplication
- Risk excessive autonomy
- Fragmentation and low cooperation

9.2.3 The matrix structure

A matrix structure combines different structural dimensions (axes) simultaneously, for example product divisions and geographical territories or product divisions and functional specialisms.[2] In matrix structures, staff typically report to two managers rather than one.

Matrix structures are potentially attractive as they can combine the advantages of different dimensions at the same time. Thus, Figure 9.3 shows how a school might combine separate subject specialisms with particular age cohorts of pupils. Similarly, a consulting firm might have both sector heads who understand clients in particular markets, for example heads of energy or retail, and heads of expert groups, for example heads of information technology or strategy: an individual consultant might report to the heads of both energy and strategy. In each case, the organisation benefits from specialised expertise, at the same time as being responsive to particular client needs.

However, replacing single lines of authority with cross-matrix relationships can bring at least two problems. There may be conflict because staff find themselves responsible to managers from two structural axes: as above, the energy head may want different things to the strategy head. Also, it will typically take longer to reach decisions because of bargaining between the managers of different axes. If conflict and delays proliferate, matrix organisations can be both inefficient and inflexible.

Figure 9.3 Two examples of matrix structures

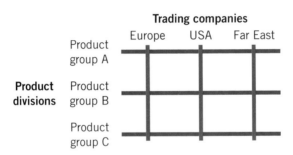

(a) Multinational organisation

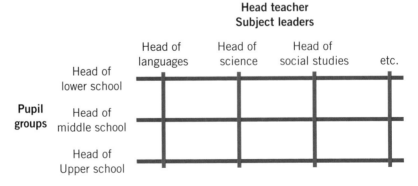

(b) School

Advantages:
- Allows specialisation
- Responsive to different needs

Disadvantages:
- Conflict between structural dimensions
- Slow decision-making

9.2.4 Multinational/transnational structures

Operating internationally adds an extra dimension to the structural challenge. As in Figure 9.4, there are essentially four structural designs available for multinationals:

- *International divisions.* An international division is a standalone division added alongside the structure of the main home-based business. This is often the kind of structure adopted by corporations with large domestic markets (such as in the USA or China), where an initial entry into overseas markets is relatively small scale and does not require structural change to the original, much bigger, home businesses. For example, a Chinese car, truck and motor-bike manufacturer might have separate divisions for each of its product areas in its home market of China, but manage its overseas businesses in a separate 'international division' combining all three product areas together. The international division is typically run from headquarters, but not integrated with the domestic business. As in Figure 9.4, the international division is centralised, but not highly coordinated with other parts of the business.

- *Local subsidiaries.* These subsidiaries typically have most of the functions required to operate on their own in their particular local market, for example design, production and marketing. They are thus a form of geographic divisional structure. They have high local responsiveness and are loosely coordinated. A local subsidiary structure is very common in professional services such as law, accounting and advertising, where there are few economies of scale and responsiveness to local regulations, relationships or tastes is very important.

- *Global product divisions.* This kind of structure is often used where economies of scale are very important. Organising the design, production and marketing on the basis of global divisions rather than local subsidiaries typically maximises cost efficiency. It also helps direct central resources to targeted markets and facilitates cross-subsidisation of unprofitable geographical markets. To return to the Chinese car, truck and motorbike manufacturer, there would be just three divisions, each responsible for its particular product area across the whole world, China included. There would be very little scope for adaptation to local tastes or regulations in particular markets. In global product divisions, local responsiveness would typically be very low.

Figure 9.4 Multinational structures

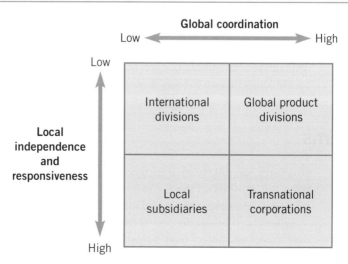

- *The transnational structure.* This structure tries to integrate the advantages of the local subsidiary structure with those of the global product divisional structure. In terms of Figure 9.4, the *transnational structure* combines local responsiveness with high global coordination.[3] Transnational structures are similar to matrices, and have some similar problems. However, they do have advantages for cross-border knowledge-sharing, specialisation and network management. Local subsidiaries tend to specialise in particular activities, becoming 'centres of excellence' that use networks to share their expertise across the whole organisation. In other words, knowledge leadership is not necessarily centralised at headquarters, but goes to wherever in the world that the best people are.

9.2.5 Project-based structures[4]

Many organisations rely heavily on project teams with a finite life span. A project-based structure is one where teams are created, undertake a specific project and are then dissolved. This can be particularly appropriate for organisations that involve goods or services that are large and take time to deliver (infrastructure, information systems, films) and those delivering time-limited events (conferences, sporting events or consulting engagements). The organisation structure is a constantly changing collection of project teams created, steered and glued together loosely by a small corporate group.

The project-based structure can be highly flexible, with projects being set up and dissolved as required. Because project teams should have clear tasks to achieve within a defined period, accountability and control are good. As project team members will typically be drawn from different departments within the firm, projects can be effective at knowledge exchange. Projects can also draw on members internationally and, because project life spans are typically short, project teams may be more willing to work temporarily around the world. There are disadvantages, however. The constant breaking up of project teams can hinder the accumulation of knowledge within specialisms. Every project requires investment in team-building before actually starting work. Consequently, without careful management, project-based structures can be inefficient.

As can be seen, every structure has its advantages and disadvantages. Successful strategy implementation depends on choosing the right structure for the particular strategy. For example, diversified strategies tend to demand divisional structures. One of the first strategy theorists, Alfred Chandler, documents how major corporations such as DuPont and General Motors nearly went bankrupt: the reason was not badly chosen strategies, but a misfit between their centralised structures and their diversified strategies (DuPont made a wide range of chemicals; General Motors made cars, trucks and tractors).[5] Chandler famously concluded: structure follows strategy.

9.3 Systems

Structures can only work if they are supported by formal and informal organisational systems, the 'muscles' of the organisation. This section considers four systems: planning, performance targeting, culture and internal markets.

Systems can be subdivided in two ways. First, systems tend to emphasise either control over *inputs* or control over *outputs*. Input control systems concern themselves with the resources consumed in the strategy, especially financial resources and human commitment. Output control systems focus on ensuring satisfactory results, for example the meeting of targets or achieving market competitiveness. The second subdivision is between *direct* and

Table 9.1 Types of control systems

	Input	Output
Direct	Planning systems	Performance targeting
Indirect	Cultural systems	Internal markets

indirect controls. Direct controls involve close supervision or monitoring. Indirect controls are more hands-off, setting up the conditions whereby desired behaviours are achieved semi-automatically. Table 9.1 summarises how the four systems of planning, performance targeting, culture and internal markets each emphasise input or output controls and direct or indirect controls. Organisations normally use a blend of these control systems, but some will dominate over others according to circumstances.

9.3.1 Planning systems

Planning systems govern the allocation of resources and monitor their utilisation. The focus is on the direct control of inputs. These might be simple financial inputs (as in budgeting), human inputs (as in planning for managerial succession) or long-term investments (as particularly in strategic planning). Tight control over inputs is often efficient, reducing waste. However, planning systems can be too rigid and fail to anticipate rapid change: planning therefore may sometimes reduce flexibility.

Goold and Campbell's[6] typology of *corporate strategy styles* helps to identify the advantages and disadvantages of planning systems. The strategy styles differ along two dimensions: the *dominant source of planning influence*, either top-down (from the corporate centre to the business units) or bottom-up (from the business units to the centre); and the *degree of performance accountability* for the business units, either tight or reasonably relaxed. In terms of the styles, organisations typically adopt positions more or less close to one of two opposed polar opposites:

- The *strategic planning* style is the archetypal planning system, hence its name. In the Goold and Campbell sense, the strategic planning style combines both strong planning from the corporate centre with relatively relaxed performance accountability for the business units. The logic is that if the centre sets the strategic direction, business unit managers should not be held strictly accountable for disappointing results that might be due to an inappropriate plan in the first place. In the strategic planning style, the centre focuses on inputs in terms of allocating resources necessary to achieve the strategic plan, while exercising a high degree of direct control over how the plan is executed by the businesses.

- The *financial control* style involves very little central planning. The business units each set their own strategic plans, probably after some negotiation with the corporate centre, and are then held strictly accountable for the results against these plans. This style differs from the strategic planning style in that control is against financial outputs. If the businesses devised the plans, then they should take full responsibility for success or failure. Business unit managers in the financial control style have a lot of autonomy and typically receive high bonus payments for success. But failure may easily lead to dismissal.

Thus corporate strategy styles vary with regard to their reliance on planning systems. The direct control of inputs characteristic of the strategic planning style is only appropriate in certain circumstances. In particular, it makes sense where there are large, risky and long-range investments to be allocated: for example, an oil company typically has to take the decision to

Figure 9.5 Strategy styles

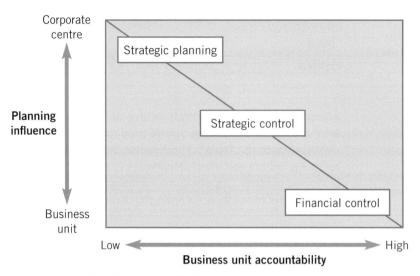

Source: Adapted from Goold, M. and Campbell, A. (1989) Strategies and Styles, Blackwell, Figure 3.1, p. 39.

invest in the ten-year development of an oilfield at the corporate centre, rather than risk delegating it to business units whose resources and time horizons may be limited. On the other hand, the financial control style is suitable where investments are small, relatively frequent and well understood, as typically in a mature, non-capital-intensive business. Many organisations end up somewhere in between these two opposite approaches, adopting what is called a *strategic control* style (see Figure 9.5). Under the strategic control style, there is more top-down planning than in the financial control style and stricter accountability than in the strategic planning style.

9.3.2 Cultural systems

Organisations typically have distinctive cultures which express basic assumptions and beliefs held by organisation members and define taken-for-granted ways of doing things (see Chapter 5). Despite their taken-for-granted, semi-conscious nature, organisational cultures can seem a tempting means of managerial control. Cultures exercise an *indirect* form of control, because of not requiring direct supervision: it becomes a matter of willing conformity or *self*-control by employees. Control is exerted on the *input* of employees, as the culture defines the appropriate effort and initiative that employees themselves choose to put into their jobs. Thus cultural mechanisms aim to standardise norms of behaviour within an organisation in line with particular objectives.

Managers often try to influence organisational culture through three mechanisms:[7]

- *Recruitment.* Employers look to recruit people who will 'fit'. Thus some employers may favour recruiting people who have already shown themselves to be 'team-players' through sport or other activities.

- *Socialisation.* Here employee behaviours are shaped by social processes once they are at work. It often starts with the integration of new staff through training, induction and mentoring programmes. People learn what it takes to get on in the organisation.

- *Reward.* Appropriate behaviour can be encouraged through pay, promotion or symbolic processes (e.g. public praise). The desire to achieve the same rewards as successful people in the organisation will typically encourage imitative behaviour.

9.3.3 Performance targeting systems

Performance targets focus on the *outputs* of an organisation (or part of an organisation), such as product quality, revenues or profits. These targets are often known as *key performance indicators* (KPIs). Targets should measure how well the strategy is being implemented. However, within specified boundaries, there is often freedom on how targets are exactly achieved.

Performance targeting can be particularly appropriate in certain situations:

* Within *large businesses*, corporate centres may choose performance targets to control their business units without getting involved in the details of how they achieve them (as in the financial control style in Section 9.3.1).

* In *regulated markets*, such as privatised utilities in the United Kingdom and elsewhere, government-appointed regulators increasingly exercise control through agreed key performance indicators (KPIs), such as service or quality levels.[8]

Many managers find it difficult to develop a useful set of targets. Two common problems are:

* *Inappropriate measures* of performance. For example, managers often prefer indicators that are easily measured or choose measures based on inadequate understanding of real needs on the ground. The result is a focus on the required measures rather than the factors that might really be essential to long-term success. For example, it is often easier to measure the costs of R&D or advertising than the benefits, with the result that these long-term investments get cut back.

* *Inappropriate target levels.* Managers are liable to give their superiors pessimistic forecasts so that targets are set at undemanding levels, which can then be easily met. On the other hand, superiors may over-compensate for their managers' pessimism, and end up setting excessively demanding targets. Unrealistically ambitious targets can either demotivate employees who see no hope of achieving them regardless of effort, or encourage risky or dishonest behaviours in order to achieve the otherwise impossible.

9.3.4 Market systems

Market disciplines (or *internal markets*) can be brought inside organisations to control activities internally. Market systems typically involve some formalised system of 'contracting' for resources or inputs from other parts of an organisation and for supplying outputs to other parts of an organisation. Control focuses on outputs, for example revenues earned in successful competition for internal contracts. The control is indirect: rather than accepting detailed performance targets, units have to earn their keep in competitive internal markets. Units have freedom to decide exactly how they will achieve required outputs, increasing adaptability on the ground. For example, a buyer–supplier relationship may be established between operating businesses and a central service unit, such as training or IT: operating businesses need only buy the services they actually want and the central service unit decides how to supply it.

Internal markets work well where complexity or rapid change makes detailed direct or input controls impractical. But market systems can create problems as well. For example, they can increase bargaining between units, consuming important management time. An overzealous use of market mechanisms can also lead to dysfunctional internal competition and legalistic contracting, destroying cultures of collaboration and relationships.

Illustration 9.2 God's work in Malaysia

Corrupt practices at Malaysia's sovereign wealth fund reveal problems with Goldman Sachs' control systems.

Lloyd Blankfein, Chief Executive of Goldman Sachs, is famous for declaring that his investment bank is 'doing God's work', so important are his bankers' activities for financing the world economy. However, in 2018, the Department of Justice in the USA charged two former Goldman Sachs bankers, Tim Leissner and Roger Ng, with misappropriating funds from the Malaysian sovereign wealth fund, 1Malaysia Development Berhad (1MDB) and paying bribes to various Malaysian officials. 1IMD appeared to be at the centre of a $2.7bn money laundering and bribery scandal, with Goldman Sachs closely involved. Malaysia's Prime Minister demanded reparations from Goldman Sachs of $600m. It was revealed that Lloyd Blankfein himself had met the Malay financier at the heart of the illegal dealings, Jho Low, at least twice.

1MDB was founded by the Malaysian government in order to stimulate long-term investment in Malaysia, for instance through the financing of large-scale energy projects. In the early years of this decade, Goldman Sachs was earning about $85m annually in fees from IMDB. The most spectacular fee came in 2012, when Goldman Sachs helped IMDB to raise $6.5bn in debt intended to fund the wealth fund's various investment projects. The fee for this transaction alone was nearly 10 per cent, $600m.

The bankers at the heart of this lucrative business were senior managers within Goldman Sachs. The man responsible for originating many of the deals, Andrea Vella, had been co-head of investment banking in Asia-Pacific ex-Japan (he was demoted and suspended by Goldman Sachs in 2018). Tim Leissner was the bank's chairman of south-east Asia as a whole. Roger Ng had been in charge of South-East Asian sales in Goldman Sachs' fixed-income, currencies and commodities unit.

Goldman Sachs is well-known for its aggressive, bonus-driven culture. It saw the growing South East Asian economies as key to its own continuing expansion. Crucial to this strategy was Andrea Vella. According to the *International Financial Review*, Vella was 'a veritable magician' in financial deals. He was also well-known for ostentatious living, with his wife famous for driving around Hong Kong in a top-end Maserati.

Explaining how the complex Malaysian deals got past the bank's internal controls, Tim Leissner admitted to a New York court: 'I conspired with other employees and agents of Goldman Sachs very much in line with the [Goldman Sachs] culture to conceal facts from [the company's] compliance and legal employees.' Formally, all deals, including those with 1MDB, are approved by Goldman Sachs' capital and client suitability committees. At the time, these were organised on a regional basis, reporting finally to a central committee in New York. Members of deal teams typically remained in committee meetings even though they would abstain from voting. Committees tended to review or approve most proposed deals by consensus. The bank preferred deal teams to attend committee discussions so they could respond immediately to any questions raised by other committee members.

The Federal Reserve Bank of the United States has queried why the Asia Pacific capital committee, which initially reviewed the first 1MDB deal in 2012, seemed to reject very few deals for being too risky or inappropriate. The Asia Pacific committee typically met in Hong Kong with Eugene Leouzon, Goldman's global chief underwriting officer, acting as co-chair with Tim Leissner. An inside observer recalled standard practice: 'Tim Leissner and Roger Ng would do the pitch and Leouzon would say, "That is interesting," then Vella would walk in like a rock star.' Apparently, Andrea Vella had been the most influential figure within the Asia Pacific committee in securing approval for the first 1MDB deal, despite being its originator. Although Vella formally abstained from the decision, he remained in the room and took part in the discussion of the key $6.5bn deal.

Sources: Financial Times, 23 November and 11 December 2018.

Questions

1 Which control systems did Goldman Sachs' primarily rely on? (see Section 9.3). How did the systems support the growth strategy and in what respects did they fail with regard to the Malaysian business and more generally?

2 What reforms to these systems would you recommend? What downsides to these reforms might there be?

9.4 Strategic leadership

Putting strategy into action relies not only on structures and systems, but also on leadership. As in the definition at the start of this chapter, strategic leadership involves influence, not just command. As such, there are leadership roles for both top managers and middle managers. Three roles are particularly important for top managers:

- *Envisioning future strategy.* There is a need to ensure there exists a clear and compelling vision of the future and to communicate clearly a strategy to achieve it both internally and to external stakeholders.

- *Aligning the organisation to deliver the strategy.* This involves ensuring that people are committed to the strategy, motivated to make the changes needed and empowered to deliver those changes. This typically involves establishing structures and systems. However, leaders also need the trust and respect of their 'followers'.

- *Embodying change.* A strategic leader will be seen by internal and external stakeholders as intimately associated with the organisation's strategy. They must act as symbols and role models for the strategy therefore.

However, middle managers also have important leadership roles to play, for example as:[9]

- *Champions of strategic issues.* Middle managers are often the closest to market or technological shifts that might signal the need for strategic change. Accordingly, middle managers must gain top management attention for strategic issues that might otherwise be missed and win commitment to appropriate strategic actions.

- *'Sense makers' of strategy.* Top management may set a strategic direction, but it is often up to middle managers to explain its implications to other employees in specific contexts (e.g. a region of a multinational or a functional department).[10]

- *Adapters to unfolding events.* Middle managers are uniquely qualified to reinterpret and adjust strategy because they have day-to-day responsibility for implementation.

Leaders tend to adopt characteristic 'styles' of behaving and intervening. These leadership styles are often categorised in two broad ways:

- **Transformational (or charismatic) leaders emphasise building a vision for their organisations**, creating an organisational identity around collective values and beliefs to support that vision and energising people to achieve it. Organisational founders are often particularly charismatic (i.e. personally inspiring). Evidence suggests that this approach to leadership is beneficial for people's motivation and job performance,[11] and is particularly positive for wider business performance when organisations face uncertainty.[12]

- **Transactional leaders emphasise 'hard' levers of change such as designing systems and controls.** The emphasis here is more likely to be on changes of structures, setting targets to be achieved, financial incentives, careful project management and the monitoring of organisational and individual performance.

In practice, transformational and transactional leadership styles are two ends of a continuum, with many feasible points between. Leaders typically combine elements of the two styles, rather than identifying exclusively with one (see Illustration 9.3). Indeed, the notion of **situational leadership encourages strategic leaders to adjust their leadership style to the context they face.**[13] In other words, there is not just one best way of leading: the appropriate leadership style depends on the specific demands of the situation. As in the next section, one important aspect of the situation is the type of strategic change being enacted.

Illustration 9.3 Leadership styles

Successful top executives talk about their leadership styles.

Miki Agrawal, CEO of Thinx, Fast Company

Source: Robin Marchant/Getty Images Entertainment/Getty Images

Fire fast

'Lessons that will continue to inform my leadership for next year: Hire slow, fire fast. My job is not to spend my time policing people and their work ethic, positive attitude, and focused execution – it's to bring in people that just have it in them. Then we can simply focus on what matters: growing the business!'

Miki Agrawal, founder and CEO of period-proof underwear startup Thinx, Fast Company, 27 December 2016.

Go with your gut

'As a leader, I have always aimed to inspire, mentor, lead – and protect. But when I became a CEO, I faced a difficult situation where I learned that not every important move could be coached or arrived at through consensus. Sometimes, you need to just go with your gut, make a decision and tell people the plan. When we had to make the tough decision [to change the technology platform], it just needed to get done. I didn't have time to dive into a 30-minute discussion and get people on board. They may not have agreed, but it didn't matter. I had to tell them what to do, and they needed to do it because I was telling them.'

Heidi Zak, co-founder and co-CEO of ThirdLove, a lingerie company. MakeIt, 19 November 2018.

Vision and grit

'A leader should never compare his technical skills with his employee's. Your employee should have superior technical skills than you. If he doesn't, it means you have hired the wrong person.

What, then, makes the leader stands out?

1. A leader should be a visionary and have more foresight than an employee.
2. A leader should have higher grit and tenacity, and be able to endure what the employees can't.
3. A leader should have higher endurance and ability to accept and embrace failure.

Jack Ma, Founder of Chinese eCommerce giant, Alibaba, *Vulkan Post*, 25 February 2015

Confidence when you don't know

'One of my favourite episodes of "Star Trek: The Next Generation" is when the captain and the doctor are stranded alone on this planet, and their brains are linked by some kind of alien device so they can read each other's thoughts. They're trying to get somewhere and the captain says, "We're going this way." And the doctor says, "You don't know which way to go, do you?" Because she can read his thoughts.

'He explains to her that sometimes part of being a leader is just picking a way and being confident about it and going, because people want to be led. I remember that episode, because it rang really true to me. Sometimes you just have to lead, even if you don't have all the answers. In fact, you shouldn't have all the answers. If you think you have all the answers, then you're probably doing something wrong. Good leadership means being willing to have the confidence to move forward, even if you don't have all the answers.'

Biz Stone, Founder of Twitter, 27 May 2014, *Washington Post*

Questions

1 Which leaders are more transformational, which more transactional and which situational (see Section 9.4)?

2 Compare the different views of leadership, particularly with regard to knowledge, courage and people. What are the commonalities and differences?

9.5 Types of strategic change

Leadership is associated particularly with strategic change. Harvard Business School's John Kotter argues that 'good management' is about bringing order and consistency to operational aspects of organisations, such as the quality and profitability of products and services. Leadership, 'by contrast is about coping with change'.[14] There are four generic types of strategic change.[15] The axes in Figure 9.6 are concerned with (i) the *extent* of change, in other words the desired end-result and (ii) the *nature* of the change process, particularly the speed.

In terms of the *extent* of change, change that occurs in line with the current business model and culture is considered a *realignment* of strategy. A business may launch new products without requiring fundamental changes in the business model or organisational culture. More extensive change, going beyond the current business model or culture, is *transformational* change (this does not necessarily imply transformational *leadership*). For example, *digital transformation* typically implies not just the introduction of new information technology and distribution channels, but deep changes in culture and skills (see Illustration 9.4 on la Redoute's digital transformation).[16]

On the other axis in Figure 9.6, the nature of change is concerned with the speed at which change needs to happen. Arguably, it is often beneficial for change in an organisation to be *incremental* since this allows time to build on the skills, routines and beliefs of those in the organisation. It also allows for learning as the change proceeds, allowing for adjustments to be made in the light of experience. However, if an organisation faces crisis or needs to change direction fast, a *rapid* approach to change might be needed: here everything is attempted all at once.

Together, Figure 9.6's two axes of extent of change and speed of change define four basic types of strategic change, as follows.

9.5.1 Adaptation

Adaptation in Figure 9.6 is incremental. Change is gradual, building on what the organisation has been doing in the past and in line with the current business model and organisational culture. This might include changes in product design or methods of production, launches of new products or related diversification. This is the most common form of change in organisations.

Figure 9.6 Types of change

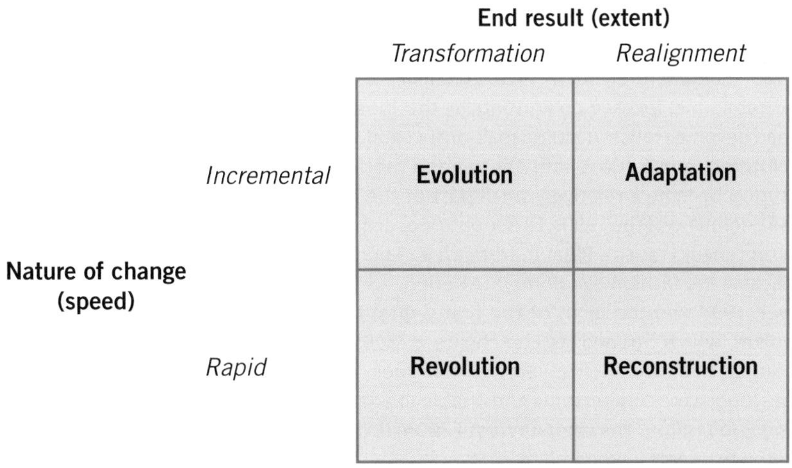

Source: Adapted from Balogun, J. and Hope Hailey, V. (2016) Exploring Strategic Change, 4th edn, Prentice Hall.

Illustration 9.4 Digital transformation at La Redoute

In four years, the struggling old-style mail order business has been transformed into one of France's leading ecommerce businesses.

Source: Sefa Karacan/Anadolu Agency/Getty Images

Founded in 1837, La Redoute has undergone at least two major transformations in its history. Originally it had been a simple wool manufacturer, but in 1928 it launched its first mail-order catalogue, focused on knitting. By the 1960s, La Redoute had become France's leading mail-order catalogue, offering clothing, home-furnishing and related products. Manufacturing became a relatively small part of the business. At the beginning of the 1990s, La Redoute was acquired by the entrepreneur Francois Pinault, forming a major part of what became the fashion conglomerate Kering.

However, 1994 saw the birth of the first digital retail giant Amazon, which opened its French site in 2000. By comparison, La Redoute's twice-yearly catalogues, each 1,300 pages long, were cumbersome and unable to adapt to rapid changes in fashion. The company lost €300m (£260m; $340m) in the five years leading up to 2014.

In 2014, Kering sold 51 per cent of La Redoute to two senior managers, Nathalie Balla and Eric Courteille for one Euro. The rest of the company was sold to 50 senior managers and employees (by 2017, two-thirds of employees were shareholders). Kering also paid the €500m cost of a major redundancy programme involving 1,200 out of the 3,400 employees at the time.

Balla and Courteille embarked on a digital transformation programme that touched nearly every part of the organisation. One of their senior managers recalls: 'It was above all a cultural shock... La Redoute was very old. It had undergone both the industrial revolution and the internet revolution. We were used to being under the protection of a large group... I like to say that we are not a start-up but a restart-up...'. This meant a radical change in mentality. La Redoute had actually launched its first internet site in 1994, but failed to follow through. The manager explained: 'We were slow to go all in on the transformation. We had to understand that our old mail-order business was finished.'

La Redoute reduced its product range, focusing on women's and children's fashion, household linens and furniture. 80 per cent of the products would be own-brand, using the company's own designs. The sport, toys, beauty and domestic appliance products that had been part of their own range now came from other suppliers through the marketplace part of their platform. Instead of two fat catalogues per year, La Redoute switched to 10 or 11 shorter catalogues annually, refreshed each time. By 2018, 30 per cent of sales were via mobile phone rather than personal computer. Sourcing moved from India and China to Turkey and Morocco to improve responsiveness to changing demand. The warehouse was radically automated, with staff reduced from 2,500 to just 550. The time from receipt of order to despatch from the warehouse fell from 36 hours to two hours.

By 2018, La Redoute was on track to profitability. The retail conglomerate Galeries Lafayette purchased Balla and Courteille's shares for an undisclosed but substantial sum. And Balla won the prestigious Veuve Cliquot prize of Frances' Businesswoman of the Year.

Sources: Capital, 16 May 2016; Culture Formation, 15 September 2017; *Les Echos*, 16 November 2018.

Questions

1 In terms of Figure 9.6, what type of change did La Redoute undertake with its digital transformation?

2 Returning to Section 9.3, what kind of leadership style might have been required of Balla and Courteille? What kinds of leadership actions would you have expected them to undertake?

9.5.2 Reconstruction

Reconstruction (sometimes associated with 'turnarounds') is rapid change involving a good deal of upheaval in an organisation, but which still does not fundamentally change the culture or the business model. Thus reconstruction might include changes in organisational structure, changes in financing (reduction of debt for instance), cost savings or the sale of a subsidiary or division. These would all be significant changes, but might still be compatible with the basic business model and organisational systems, for example its culture.

9.5.3 Revolution

Revolution is change that requires rapid and major strategic *and* cultural change. Revolution could be pursued in circumstances where the strategy has been so bounded by the existing culture that, even when environmental or competitive pressures might require fundamental change, the organisation has failed to respond. This might have occurred over many years and resulted in circumstances where pressures for change are extreme – for example, when a takeover threatens the continued existence of a firm. Revolutionary change therefore differs from reconstruction in the need for deep cultural change.

9.5.4 Evolution

Evolution is change in strategy that results in transformation, but gradually. Arguably this is the most challenging type of strategic change since it is typically not motivated by a crisis. One approach to cultivating evolutionary change is to cultivate organisational ambidexterity.

Human ambidexterity is the ability to use both hands equally well. **Organisational ambidexterity is the capacity both to exploit existing capabilities and to explore for new capabilities.** It is, of course, appropriate for an organisation to exploit the capabilities it has built up over time in order to achieve and sustain competitive advantage. However, *exploitation* will tend to allow only incremental change, since strategy is being built on established ways of doing things. If transformational change is to be achieved, there needs also to be *exploration* in order to innovate and build new capabilities. Organisational ambidexterity can be built in three ways relevant to this chapter:

- *Structural ambidexterity.* Organisations may keep the core of the business devoted to exploitation using tight control but create separate units for exploration. These exploratory units will be smaller in size, less tightly controlled with much more emphasis on learning and processes to encourage new ideas.[17] For example Alphabet restructured in 2015 to place its large and mature search and advertising businesses in the Google subsidiary, while keeping its more exploratory activities apart in the separate Ventures and X subsidiaries.

- *Tight and loose systems.* There needs to be a balance between 'tight' systems of strategy development that can exploit existing capabilities – perhaps employing the disciplines of strategic planning – and 'looser' systems that encourage new ideas and experimentation. This combination of loose and tight systems can be given coherence so long as there is some overall common 'glue', perhaps in the form of an organisational mission or vision that allows different units to express the organisation's overall purpose in different ways.

- *Leadership.* Leaders need to encourage and value different views rather than demanding uniformity.[18] This may mean running with new ideas and experiments to establish just what makes sense and what does not. However, they also need the personal authority to stop such experiments when it becomes clear that they are not worthwhile.

Following the logic of situational leadership, appropriate leadership styles are likely to vary according to the types of change being sought. Urgent and limited change – especially reconstruction – tends to require more emphasis on the transactional approach, focused on short-term targets and tight monitoring of performance. Transformational leadership styles are usually more important in broad and longer-term evolutionary change, though they also play a role in the cultural elements of revolutionary change.

9.6 Steps for strategic change: Kotter's Change Model

Sometimes levers for change are presented as a sequence. Kotter's Eight Steps for Change is a very popular framework and describes a process of change as a series of steps that lead eventually to the institutionalisation of change (Figure 9.7). These steps are:

1. *Establish a sense of urgency*: help others see the need for change through an aspirational statement that communicates the importance of acting immediately.

2. *Form a powerful guiding coalition*: create an influential team to coordinate and communicate change.

3. *Create a vision*: explain how the future will be different from the past and how this can be made a reality through initiatives.

4. *Communicate the vision*: communicate frequently and powerfully and 'walk the talk'.

5. *Empower others to act on vision*: remove barriers to change and recognise and reward people for making change happen.

6. *Create short-term wins*: these must be recognised as success energises participants.

7. *Consolidate gains and build more change*: victory can be declared too early, so keep looking for improvements and keep setting goals to maintain momentum.

8. *Institutionalise the new approaches*: explain the connections between new behaviours and organisational success. Continue until old habits have been replaced.

These eight steps may provide leaders with a clear progression in managing change. In practice, many of these levers are likely to be used simultaneously rather than in the kind of logical sequence shown in Figure 9.7.

Figure 9.7 Kotter's Eight Steps for Change

Source: Adapted from Kotter J. (1996), Leading Change: Why Transformation Efforts Fail, Harvard Business Review, March-April, p. 61.

Summary

- This chapter introduces organisational *structure* and *systems* as key factors in strategy *implementation*.

- There are five main *structural types* (e.g. functional, divisional, matrix, transnational and project). Structure should fit strategy.

- There are four different organisational *systems* to facilitate and control strategy: planning, cultural, performance targeting and internal markets. These systems can focus on either *inputs* or *outputs* and be *direct* or *indirect*.

- There are two main types of leadership style, *transactional* and *transformational*. *Situational leadership* suggests that leaders need to adapt their sty*les* according to different types of change.

- The *types of strategic change* can be thought of in terms of the *extent* of change required and its *speed* – whether it can be achieved through incremental change or requires rapid action.

- *Steps* in managing strategic change include building a compelling case for change, challenging the taken for granted, changing operational processes, routines and symbols, political processes, timing and quick wins.

Recommended key reading

- The best single coverage of structural and systems issues is in R. Daft, J. Murphy and H. Willmott, *Organization Theory and Design: an International Perspective*, 3rd edition, Cengage, 2017. A good textbook on leadership and change is Balogun and V. Hope Hailey, *Exploring Strategic Change*, Prentice Hall, 4th edn, 2016.

References

1. A good review of organisation structure is J.R. Galbraith, 'The future of organization design', *Journal of Organization Design*, vol. 1, no. 1 (2012), pp. 3–6.
2. For recent experience with matrix structures, see Worren, N. 'The matrix as a transitory form: the evolution of FMC technologies 2001–2016', *Journal of Organization Design*, vol. 6, no. 1. (2016), pp. 1–14.
3. Bartlett, C.A. and Beamish, P.W. *Transnational Management: Text and Cases in Cross-border Management*, Cambridge University Press, 2018.
4. The classic article on project-based organisations is by R. DeFillippi and M. Arthur, 'Paradox in project-based enterprise: the case of film-making', *California Management Review*, vol. 40, no. 2 (1998), pp. 125–45.
5. A.D. Chandler, *Strategy and Structure*, MIT Press, 1962.
6. M. Goold and A. Campbell, *Strategies and Styles*, Blackwell, 1987.
7. For the socialisation of graduate trainees, see A.D. Brown and C. Coupland, 'Sounds of silence: graduate trainees, hegemony and resistance', *Organization Studies*, vol. 26, no. 7 (2005), pp. 1049–70.
8. The value of goals and performance targets have been debated vigorously: see L. Ordonez, M. Schweitzer, A. Galinksy and M. Bazerman, 'Goals gone wild: the systematic side effects of overprescribing goal setting', *Academy of Management Perspectives*, vol. 23, no. 1 (2009), pp. 6–16.
9. See S. Floyd and W. Wooldridge, *The Strategic Middle Manager: How to Create and Sustain Competitive Advantage*, Jossey-Bass, 1996.
10. See for example J. Balogun and L. Rouleau, 'Strategy-as-practice research on middle managers and sensemaking', *Handbook of Middle Management Strategy Process Research*, Cambridge University Press, 2017.

11. See T.C. Bednall, A.E. Rafferty, H. Shipton, K. Sanders, K. and C.J. Jackson, 'Innovative behaviour: how much transformational leadership do you need?' *British Journal of Management*, vol. 29, no. 4 (2018), pp. 796–16.

12. For this evidence see D.A. Waldman, G.G. Ramirez, R.J. House and P. Puranam, 'Does leadership matter? CEO leadership attributes and profitability under conditions of perceived environmental uncertainty', *Academy of Management Journal*, vol. 44, no. 1 (2001), pp. 134–43.

13. A discussion on different approaches of strategic leaders and evidence for the effectiveness of the adoption of different approaches can be found in D. Goleman, 'Leadership that gets results', *Harvard Business Review*, vol. 78, no. 2 (March–April 2000), pp. 78–90.

14. Kotter, 'What leaders really do', *Harvard Business Review* (December 2001), pp. 85–96.

15. This part of the chapter draws on Chapter 3 of *Exploring Strategic Change* by J. Balogun and V. Hope-Hailey, 3rd edn, Prentice Hall, 2008.

16. G. Brooks, M. Smets and A. Stephen, *Understanding Chief Digital Officers: Paradoxical Protagonists of Digital Transformation*, Said Business School research report, University of Oxford, 2018.

17. Friesl, L. Garreau and L. Heracleous L., 'When the parent imitates the child: strategic renewal through separation and reintegration of subsidiaries', *Strategic Organization*, vol. 17, no. 1 (2019), pp. 62–94.

18. C.A. O'Reilly and M.L. Tushman, 'Organizational ambidexterity in action: how managers explore and exploit', *California Management Review*, vol. 53, no. 4 (2011), pp. 5–22.

Case example
Tencent: Third Time Lucky?

Pony Ma, founder of Tencent
Source: Jerome Favre/EPA/Shutterstock

Ma Huateng ('Pony' Ma) founded Tencent in 1998 as a provider of Internet-enabled instant messaging in China. Twenty years later, Tencent had become Asia's most valuable company, active in investment, messaging, gaming, entertainment and cloud services. In 2018, Pony Ma was still Chairman and Chief Executive. He was also China's richest man, owning just under 10 per cent of Tencent's shares.

But Tencent's twentieth anniversary year proved a hard one, the company's share price falling by one-third. Poor internal coordination, new competition and a slow move into cloud services were among the reasons given for the company's troubles. Tencent's solution to its challenges was a major reorganisation, the third in its 23-year history. The reorganisation was hailed by the company as 'a new beginning for the next twenty years'.

Earlier reorganisations

Tencent's two previous reorganisations had each confronted different problems. The company's first major reorganisation came in 2005, when Tencent was approaching a scale of 4,000 people. By training, Pony Ma was an engineer and product manager, always inclined to examine the details of the company's new products. However, the businesses were getting too big and complex for him to manage directly anymore, and internal coordination was falling down. The solution in 2005 was to divide the organisation essentially into two independent business groups, 'Business' and 'Platform Development', each led by their own senior managers, with a series of business units reporting to them.

The second reorganisation had come in 2012. Tencent's original messaging service (QQ) had been struggling for some time. One of the problems was how QQ was spread over three different business units (PCs, wireless and internet), themselves in different business groups (business or platform development). One result was a slow response to the rise of smartphones, particularly the Apple iPhone which was becoming very popular in China.

In a sense, QQ's sluggishness provided an opportunity for Tencent's next great product success, WeChat (Weixin), a multi-purpose messaging, social media and (from 2013) mobile payment app. WeChat originated through Tencent's characteristic process, internal competition between rival projects. Faced by the rise of smartphones, Pony Ma described the two-month development process as 'a matter of life or death' for the company. WeChat was the winning project and, released in 2011, acquired 100 million users within a year (by 2018 it had a billion users). However, WeChat's success – and other developments – created what Pony Ma called 'big company illness'. By 2012, Tencent had 24,000 employees. Ma asked in an email: 'When the size of the team grows bigger, it is easy to breed big business problems. How can we overcome the big business problem and build a world-class Internet company?' His answer was the 2012 reorganisation, a split into seven distinct business groups: Interactive Entertainment, Online Media, Mobile Internet, Social Networking, WeChat and Technology and Engineering.

The 2018 reorganisation

2018 was not only an anniversary year for Tencent: it was also a transitional year in the development of the internet business. Pony Ma explained:

> **'The second half of the Internet belongs to the industrial Internet. In the first half, Tencent provided users with high-quality services by connecting people. In the second half, building from this foundation, we will support industries and consumers to form more openly connected ecosystems. As an Internet-based technology and culture company, technology is Tencent's most solid underlying infrastructure... Tencent will use technology as the driving engine to explore the next generation of social and content convergence.'**

Pony Ma distinguishes here between two halves of the internet era: the first half was characterised by the rapid growth in consumer internet usage, firstly in desktop and later in mobile technologies; the second industrial half refers to a maturing of the consumer market and a period when growth will come from collaborating directly with other businesses to digitalise their industries, helping them link to consumers as well. This shift to the second half of the internet had organisational consequences for Tencent. As Pony Ma put it: 'From the management side, the biggest challenge we face is internal organization. Right now, Tencent needs to get better at doing B2B (business to business services).'

B2B services have indeed been a problem for Tencent. An illustration of the issue is Tencent's performance in cloud services (platforms offering computer power, database storage, applications, and other IT resources, especially to business). Alibaba, a powerful peer in China's technology sector (see Chapter 2 end case), had been an early entrant into cloud services in 2010, and had captured about one third of the Chinese market by 2017. Tencent hesitated till 2011, with the result that its market share was about a fifth. As Pony Ma said above, it would be very important to create openly connected ecosystems joining consumers and industries. However, although it was developing industry applications, WeChat retained its historical focus on consumers.

Tencent's 2012 structure reinforced a 'silo culture' that did not help in fostering connections. Each business unit was responsible for its own business, encouraging a narrow focus on its specific opportunities, each standing apart like the tall grain silos of America. The consequence has been difficulties in sharing ideas, data and even lines of code. Cross-selling to the same client from one part of the business to another has also suffered. Geography exacerbates some of these problems: the business serving iPhones is based in Shenzhen (Tencent's head-office location), while the iPad business is in Beijing, more than 2,000 kilometres away. The WeChat team is mostly located in Guangzhou, 140 kilometres from Shenzhen. Again, internal competition also plays a role. One expert

on Tencent, Matthew Brennan, observes of Tencent's system: 'It's called saima, like a horse race – the concept of putting several teams to attack the same opportunity.' When a Chinese competitor, ByteDance enjoyed great success with its short video apps, Tencent responded by launching a new video app, Yoo, in competition not just with ByteDance but with its own Weishi app. On top of all this, Tencent had grown from 24,000 employees in 2012 to 45,000 in 2017.

Addressing these issues, Tencent moved in 2018 to a new organisational structure based on six groups rather than seven: now there would be interactive entertainment, platforms and content, cloud and smart industries, corporate development, WeChat and technology and engineering (see Figure 1). Although the WeChat Group and the Technology and Engineering Group had been left basically untouched, there was also a lot of movement of businesses between the other groups. Three old business groups – Online Media, Social Networking and Mobile Internet – were entirely disbanded with their businesses absorbed into either the new Cloud and Smart Industries Group (CSIG) or Platforms and Content Group (PCG). CSIG combines a number of businesses aimed at B2B services: Tencent Cloud, Internet +, Smart Retail, Education, Medical, Safety & Location Based Services and Industry Solutions. PCG is aimed at countering competitors like ByteDance, combining all of Tencent's largest content-centric mobile apps and platforms in a single Group. All non-WeChat platforms and content are now combined within PCG, with the hope of improved sharing of data and content. The Corporate Development Group serves as an incubator for new businesses. Overseeing the various Groups in the 2018 structure is a new Tencent Technical Committee. This committee is intended to foster the sharing of data, key for the development of AI (artificial intelligence) and algorithms, seen as crucial for the delivery of personalised consumer content, amongst much else. Nonetheless, Tencent retains three separate

Figure 1 Simplified from: https://www.tencent.com/en-us/structure.html

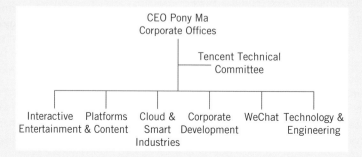

AI teams, one in the Cloud and Smart Industries Group, another in the Technology and Engineering Group and a third in WeChat. More generally, it was not yet evident how the Technical Committee would work with the Technology and Engineering Group.

In a declining market, the two weeks following Tencent's 2018 reorganisation announcement saw a 10 per cent drop in the company's share price (larger than the falls of fellow Chinese technology giants Alibaba and Baidu). Nonetheless, at the annual staff meeting soon after the announcement, Pony Ma re-emphasised the importance of internal connectedness: 'It is precisely because we hold extensive connections in the consumer internet that we can better serve business (to B) and government (to G) customers. This ability is our magic weapon for our future competitive advantage.'

Main sources: M. Brennan, A Deep Dive into Tencent's Restructuring, *ChinaChannel*, 3 October 2018; *Financial Times*, 18 and 25 October 2018.

Questions

1 Explain the strategic reasons behind each of the reorganisations (2005, 2012 and 2018) undertaken by Tencent.

2 How adequate is the 2018 reorganisation to Tencent's various challenges at that point? What else might be necessary?

3 In terms of Figure 9.6, what type of change is being undertaken in 2018? What kind of leadership style would you suggest is most relevant for this change?

Glossary

Acquisition is achieved by purchasing a majority of shares in a target company (p. 148)

BCG matrix uses market share and market growth criteria to determine the attractiveness and balance of a business portfolio (p. 145)

Business-level strategy how an individual business competes in its particular market(s) (p. 9)

Business model describes a value proposition for customers and other participants, an arrangement of activities that produces this value, and associated revenue and cost structures (p. 120)

Competitive advantage how a company, business unit or organisation creates value for its users both greater than the costs of supplying them and superior to that of rivals (p. 110)

Competitive strategy how a company, business unit or organisation achieves competitive advantage in its domain of activity (p. 110)

Complementor(s) an organisation is your complementor if it enhances your business attractiveness to customers or suppliers (p. 49)

Corporate governance is concerned with the structures and systems of control by which managers are held accountable to those who have a legitimate stake in an organisation (p. 93)

Corporate-level strategy is concerned with the overall scope of an organisation and how value is added to the constituent businesses of the organisation as a whole (p. 9)

Corporate social responsibility the commitment by organisations to behave ethically and contribute to economic development while improving the quality of life of the workforce and their families as well as the local community and society at large (p. 96)

Cost-leadership strategy involves becoming the lowest-cost organisation in a domain of activity (p. 111)

Cultural web shows the behavioural, physical and symbolic manifestations of a culture (p. 99)

Differentiation strategy involves uniqueness along some dimension that is sufficiently valued by customers to allow a price premium (p. 114)

Diffusion is the process by which innovations spread among users (p. 164)

disruptive innovation creates substantial growth by offering a new performance trajectory that, even if initially inferior to the performance of existing technologies, has the potential to become markedly superior (p. 169)

Distinctive resources and capabilities are required to achieve competitive advantage (p. 68)

Diversification (related and unrelated/conglomerate) increasing the range of products or markets served by an organisation (p. 133)

Dominant logic the set of corporate-level managerial competences applied across the portfolio of businesses (p. 138)

Dynamic capabilities an organisation's ability to renew and re-create its strategic capabilities to meet the needs of changing environments (p. 80)

Economies of scope efficiency gains made through applying the organisation's existing resources or competences to new markets or services (p. 138)

Ecosystem consists of a group of mutually dependent and collaborative partners that need to interact to create value for all (p. 163)

Entrepreneurship is a process by which individuals, start-ups or organisations identify and exploit opportunities for new products or services that satisfy a need in a market (p. 155)

Exploring Strategy **Framework** includes understanding *the strategic position* of an organisation (context); assessing *strategic choices* for the future (content); and managing *strategy in action* (process) (p. 10)

First-mover advantage exists where an organisation is better off than its competitors as a result of being first to market with a new product, process or service (p. 167)

Focus strategy targets a narrow segment or domain of activity and tailors its products or services to the needs of that specific segment to the exclusion of others (p. 115)

Forecasting takes three fundamental approaches based on varying degrees of certainty: single-point, range and multiple-futures forecasting (p. 32)

Functional strategies are concerned with how the components of an organisation deliver effectively the corporate- and business-level strategies in terms of resources, processes and people (p. 9)

Game theory encourages an organisation to consider competitors' likely moves and the implications of these moves for its own strategy (p. 118)

Global–local dilemma the extent to which products and services may be standardised across national boundaries or need to be adapted to meet the requirements of specific national markets (p. 147)

Governance chain shows the roles and relationships of different groups involved in the governance of an organisation (p. 94)

Implementation refers to the translation of a chosen strategy into organisational action in order to achieve strategic goals and objectives (p. 178)

Industry a group of firms producing products and services that are essentially the same (p. 42)

Inimitable resources and capabilities are those resources and capabilities that competitors find difficult and costly to imitate or obtain or substitute (p. 70)

Innovation the conversion of new knowledge into a new product, process or service *and* the putting of this new product, process or service into actual commercial use (p. 155)

Key drivers for change are the environmental factors likely to have a high impact on industries and sectors, and the success or failure of strategies within them (p. 30)

Leadership the process of influencing an organisation (or group within an organisation) in its efforts towards achieving an aim or goal (p. 178)

Macro-environment broad environmental factors that impact to a greater or lesser extent many organisations, industries and sectors (p. 22)

Market a group of customers for specific products or services that are essentially the same (e.g. a particular geographical market) (p. 42)

Market development involves offering existing products/services to new markets (p. 136)

Market penetration implies increasing share of current markets with the current product or service range (p. 134)

Market segment a group of customers who have similar needs that are different from customer needs in other parts of the market (p. 57)

Mission statement aims to provide the employees and stakeholders with clarity about what the organisation is fundamentally there to do (p. 6)

Network effects there are network effects in an industry when one customer of a product or service has a positive effect on the value of that product for other customers (p. 49)

Objectives are statements of specific outcomes that are to be achieved (often expressed in financial terms) (p. 7)

Open innovation involves the deliberate import and export of knowledge by an organisation in order to accelerate and enhance its innovation (p. 163)

Organic growth is achieved by building on and developing an organisation's own capabilities (p. 148)

Organisational ambidexterity the ability of an organisation simultaneously to exploit existing capabilities and to search for new capabilities (p. 193)

Organisational culture the taken-for-granted assumptions and behaviours of an organisation's members (p. 98)

Outsourcing activities that were previously carried out internally are subcontracted to external suppliers (p. 140)

Paradigm is the set of assumptions held in common and taken for granted in an organisation (p. 99)

Parenting advantage is the value added to businesses by corporate-level activities (p. 132)

PESTEL framework categorises environmental influences into six main types: political, economic, social, technological, environmental and legal (p. 23)

Porter's Five Forces Framework helps identify the attractiveness of an industry in terms of five competitive forces: the threat of entry; the threat of substitutes; the power of buyers; the power of suppliers; and the extent of rivalry between competitors (p. 43)

Product and service development is where organisations deliver modified or new products (or services) to existing markets (p. 134)

Rare resources and capabilities are those resources and capabilities that are possessed uniquely by one organisation or by a few others (p. 69)

Resource-based view states that the competitive advantage and superior performance of an organisation is explained by the distinctiveness of its capabilities (p. 65)

Situational leadership encourages strategic leaders to adjust their leadership style to the context they face (p. 189)

Stakeholder mapping identifies stakeholder expectations and power, and helps in the understanding of political priorities (p. 89)

Stakeholders those individuals or groups that depend on an organisation to fulfil their own goals and on whom, in turn, the organisation depends (p. 87)

Statements of corporate values communicate the underlying and enduring core 'principles' that guide an organisation's strategy and define the way that the organisation should operate (p. 6)

Strategic alliance where two or more organisations share resources and activities to pursue a common strategy (p. 148)

Strategic business unit supplies goods or services for a distinct domain of activity (p. 109)

Strategic change involves either organisational transformation or realignment in the pursuit of a new or adjusted strategy (p. 178)

Strategic choices involve the options for strategy in terms of both the *directions* in which strategy might move and the *methods* by which strategy might be pursued (p. 12)

Strategic groups organisations within an industry or sector with similar strategic characteristics, following similar strategies or competing on similar bases (p. 56)

Strategic position the impact on strategy of the external environment, the organisation's strategic capability (resources and competences), and the organisation's goals and culture (p. 11)

Strategy the long-term direction of an organisation (p. 2)

Strategy in action is about how strategies are formed and how they are implemented (p. 13)

Strategy statements should have three main themes: the fundamental *goals* that the organisation seeks, which typically draw on the organisation's stated mission, vision and objectives; the *scope* or domain of the organisation's activities; and the particular *advantages* or capabilities it has to deliver all of these (p. 7)

Structures give people formally defined roles, responsibilities and lines of reporting (p. 178)

SWOT provides a general summary of the Strengths and Weaknesses explored in an analysis of resources and capabilities and the Opportunities and Threats explored in an analysis of the environment (p. 76)

Synergy the benefits gained where activities or assets complement each other so that their combined effect is greater than the sum of their parts (p. 139)

Systems support and control people as they carry out structurally defined roles and responsibilities (p. 178)

Three horizons framework suggests organisations should think of themselves as comprising three types of business or activity, defined by their 'horizons' in terms of years (p. 3)

Threshold resources and capabilities those that are needed for an organisation to meet the necessary requirements to compete in a given market and achieve parity with competitors in that market (p. 66)

Transactional leaders emphasise 'hard' levers of change such as designing systems and controls (p. 189)

Unrelated diversification involves moving into products or services with no relationships to existing businesses (p. 133)

Value chain describes the categories of activities within an organisation which, together, create a product or service (p. 74)

Vertical (forward and backward) integration entering into activities where the organisation is its own supplier or customer (p. 139)

vision statement is concerned with the future the organisation seeks to create (p. 6)

VRIO analysis helps to evaluate if, how and to what extent an organization or company has resources and capabilities that are (i) valuable, (ii) rare, (iii) inimitable and (iv) supported by the organisation (p. 73)

Name index

General index

Bold locators are used for glossary entries

Publisher's acknowledgements

Text credits

3 MIT Press: (Figure 1.1) A.D. Chandler, *Strategy and Structure: Chapters in the History of American Enterprise*, MIT Press, 1963, p. 13; M.E. Porter, 'What is strategy?', *Harvard Business Review*, November–December 1996, p. 60; P.F. Drucker, 'The theory of business', *Harvard Business Review*, September–October 1994, pp. 95–106; H. Mintzberg, *Tracking Strategies: Towards a General Theory*, Oxford University Press, 2007, p. 3; **4 Martin Eberhard:** Quoted by Martin Eberhard; **4 Insider Inc.:** D. Baer, 'The making of Tesla: invention, betrayal, and the birth of the Roadster', *Business Insider*, 11 November 2014; **5 Texere Publishers:** (Figure 1.2) Adapted from M. Baghai, S. Coley and D. White, *The Alchemy of Growth*, Texere Publishers, 2000. Figure 1.1, p. 5; **7 Tesla, Inc.:** Tesla, Inc.; **8 SAMSUNG:** Samsung Electronics; **9 Inter IKEA Systems B.V.:** Used with permission of Inter IKEA Systems B.V.; **14 Pearson Education:** (Table 1.1) A practical introduction to strategic planning is V. Evans, FT Essential Guide to Developing a Business Strategy: How to Use Strategic Planning to Start Up or Grow Your Business, FT Publishing International, 2013; **19 Brian Cesky:** Quoted by Brian Cesky, Founder and CEO at Airbnb; **19 Joseph Gebbia:** Quoted by Joseph Gebbia; **19 Airbnb:** Written by Airbnb, http://blog.airbnb.com/belong-anywhere/; **28 Avi Hasson:** Quote by Avi Hasson published in Orpaz, Inbal. The secret to high-tech success? This elite Israeli army unit, 18 April 2014, Haaretz.com; **29 IEEE:** (Figure 2.5) Drawn from data extracted from the International Roadmap for Devices and Systems, 2018 edition, Institute for Electronics and Electrical Engineers; **31 JUUL Labs, Inc.:** Used by permission from JUUL Labs, Inc.; **31 Forbes Media LLC:** Chaykowski, Kathleen. The Disturbing Focus of JUUL's Early Marketing Campaigns, 16 November 2018, Forbes Media LLC; **35 Deloitte:** (Illustration 2.4) 'The world remade by Covid-19: scenarios for resilient leaders', 6 April 2020, Deloitte; **43 Simon & Schuster Inc.:** (Figure 3.1) Adapted from *Competitive Strategy: Techniques for Analyzing Industries and Competitors*, The Free Press by Michael E. Porter, copyright © 1980, 1998 by The Free Press. All rights reserved.; **46 Hannah Nixon:** Quote by Hannah Nixon; **46 Andrew Bailey:** Quote by Andrew Bailey published in New Bank Start-up Unit launched by the financial regulators, 20 January 2016, The Bank of England; **46 Deloitte Touche Tohmatsu Limited:** Digital disruption: Threats and opportunity for retail financial services, 2014, Deloitte; **46 THE FINANCIAL TIMES LTD:** Cumbo, Josephine. (2015) Banks need to adapt to new breed of rival, 7 December 2015. © The Financial Times Limited 2015. All Rights Reserved; **50 Mark Zuckerberg:** Quote by Mark Zuckerberg published by Economy, Peter. Mark Zuckerberg: 19 Inspiring Power Quotes for Success, Manuseto Ventures; **60 Peter Cardwell:** (Case Example) Reprinted with permission from Peter Cardwell; **61 Zenith:** (Table 1) Zenith Media, Statista, December 2018; **61 WPP:** (Table 2) WPP, Omnicom, Publicis Groupe, IPG, Dentsu; **62 Zenith:** (Table 3) Zenith Media, Statista, December 2018; **63 eMarketer, Inc.:** (Table 4) US Mobile Ad Spending, In-App vs. Mobile Web, 2015-2019, eMarketer Inc., ; **67 Australian Red Cross:** Australian Red Cross Capability Framework, http://www.redcross.org.au/files/Red_Cross_Capa-biity_Framework_2015; **67 AstraZeneca:** AstraZeneca Annual Report 2017, pp 4-32; **67 S. D. Shibulal:** Quoted by S. D. Shibulal; **67 Skilling India:** Skilling India; **69 Pearson Education:** (Figure 4.1) The VRIO criteria were introduced by Jay Barney in J.B. Barney, *Gaining and Sustaining Competitive Advantage*, Addison-Wesley, 1997; **72 Dow Jones & Company, Inc.:** Raice, Shayndi, Groupon and It's 'Weird' CEO, 31 January 2012. *The Wall Street Journal*; **72 Crain Communications, Inc.:** Crains Chicago Business, 9 March 2018 (John Pletz: 'What's this? Groupon is now profitable') Groupon Shares Crumble After Company Names New CEO, 3 November 2015, Forbes; **74 Pearson Education:** (Table 4.2) Adapted with the permission of J.B. Barney and W.S. Hesterly, *Strategic Management and Competitive Advantage*, Pearson, 2012.; **75 Simon & Schuster Inc.:** (Figure 4.3) Adapted from *Competitive Advantage: Creating* *and Sustaining Superior Performance* by Michael E. Porter. The Free Press, a Division of Simon & Schuster, Inc.; **77 Jill Shepherd:** (Illustration 4.3) Prepared by Jill Shepherd, Segal Graduate School of Business, Simon Fraser University, Vancouver, Canada; **83 THE FINANCIAL TIMES LTD:** Davies, Sally. (2014), Rocket Internet's Oliver Samwer responds to critics ahead of IPO, July 15 © The Financial Times Limited 2014. All Rights Reserved.; **84 Venture Village:** Kaczmarek, J. (2012) 'An inside look at Rocket Internet', 18 November 2012, VentureVillage.com; **84 Alexander Kudlich:** Alexander Kudlich; **84 Florian Heinemann:** Florian Heinemann; **84 Dow Jones & Company, Inc.:** Rooney, B. (2012) Rocket Internet leads the clone war, 14 May 2012, *The Wall Street Journal*; **84 Marc Samwer:** Quote by Marc Samwer published in Crampton, Thomas (2006), German brothers break the mold, 2 December 2006, *NY Times*; **85 Thomson Reuters Corporation:** Thomasson, E. and Schimroszik, N. (2018) Rocket Internet CEO says ready to pounce with cash pile, January 11, Reuters Business News; **88 Cambridge University Press:** (Figure 5.1) Adapted from R.E. Freeman, *Strategic Management: A Stakeholder Approach*, Pitman, 1984. Copyright 1984 by R. Edward Freeman.; **90 Guardian News & Media Limited:** Aitkenhead, D. and Beaumont, P. (2018) Oxfam chief accuses critics of 'gunning' for charity over Haiti sex scandal claims, February 16, Guardian News & Media Limited; **90 Oxfam International:** Haiti Investigation Final Report, 2018, Oxfam; **91 Taylors & Francis Group:** (Figure 5.2) Newcombe, R. (2003) From client to project stakeholders: a stakeholder mapping approach, Construction Management and Economics, 21.8, pp. 841-848; **95 THE FINANCIAL TIMES LTD:** Edmonds, Mark. (2018) Jamie Oliver: 'We had simply run out of cash', August 30 © The Financial Times Limited 2018. All Rights Reserved; **98 John Wiley & Sons, Inc.:** Schein, E. (2004) *Organisational Culture and Leadership*, 3rd edn, Jossey-Bass, John Wiley; **98 Pearson Education:** Deal, T.E and Kennedy, A.A. (1982) *Corporate Cultures: The Rites and Rituals of Corporate Life*, Addison-Wesley Publishing; **100 Harvard Business School Publishing:** Fairclough, Rushton. (1916) Virgil: Eclogues-Georgics-Aeneid Books I- (Loeb classical library) Harvard University Press, 1916; **100 University of Bath:** University of Bath; **100 Guardian News & Media Limited:** Adams, R. (2017) Could Bath University vice-chancellor's latest pay controversy be her last? November 24, Guardian News & Media Limited; **100 Eve Alcock:** Quoted by Eve Alcock; **106 Susan Fowler:** Fowler, S. (2017) Reflecting on One Very, Very Strange Year at Uber, February 19, https://www.susanjfowler.com; **106 Dara Khosrowshahi:** Quoted by Dara Khosrowshahi; **106 Uber Technologies Inc.:** Khosrowshahi, D. (2017) Uber's new cultural norms, 7 November 2017, Uber Technologies Inc.; **106 The New York Times Company:** Fitzsimmons, E. (2018) Meet the Man Tasked With Expanding Uber's Business in New York, with a smile, 30 November 2018, *New York Times*; **107 Business Insider:** Bort, J. (2018) 'We have screwed up': Uber CEO Dara Khosrowshahi admits in an all-hands meeting that the company deserves some fault after its self-driving car killed a pedestrian, 29 November, *Business Insider*; **110 Simon & Schuster Inc.:** (Figure 6.1) Adapted from Competitive Advantage: Creating and Sustaining Superior Performance by Michael E. Porter. The Free Press, a Division of Simon & Schuster, Inc.; **113 THE FINANCIAL TIMES LTD:** Oakley, D. (2015) Vanguard's march to Europe tracks ECB's quantitative easing, 4 March 2015 © The Financial Times Limited 2015. All Rights Reserved; **113 THE FINANCIAL TIMES LTD:** Foley, S. (2014) Vanguard turns firepower on shake-up of financial advice market, 8 December 2014 © The Financial Times Limited 2014. All Rights Reserved; **116 THE FINANCIAL TIMES LTD:** Leahy, J. (2009) Volvo takes a lead in India, 31 August 2009, © The Financial Times Limited 2009. All Rights Reserved; **116 ETAuto.com:** Mathur, S. (2017) Interview with Kamal Bali, President and Managing Director, Volvo Group India, 19 May, ETAuto.com; **121 Verizon Media:** Korosec, K. (2018) Uber CEO: ride hailing will be eclipsed by scooters, bikes and even flying taxis, 7 September, Verizon Media; **126 Neil Saunders:** Quoted by Neil Saunders; **126, 127 Anders Dahlvig:** Quoted by Anders Dahlvig; **128 Fortune Media IP Limited:** B. Kowitt, 'How Ikea took over the world', *Fortune*, March 10 2015, Fortune Media IP Limited; **129 Inter IKEA Systems B.V.:** IKEA yearly report FY15; **129 Inter IKEA Systems B.V.:** IKEA yearly summary FY18; **134 Penguin Random House:** (Figure 7.2) Adapted from H.I. Ansoff, *Corporate Strategy*, Penguin, 1988, Chapter 6. Ansoff originally had a matrix with four separate boxes, but in practice strategic directions involve more continuous axes. The Ansoff matrix itself was later developed – see reference 1; **137 Telegraph Media Group Limited:** Curtis, S. (2015) TomTom: from satnavs to driverless cars, 5 May, Telegraph Media Group; **143 Bloomberg L.P:** Chipotle: the definitive oral history; http://www.bloomberg.com/graphics/2015-chiptole-oral-history; **150 Peter**

Barton: (Case Example) Peter Barton; **150 Del Vecchio:** Quoted by Del Vecchio; **151 Striano:** Quoted by Striano; **151 INFORMS:** B.S. Vanneste, 'How much do industry, corporation and business really matter? A meta-analysis', *Strategy Science*, vol. 2, no. 2 (2017) pp. 121–39.; **151 Grand Vision:** (Figure 1) Key Figures, https://investors.grandvision.com/key-figures; **152 Jonathan Lawson:** Quoted by Jonathan Lawson; **153 THE FINANCIAL TIMES LTD:** Stothard, Michael. (2017) Hubert Sagnières, Essilor CEO, on an eyewear megamerger, 11 June 2017 © The Financial Times Limited 2017. All Rights Reserved; **153 Norbert Gorny:** Quoted by Norbert Gorny; **158 Pearson Education:** (Figure 8.2) Adapted from B.R. Barringer and R.D. Ireland, *Entrepreneurship – Successfully launching New Ventures*, 4th edn, 2012, Pearson.; **159 The Slate Group LLC.:** Beam C. (2010) The Other Social Network, 29 September, The Slate Group; **159 BBC News:** Cellan-Jones, R., 'Wayne Ting, nearly a billionaire. Or how Facebook won', 21 December 2010, BBC News; **162 Elsevier:** (Figure 8.4) Adapted from J. Abernathy and W. Utterback, 'A dynamic model of process and product innovation', *Omega*, vol. 3, no. 6 (1975), pp. 639–56; **169 Harvard Business School Publishing:** (Figure 8.6) From The Innovator's Solution by C. Christensen and M.E. Raynor. Boston, MA (2003). Copyright © 2003 by the Harvard Business School Publishing Corporation. All rights reserved.; **173 Mikael Hed:** Mikael Hed; **174 CNBC LLC:** Choudhury, S. 'Angry Birds creator talks about the movie and future of the popular game', 5 June 2018, CNBC; **176 Kati Levoranta:** Quote by Kati Levoranta, CEO Rovio Entertainment; **176 Ville Heijari:** Ville Heijari, Rovio's Chief Marketing Officer; **180 Elon Musk:** Quoted by Elon Musk; **183 Harvard Business School Publishing:** (Figure 9.4) *Managing Across Borders: The Transnational Corporation*, 2nd edition by C.A. Bartlett and S. Ghoshal, Boston, MA, 1998. Copyright © 1998 by the Harvard Business School Publishing Corporation. All rights reserved. Reprinted by permission of Harvard Business School Press; **186 John Wiley & Sons, Inc.:** (Figure 9.5) Adapted from Goold, M. and Campbell, A. (1989) *Strategies and Styles*, Blackwell, Figure 3.1, p. 39; **186 Harvard Business School Publishing:** E.C. Wenger and W.M. Snyder, 'Communities of practice: the organized frontier', *Harvard Business Review*, vol. 78, no. 1 (2000), pp. 139–46.; **188 Tim Leissner:** Quoted by Tim Leissner; **190 Miki Agrawal:** Miki Agrawal, founder and CEO of period-proof underwear startup Thinx, *Fast Company*, 27 December, 2016.; **190 Heidi Zak:** Zak, Heidi (2018) Google alum turned start-up CEO: This tough moment helped me find my voice, 19 November, CNBC; **190 Jack Ma:** Jack Ma, Founder of Chinese eCommerce giant, Alibaba; **190 Biz Stone:** Quote by Biz Stone published in Cunningham, Lillian. (2014) Biz Stone on leadership (and Star Trek), *Washington Post*; **191 Harvard Business School Publishing:** J. Kotter, 'What leaders really do', *Harvard Business Review* (December 2001), pp. 85–96.; **191 Pearson Education:** (Figure 9.6) Adapted from Balogun, J. and Hope Hailey, V. (2016) *Exploring Strategic Change*, 4th edn, Prentice Hall; **192 La Redoute:** Quoted by La Redoute; **194 Harvard Business School Publishing:** (Figure 9.7) Adapted from Kotter J. (1996), Leading Change: Why Transformation Efforts Fail, *Harvard Business Review*, March-April, p. 61; **197, 198 Pony Ma:** Quoted by Pony Ma, Tencent CEO; **198 Tencent:** (Figure 1) Simplified from: https://www.tencent.com/en-us/structure.html.

Photo Credits

4 Alamy Stock Photo: Jim West/Alamy Stock Photo; **17 Shutterstock:** AlesiaKan/Shutterstock; **38 Shutterstock:** Eugenio Loreto/EPA-EFE/Shutterstock; **50 Alamy Stock Photo:** Robert Galbraith/Reuters/Alamy Stock Photo; **60 Shutterstock:** PixieMe/Shutterstock; **83 Dieter Mayr Photography:** Dieter Mayr Photography; **105 Shutterstock:** Justin Lane/EPA/Shutterstock; **121 Shutterstock:** Narapirom/Shutterstock; **128 Alamy Stock Photo:** Kevin Foy/Alamy Stock Photo; **135 Getty Images:** Daniel Leal-Olivas/AFP/Getty Images; **135 Getty Images:** Bloomberg/Getty Images; **150 LUXOTTICA GROUP:** List of Luxottica brands: http://www.luxottica.com/en/eyewear-brands; **151 Safilo Group:** List of Safilo brands: http://www.safilogroup.com/en/2-licensed-brands; **164 Shutterstock:** Zapp2Photo/Shutterstock; **176 Alamy Stock Photo:** Collection Christophel/Alamy Stock Photo; **190 Getty Images:** Robin Marchant/Getty Images Entertainment/Getty Images; **192 Getty Images:** Sefa Karacan/Anadolu Agency/Getty Images; **197 Shutterstock:** Jerome Favre/EPA/Shutterstock.